THE *Eugenia Price*
Trilogy

Books by Eugenia Price

FICTION
Margaret's Story
Maria
Don Juan McQueen
The Beloved Invader
New Moon Rising
Lighthouse

NONFICTION
At Home on St. Simons
Diary of a Novel
St. Simons Memoir
No Pat Answers
Leave Yourself Alone
Learning to Live from the Acts
Learning to Live from the Gospels
The Unique World of Women
Just As I Am
Make Love Your Aim
The Wider Place
God Speaks to Women Today
What Is God Like?
Find Out for Yourself
A Woman's Choice
Beloved World
Woman to Woman
Share My Pleasant Stones
Early Will I Seek Thee
Never a Dull Moment
The Burden Is Light
Discoveries

THE *Eugenia Price* *Trilogy*

A COLLECTION INCLUDING

Discoveries

The Burden Is Light

Early Will I Seek Thee

Printed in the United States of America

ISBN: 0-7394-3185-4

Contents

Discoveries

To

Ellen Riley Urquhart

. . . the one through whom He found me

Contents

Acknowledgment

Some of the material included in this book has appeared in the column "The Way Out," written each month by Eugenia Price for the *Christian Patriot*, which was the official publication of the Christian Amendment Movement.

Preface

To my readers who do NOT follow Jesus Christ:

These pages may seem to be written only for those who follow Christ. They are not. They are written for you, too, if (as I did not, a few short years ago) you do not believe He is who He says He is. Perhaps you do not (as I did not, a few short years ago) believe in God at all. These pages are written for you, too. And this is why: to give you license to watch and check on those of us who say we do believe and follow Christ.

Why do I want you to watch us? For His sake. Too often, His followers do not remember that they have the reputation of their Lord in their hands every minute of every hour they are alive on this earth.

You may not be impressed favorably by what you see when you scrutinize us as Christians. But please do it anyway, and then go on beyond us to Jesus, Himself! For your own sake and for His sake, I beg you not to let us stop you, no matter what you see. He will work His miracles in His followers only as rapidly as they permit Him to work. And so, what you may see in many Christians that seems to be unlike Jesus Christ will be unlike Jesus Christ. In fairness, do not blame Him for that. Rather, be bold and kind enough to let us know that you have found us wanting in Christian personality. And if we defend ourselves, remind us that if we do follow this Christ of the Cross, we have no right to defend ourselves. We have no rights left if our surrender has been complete. You who do not follow Christ, however, still have all your rights in your own possession. You are not free, because rights are jailers. But you are entitled to your rights because they are still yours.

Scrutinize us carefully if we profess to have been touched and transformed by the person of the Holy Spirit of the Christ of the Cross and the open tomb. If we defend ourselves, remind us of His words from that Cross about forgiveness. Remind us of His attitude toward His accusers. And it is my sincere prayer that your scrutiny will remind us that when we act just like non-believers, our Lord takes the blow!

There is still another reason why these pages are written for you who do not know Jesus Christ personally: to dare you to read the book through and not hear His voice speaking to you once as He spoke to me all the while I wrote it. If you can do this, I hope you will let me know. Thank you.

EUGENIA PRICE
Chicago, Illinois
February, 1953

Introduction

"All the best part of experience," wrote C. E. Montague, "consists in discovering that perfectly trite pieces of observation are shiningly and exhilaratingly true."

Our Christian beliefs, at least for throngs of Americans, are not in jeopardy because they are suspected of being false; they are in danger only because they are suspected of being trite, flat, unreal, unexciting.

I revel in what Eugenia Price has released from her radiant soul in these pages, for here are DISCOVERIES that seem to say to us: "Why didn't somebody tell me sooner? I have found that the things they have long said about Jesus Christ are, after all, 'shiningly and exhilaratingly true.'"

The evening that Miss Price told me, in part, the story of what preceded and what has followed her transforming encounter with Christ is one that I treasure among the brightest of hours. No stuffiness, no staginess, no conventionality (not even in vocabulary), just sheer joy in Christ and the infectious longing to share that joy with others!

Christianity has two very different types of apologetics which, in spite of their difference, ought to be in evidence all the time. One is the apologetic of the informed scholar; the other the apologetic of the transformed sinner. The disciplined scholar is

Christianity's intellectual defense, but it is the delivered sinner who constitutes Christianity's practical defense. Miss Price is a convincing example of the latter.

The late Bishop William McDowell once wrote: "We are saved by a Person, and only by a Person, and only by one Person!" Here, on these glowing pages which it is a pleasure to introduce, you will find Eugenia Price's "testament of devotion" to that one Person!

PAUL S. REES
Minneapolis, Minnesota

DISCOVERIES
... *Concerning Discipleship*

1

His Viewpoint or Mine?

I was led into a personal walk with Jesus Christ by a disciple of Jesus Christ, who immediately set about fulfilling the command of her Lord, to make a disciple of me!

Jesus did not say, just before He went to sit at the right hand of the Father, "Go and save men." He said: "Go and make disciples of men!" As I see it, a disciple is one who learns. One who puts himself in position to learn, and above all, one who is willing to learn. Does that include us? Are we in position to learn about Him? Or are we locked up, bolted down within the rigid confines of our own creed and unable to see beyond it into the breath-taking distances of God? Are we devoted to the task of bringing others into a personal relationship with Jesus Christ? Or are we bound and determined to bring them into agreement with ourselves?

Jesus said: "When the Spirit of truth comes, He will guide you into all the truth." Do we really trust the Spirit of Truth or do we merely trust what we understand about Him?

Are we dogmatic clingers to our doctrines? Or are we held in the everlasting arms of Him who promised that He would never leave us nor forsake us? Are we believers in the things we know about Jesus Christ? Or are we believers in Jesus Christ Himself? Are we disciples? Are we learners? *Are we?*

What does it mean to be a disciple? Quite simply, from my own experience and from having been privileged to watch a few of God's real disciples live their daily lives, I would venture to say that if one is to become a disciple of Jesus Christ, one must have the viewpoint of Jesus Christ.

We all think in the language which we speak. I don't think too well on certain subjects without my dictionary. And so, together let's tip our hats toward Mr. Webster right now and see what he has to say about the meaning of the word "view," since "viewpoint" is a noun meaning point of view. When we look at his definition of the word "view," doors begin to open in our minds! Our "view" is widened. As we carry the definition of a disciple as one who has the viewpoint of Christ into Webster's rather complete defining of the word "view," one horizon after another collapses and we see out and away into still more of the distances of God.

First of all, "view" means the "very act of seeing." *Do* we see what Christ sees in the people around us?

Secondly, "view" means "a mental survey; a just view of the arguments." *Do* we have Christ's "just view" of the arguments (rational and irrational), which we hear going on about us even among Christians?

Thirdly, Mr. Webster says that "view" means "power of seeing; reach or range of sight." Do we have Christ's "power of seeing" those whom He sends us to help? Do we have His "range of sight" into their needs and the causes of their separation from Him?

Mr. Webster further defines the word "view" as "mode of looking at anything; judgment; as to state one's view of policy." Do we look through the eyes of Christ at His sheep and their predicaments? Or do we judge for ourselves as we scoff and condemn silently, the while we deceive even ourselves into believing we are leaving the judgment to Him? And the last half of that particular definition of the word view embraces the stating of one's view of a policy! How Christlike are we in our view of our Christian brother's policy when it happens to disagree with our own?

"Viewpoint": a commonly used word with uncommon depths of meaning when we as believers in Jesus Christ dare to examine our own discipleship in the light of whether or not we live and operate from the viewpoint of the One in whom we believe.

For the next few pages we are going to go into some of the implications of having the viewpoint of Christ. Again, I confess to sharing my brand-new understanding of these things. Perhaps the reader's years of experience in walking with God will far over-shadow my new entrance into the brightness of the life for which we were born. But no matter how new the Christian follower, Jesus Christ was "in the beginning." And His viewpoint has and always will be without variation. For He is the Rock on which our every premise may rest, and from which we may safely project our flights of understanding. If our discoveries are real and if they are true, they will return to rest upon the Rock. They will be checked and re-checked and directed and patiently redirected by the Spirit of Truth who, thank God, has come and does dwell within us if we but invite Him.

I have invited Him to come in. I have given myself over to Him. He is mine and I am His. I want to share with you what I believe He is teaching me concerning true discipleship. I want to confess my stumblings and share with you my victories and rejoice the while in my Lord, whom to know is life eternal; whom to know is to belong to and to love—forever.

2

No Condemnation

We have dwelt at some length on what it means to have the viewpoint of Jesus Christ. We stated that it is impossible for a Christian to be a true disciple unless he possesses the viewpoint of Christ as his own. I have found this to be invariably true of my own personal life. Unless we view a dilemma in another's life as Christ views it, we are not able to help that person to a lasting solution of the problem. Unless we face the problems that arise in our own life from the viewpoint of the One who has redeemed us, we do not find their workable solutions.

But even more important than seeing problems from the viewpoint of Christ is the absolute necessity of looking at other people—whether believers or non-believers—as Jesus Christ looks at them. To do this, we must stay out of the picture completely. With mere human perception, no matter how educated or how keen that perception, we simply cannot see others as Jesus Christ sees them. We see them smudged by our own shortcomings. We see them cracked and splintered around the edges because too often we look from the viewpoint of self-justification, especially if we happen not to have been burdened with one of the particular faults or sins under which our neighbor labors. We see them blurred through our own self-righteousness. We see them bent and shapeless because they happen to have fallen into a particular pit which, by the grace of God, we passed over.

Or, we see them as strangers, out of our world, beyond our comprehension; and therefore well-nigh impossible to help, because we have not shared in their specific trouble or sin. For example, if we have not drunk excessively or at all, we look in wide-eyed amazement at the alcoholic who simply will not drop the bottle even when he or she sees the damage the bottle is causing!

We, being human, will distort our fellow men through our own spiritual eyes, unless and until we have the viewpoint of Christ. And we can only have this at last, by a complete and entire surrender of our selves (including our precious viewpoints) into the hands of the living God! Christ, alone, through His Holy Spirit, can give us the viewpoint which He has.

We believe the viewpoint of Christ must begin at the Cross of Christ. We cannot look at our fellow human beings with the viewpoint of Christ unless we can see them as He saw them—from the Cross! And the viewpoint of the Christ of the Cross is summed up in His own words spoken from that wrack of torture: "Father, forgive them, for they know not what they do!"

The viewpoint of Christ, then, must be one of no condemnation; because a viewpoint of condemnation implies only one thing—self-righteousness within the heart of the one who condemns. And self-righteousness within the believer implies only one thing—the viewpoint of the believer, rather than the viewpoint of the One in whom he believes!

The circle is vicious and subtle.

But let us look at the pattern of the earthly life of our Lord for a moment. He was born in the lowest place a man can be born. I believe the Father picked out a stable for His Son's birthplace so no human being in all the ages after could say, "My background isn't good enough for me to become a Christian." No one . . . no one can be born in more meager surroundings than was our Lord.

From the point of view of His birth and the conditions surrounding it, can we condemn anyone among our fellow men no matter what their beginnings?

Or, let us look at the baptism of Jesus of Nazareth. "Then cometh Jesus from Galilee to Jordan unto John, to be baptized by him." To be baptized by John the Baptist, the people stood in line along the bank of the Jordan River. Can you picture Him, "The Lamb of God who taketh away the sin of the world," standing there patiently in line between a repentant thief and a woman of the streets, waiting His turn to be baptized with the others? We can picture Him doing nothing else. For He came to serve, not to be served. To save, not to condemn.

I testify from my own experience that if the one whom God used to lead me into a personal relationship with Jesus Christ had in any way, by the merest shadow of inference, chanced to condemn me during those first tense days as the Holy Spirit worked within my heart, I would not be writing these lines now! I know now how difficult it was for her. It is not easy for one who loves Jesus above all else to sit and hear His Name blasphemed and used carelessly to punctuate casual conversation. It is not easy to have one's Reason for Living ridiculed. It is not easy to be ridiculed for Christ's sake.

But neither was it easy for Him to hang there hearing His own blood drain from His pain-wracked body and pray for the forgiveness of those who crucified Him! It did not take the usual dozen men to hold Jesus as they laid Him flat on the rude cross beam of the Cross. He lay there offering no resistance, making no move in self-defense as the blunt nails were driven into His outstretched hands and feet. When the Cross was lifted up and dropped into the excavation in the ground, He made no cry of protest. He prayed for forgiveness for those who lifted Him up! In this viewpoint of Christ from the Cross is the open secret of the victorious life of discipleship available to you and to me.

If we are to have the viewpoint of Christ we cannot condemn, we can only care.

3

No Hopeless Cases

When one true disciple of Jesus Christ thought on the vast, unending resources of the One whom he followed, he wrote: " . . . him that is able to do exceeding abundantly above all that we ask or think, according to the power that worketh in us!"

The disciple, of course, was St. Paul. One who had, beyond the shadow of a doubt, the viewpoint of Jesus Christ. And, because he had this viewpoint, Paul knew for a fact that if he stayed sufficiently out of the way, the Holy Spirit of God could and would do through him (Paul) "exceeding abundantly above all that we ask or think."

Do we as followers of Jesus Christ really believe this? We say we believe the Bible to be the holy inspired Word of God. We say we believe the Pauline epistles, but do we actually believe that Jesus Christ can do exceedingly abundantly above all that we ask or think? If we do, then why don't we act like it by acting on that promise?

Do we or do we not believe that there are any hopeless cases where Jesus Christ is concerned? I am constrained to repeat that question—not for our sakes, but for His sake:

Do we or do we not believe that there are any hopeless cases where Jesus Christ is concerned?

What about the alcoholic or the inveterate liar or the gambler or the prostitute over whose darkened, frenzied, anxious lives have passed year after year of despair and failure? What about these people? As I write these lines I am half-listening for my telephone to ring, hoping against hope that a warm-hearted, gentle-mannered but seemingly hopeless alcoholic will call from somewhere in the cold, rainy shadows of this night along Chicago's Skid Row. I am trusting God that this boy will at last begin to act upon the knowledge he already possesses about his own "hopeless" case. This boy has known for ten years what he must do. He knows he must surrender one last thing to Christ. My friend and I have been praying and trying again with him for more than two years. His Christian mother in Little Rock, Arkansas, prays with us and believes with us that even though the years are piling up over her son's head, there is no such thing as a hopeless case with Jesus Christ!

There are no hopeless cases in Christ. If we believe there are, we are looking at the sin in the so-called hopeless case, or at the sinner. We simply are not looking at Christ and His resources. There are no hopeless cases with "him that is able to do exceeding abundantly above all that we ask or think."

A Christian believer shook my hand after a speaking engagement not long ago and wonderingly shook her head too as she asked: "How do you dare stand up there and promise that there are no hopeless cases when you've only been a Christian for such a short time? My brother-in-law's been an alcoholic for twenty years. We've never stopped praying that God would change him. But he's still at it. And we've just decided he's a hopeless case!"

I can stand anywhere and promise anyone that there are no hopeless cases in Christ on the full authority of the Son Himself who said: "I am come that they might have life, and that they might have it more abundantly."

I can promise that in Him there are no hopeless cases because my Lord dared say of Himself what no mere human being ever dared say: "I am the way, the truth, and the life." And He did not mean a Way of darkness and despair and sin and self-imprisonment. He meant the Way of freedom and hope and eternal life. He meant the Way out of darkness into the light of His love. And if Jesus Christ cannot back up the startling statements He made, if He cannot back up the claims He made, then He is the biggest phony who ever walked the face of this earth! If I cannot believe Him, whom can I believe?

More than that, even more than being able to put my whole weight down upon the promise of Christ, upon the spoken word of Christ, I can promise anyone, any time, anywhere that in Him are no hopeless cases because He was able to redeem me!

Quite quietly and quite calmly I stake my eternal life on the fact of my Saviour and my Lord, Jesus Christ. I know that when He looked down at me three and a half years ago, He did not see a hopeless case at all. He saw another creature of His, twisted all out of His plan and his nature by sin and self-will and hardness of heart. He saw one of His creations turned almost completely backwards to what He had intended her to be. But He did not see a hopeless case at all. Because He knew Himself. He saw me from the viewpoint of Himself. And He knew His own resources.

The true disciple, if Christ is to be able to use His resources through that disciple as he walks this old trouble tattered earth, must have the viewpoint of his Lord. And Jesus Christ knows that for Him, there are no hopeless cases.

4

Innocence Is Not Purity

*I*t may seem a presumptuous thing to do to begin a meditation by disagreeing point blank with the authority on words, Mr. Webster. And, I do not disagree in a general sense. But where two words in particular are concerned, I must disagree from the standpoint of their spiritual meaning to a true disciple of Christ.

Mr. Webster contends that they are practically synonymous. In two sections of his definition, he uses them interchangeably. Spiritually this is impossible. And yet many Christians not only use them interchangeably, to their own confusion of soul, but they also *act* upon them interchangeably, which results in the department of utter confusion for new Christians and non-believers!

What are these two pesky words? They are: "innocence" and "purity."

Spiritually, I contend, they are not the same. And I have experienced in my own life, the confusion and heartache and inner damage which result from well-meaning Christians acting as though they were one and the same.

Isn't innocence the state in which babies are born? And isn't purity an outright gift of God? Are we not made pure, because of what Jesus did for us on the Cross, only after we have been born again into that purity which comes from Him? And only from Him?

We are born innocent at our physical birth. But we are made pure by faith in Jesus Christ. And faith in Him means we dare to follow Him. "Surely he hath borne our griefs, and carried our sorrows: yet we did esteem him stricken, smitten of God, and afflicted. But he was wounded for our transgressions, he was bruised for our iniquities; the chastisement of our peace was upon him; and with his stripes we are healed. [Because] all we like sheep have gone astray; we have turned every one to his own way; and the Lord hath laid on him the iniquity of us all."

"With his stripes we are healed"—made pure! We were born physically in innocence. We are made pure by Christ.

"Well," you say, "I believe all that. I do not contend that I was born pure. I am a true believer in the redemption of Jesus Christ. I know that includes me as just another sheep who went astray. I know I can claim no purity outside that which Christ has given me. I know I have been made pure!"

All right, if we know that, then why is it that some of us do not behave as though we know it? Until she saw the true spiritual meanings of purity and innocence a well-meaning mother confused the issues in her family and in her own life by assuming that her innocence of certain sins of which her family was guilty somehow made her pure! She would shake her head prettily and say: "My goodness, I just don't see how they can drink that old stuff!" Or, "How can you swear every other breath like that?" Or "I never wanted to do those things!"

Sound familiar? Do you know someone like that? And does his very attitude seem to condemn you? Does this person's insistence that he has never even been tempted along your "disgusting lines" make you want either to bop him on his self-righteous head or run and hide your own head and give up trying to find Christ's answer to your own trouble? I know this is not a far-fetched reaction because I have had it myself. I have watched others smarting under it. I have heard Christian young people sneer and act superior with their fellow students who drink. Thus they imply, if they do not say, "I just don't see how they can do it! How can they cheapen themselves!" The fellow students smart under their criticism and go on running from Christ.

Now, please do not misunderstand. Your writer, having lived in the world of paganism for almost eighteen years, is the first to be glad and thankful when a Christian boy or girl grows all the way to maturity without sampling the world's interests. But I plead that they do just that—grow all the way to maturity! For Jesus' sake and for their own sakes! And for the sake of those whom they shut out of the kingdom by their own confusion of the spiritual meanings of the two words, "innocence" and "purity"! I contend that innocence in an adult approaches stupidity! Again, do not misunderstand my meaning here. I do not advocate that any one try the world in order to be delivered directly from worldly sins into the state of purity given only by Christ. He was without sin, and yet He reached down as far as is necessary to lift up the lowest sinner. He did not curl His lip and assume a lofty attitude and flaunt His innocence by reminding the populace that He "had never been interested in those things!"

Your writer has tried her share and more of the pleasures of the world. And yet there are things she has never tried, simply because they did not interest her. But, do I have a right to curl my lip at those who have fallen on those points? Does my innocence of their particular sin give me a sense of purity on that point? If I think it does, God forgive me! I am not allowing Jesus Christ to live through me if this is so. Jesus was pure—not pompously innocent. And I am pure because He has made me pure.

Perhaps you have never loved the taste of whiskey. Perhaps you have never stolen anything. Perhaps you have never broken up a home. But, have you never shaded the truth in a conversation? Have you never told a white lie? Have you never lost your temper? Have you never criticized a fellow human being? Have you never been quick to fly to your own defense? Have you never been jealous? Have you never felt sorry for yourself? Are these not sins? Are they not transgressions for which He was wounded? Is anyone alive completely innocent of all these sins of the disposition? No. No one. But we can be made pure, thanks be to Him who "increased in wisdom and in stature"; who grew up into the maturity of deep sympathy and understanding of the failures of men; who not only expects us to do the same, but who daily offers us His grace and strength that we might be able to do it.

5

His Purpose for Other People

*I*n my own life, I have found that if I am truly following Christ, as a disciple follows his master, I do not have to concern myself about—myself. I do not have to wonder whether or not I will be at the right place at the right time in order to accomplish a certain end. I do not have to pick my friends. I do not need, even as a Christian, to hand out solutions to others in need. I do not need to do anything but obey the One whom I profess to trust enough to follow.

It is not easy for a convinced follower of Christ to keep silent many times when the answer to another's problem seems so evident. But there are times when the problems and sorrows of humanity are too terrible for words. And sympathetic silence, deep with the presence of Christ, performs its own miracles. We must be able to express our faith in words, but actions speak louder than words every time. We must not be disturbed if we do not always have the answer. But every minute of our lives we must be the answer.

We do not need to have the answer, but we do need to be the answer.

This is simply said, but not simply done. Coming completely into the viewpoint of Jesus Christ is painful, because it means the dying out of our own points of view. But it also means the birth in us of His point of view, and that is added pain, since birth is usually more painful than death.

We must decide whether or not we are willing to "fill up that which is behind of the afflictions of Christ." Either we are willing or we are not willing. Only we can decide.

But if, as I pray will be true, you decide within your own heart that you want to "walk in the light as he is in the light," in close discipleship with the Master, on an intimate, friendship basis, then there is still another aspect of His viewpoint which you must take for your own: You must completely identify yourself with His purpose for other people.

The real meaning of this is not apparent at first. At least the apparent meaning is far from the entire meaning. At first glance we would think this means that since He said, "Go ye into all the world and make disciples," our efforts toward bringing others into the Christian life would constitute "identifying ourselves with His purpose for other people."

This is true. But it is only part of the deepest meaning of complete identification with His intent in the individual lives of those with whom we come in contact. We simply cannot help winning some if we ourselves are in complete contact with Christ. We cannot be in contact with Him, unless He indwells us and lives again on this earth in our bodies. And since He Himself said: "I, if I be lifted up . . . will draw all men unto me," we must, if His words are true, win some. Those of us who love Him and rejoice in the fullness of the wonder of the life hid with Christ in God find it difficult to keep still about this enchanted life. We don't witness because we believe it is expected of us. We simply do it because we can't help it. And so, winning others, as essential as it is, comes as a fruit of belonging entirely.

And we, who mean to go all the way with Him, must delve deeper and find still other ways of identifying ourselves with His purpose in other lives.

In my experience with this deeper delving, I have stumbled and blundered most noticeably at the times when I felt perfectly justified in using my common sense. I do not believe we can repeat too often the dust-raising truth that if common sense had been enough, Jesus Christ would not have needed to die!

Let me illustrate by a personal experience. Sometime ago after a broadcast I was asked to talk to a brilliant actor, who had struggled vainly with the bottle for years. Now, normally the opportunity to talk with anyone from my old world B.C. is one of the dear delights of my heart, but this particular request seemed to offer a few serious complications. I hesitated because a travel schedule had given me only four hours sleep the night before, the broadcast was an unusually difficult one to direct, and I was scheduled to leave town a bit after dawn the next morning for three speaking engagements in two different cities in one day.

I have long since learned that mere physical fatigue need not stop Christ's work for long. If we stay attached to the Vine, we are constantly in line to receive the continuous flow of living water. And so, trying His strength has turned into an exciting experience. I was not worried about feeling tired. But I did hesitate momentarily for this reason: what about the three congregations of people waiting to hear me the next day? Was I being fair to drag in a tired, limp excuse for a speaker when so many people were involved? Common sense would have said: "Consider the previously made engagements. This actor lives in Chicago. You can talk to him when you come back! You know it will be well after midnight before you get to bed if you get involved in a conversation of that type."

Common sense said that. But I asked Jesus what His purpose in this actor's life was—for that night! I got no answer at once. But after about ten minutes in the silence with the One in whose will I want to live every minute, I had my answer. And after our conversation that night, driving home alone, my friend, the actor, stopped his car, put his head down on the steering wheel and received Jesus as his Saviour and his Lord. Having been very much aware of Christ's complete mastership of my every action and thought that night, I had talked at length about that aspect of the Christian life. So when my friend stepped "in," he knew it meant turning his back on himself—completely. The fact that Jesus mastered me intrigued him. He came in all the way! Jesus does not always figure in numbers. And we cannot "figure" His purpose from our viewpoint. We must do our looking and our acting—every minute of every hour of every day—from the viewpoint of Christ!

6

Self-realization vs. Self-expenditure (I)

*T*here is something definitely attractive in the schools of "new thought" and the cults of self-development. Much of their positive thinking could make more victorious Christians of the true followers of the divine Son of God, Jesus of Nazareth, whom the cultists merely admire as a great man. After all, Jesus Himself said, "*Let* not your heart be troubled." That requires some positive affirming on our part. (However, it is a mystery to me how an unregenerate person, a mere imitator of Christ, *could* simply ignore the pieces and let not his heart be troubled if that heart found itself in a shattered state.) There *is* something attractive about the self-development cults. In fact, it is so attractive that they are drawing off bored, tired, nominal Christians into their ranks every day!

And what is this attraction? The bane of the Christian's existence! *Self.* But to the man outside of Christ, the most important person in the world is *himself.* And when a religion (such as Hinduism) or a new thought school (such as the various scientific pseudo-Christian movements) encourages a man to "bring out the best within" and "develop" that all important person—himself, naturally he is going to summon his fellow man and follow after the group that tells him he's going to be just fine when he gets the best in him all shined up and declared righteousness by—himself!

I repeat that reborn Christians could take some pointers here. Once we have dumped our own sinful selves into the hands of Jesus Christ our Redeemer, *then* we can expect the very best from those redeemed selves. If we cannot, in fact, if we *do* not, we underestimate our Redeemer. I believe that a "new creature," by the power of the indwelling Holy Spirit, *can* "let not" his heart be troubled! He is *enabled* to do it. He is not doing it under his own human steam; he is *enabled* to do it by Christ's indwelling presence.

None of this is new to the thoughtful disciple of Christ. But it is needed to preface what we must consider together now, as we move toward the end of our thinking on some of the characteristics of the true disciple of Jesus Christ. Here is the focal point of this last characteristic which space permits us to discuss: We must shift our perspective from *self-realization* to *self-expenditure!*

If we are to be disciples, we must have the viewpoint of Christ, and in order to have His viewpoint, we must stop trying to *realize* our *selves,* and begin *spending ourselves* for Him! Your writer, back in her B.C. days, was an accomplished spendthrift. Now, the Lord has taken that sin, turned it inside out, redeemed it, but is still *fulfilling* that desire to spend by allowing me the unspeakable joy and stimulus of *spending myself for Him!* I have found Jesus Christ to be the kind of God who never asks us to give up a single thing which He does not replace with "good measure pressed down . . . and running over"! When my dear friend, Ellen, led me into the presence of the One who transformed my life, she needed at the last moment to urge me only to this extent: "Give Him all of your life, and He will hurl all of His life back into its place!"

Could I resist an exchange like that? No, I could not. Thank God, I did not. And although the deep-down excitement that flooded my very being that day, October 2, 1949, when this eternal transaction was made between myself and my Saviour, has ebbed and flowed at times, not once have I lost sight of the fact that in the terms of that eternal transaction, *I* had promised to give Him *all of my* life. I became aware also that the transaction was continuous as well as instantaneous. As with all of us, at times I have jerked myself back from His hands, and have started "throwing cues" according to what I considered good timing. But at no time in my entire life have I known heart misery to equal my own when I have done this—even for a few minutes! And so, my soul vibrates with joy that I have been made aware that if I continue to give to Him, He continues to give to me—good measure, pressed down, and shaken together, and running over!

And when I speak of spending myself, I do not mean the long tiring trips and loss of sleep entailed by a top-heavy speaking schedule. I do not mean the nights spent in pounding the type-writer in order to meet script and book deadlines. These could easily fall into the category of *self-realization—if* my conception of self-expenditure ended there!

But, as a disciple of Jesus Christ, I believe that we have no right to be anything but door mats to every human being who does not know the *full measure* of joy we know in belonging to Jesus personally. And that statement should be examined closely, because it implies much more than it states. "Every human being who does not know the full measure of joy" might seem to mean every *non-believer.* But it means much more than that. I feel ashamed if for His sake, I am at times unwilling to be or careless about being "broken bread and poured out wine" for all Christians who have *not* found the *fullness* of the life hid with Christ in God. I have wept into my pillow many nights because of the multitudes of unhappy, unvictorious, worried, anxious Christians with whom I have spoken here and there. And because I have finally yielded my own stubborn (converted) self into the hands of Him who surrendered His life for *me,* I can only be "broken bread and poured out wine" until these anxious Christians as well as the non-believers with whom I come in contact are brought into the fullness of the life hid with Christ in God!

If we are trying to realize the best in ourselves and save our energies for our own troubles, we do not have the viewpoint of Jesus Christ. We are *saving* ourselves in the face of what He did to save us *from* ourselves! We are saving ourselves when, for love of Him, we should be *spending* ourselves!

7

Self-realization vs. Self-expenditure (II)

(I could fill the pages of an entire book with what I have discovered about the miracles that result in a redeemed human life when the will is fully surrendered to Jesus Christ. A fully surrendered will and a completely yielded life mean a life of true discipleship, with fruit hanging from every thriving branch. Christ allows the fruit to grow on the branches while He, the Vine, quietly and lovingly supports and feeds each branch with His own life!)

We continue thinking together on this essential characteristic of the true disciple: self-expenditure in place of self-realization.

We resign as masters of the universe and allow Christ to take over at conversion. But, just as the same basic law of nature that brings the bud to the apple tree for the first time continues operative between the Creator and the apple tree for the duration of the tree's life, so the same divine law that brings about our spiritual rebirth remains operative between the disciple and the Creator forever.

In the deepest sense, perhaps we could say He creates discipleship in us. Our part is to let Him do it! No human being alive prefers in his own raw, human nature, to deny himself for others. No human being prefers to lose his life in order to save it. He prefers to save his life and take his chances on finding still more!

This is not observation culled from tomes on the psychology of human nature. This is fact from your writer's own life B.C. Until Jesus Christ reached down and took me to Himself, my philosophy of life (if such I had in fact) ran something like this: "Get all I can get for myself today and then take my chances on being able to get even more tomorrow!"

This did not make me an unpleasant, greedy creature. This simply made me resemble people. I was generous and kind to those about whom I cared, or who pleased me for one reason or another; but I would not give one iota of myself for someone about whom I did not care. I was the most important person in the world to me. Period.

I probably would not have admitted it then, because indeed, in all honesty, I simply did not see myself that way. How could I? That is looking at human nature through the clear eyes of Christ. He sees anything that comes between Himself and His creatures for whom He died, as Sin. And the self in that creation is the root of all that comes between. My overdose of self blinded me to myself!

With these stinging truths in mind, examine your Christian life with me—right now, as I examine mine under the light of Him who is light. Is your cup running over? Is mine? If they are not, they should be! Jesus has plenty of living water, and if our cups are only half full it must mean they are simply not clean enough for Him to fill. He will not, He cannot pour His living water into a dirty cup.

Now, we can soil our cups and pitchers in many ways. Worry, fear, anxiety, stubbornness, jealousy, bitterness, resentment, temper, a critical nature, a sharp tongue—any or all of these and more can so smudge our lives that the living water, because of God's own holy nature, cannot be poured into them!

But the most frequent cause of smudge among Christians which I have found is this: The seemingly unthinking way in which we continue to live our own lives. When I say

35

"unthinking," I mean that it is almost as though many are innocent of the fact that they are continuing to live their own lives. We
attend our churches, work among the church groups, serve on
committees, teach classes, tithe, give religious books to non-
believers, intercede in prayer, keep our moral lives above
reproach—and yet, we are living self-lives. Our families and our
homes and our offices and our church activities are in the center
of our lives. All for the glory of God, of course, we strive to do a
better job than the other fellow did. Our churches are filled with
well-meaning, hard-working, respectable Christian men and
women who have their Christian selves in the center of their lives
and not the person of Jesus Christ!

Jesus Christ's person was magnetic and powerful enough literally to pull me out of a life of paganism and draw me to Himself.
Perhaps it is simpler (not easier, but simpler) for me to keep Him
in the center of my life. After having steamed through thirty-three
years under a full head of self-realization, I can do nothing now
but shift completely to the viewpoint of the One who gentled my
striving sinful spirit and restored me to the freedom and fulfillment He meant me to have "in the beginning."

You may spend more nights a week on church work than you
spend with your family. But what would be your reaction if an
alcoholic called you on the telephone at 3:30 A.M. and began
mumbling and mouthing at you about the tough way life treats
him? I may write half the night and speak four times the next day,
but how much of the spirit of Christ will I show when, at the close
of the last speaking date that next day (when my eye-lids are being
propped open by the grace of God), some well-rested Christian
brother comes up to me and says, "I'm glad God is no respecter of
persons and that he saved you, Miss Price, but I'm sorry you had
to sink so low first. And another thing, Miss Price, on your radio
program seven weeks ago you said that 'whosoever believeth in
him should not perish,' and it should have been 'whosoever
believeth on him!'" Will I smile at that well-meaning brother and

offer him my hand, mindful of the nail prints in the hand of the One who was no respecter of persons (thank God!) when He did reach down to save me? Will I view life from the perspective of my own touchy self, or have I truly shifted my perspective from self-realization, from self-protection, to self-expenditure?

What of the Christians who have never invited a non-believer to their homes for dinner? Who refuse to entertain a new, stumbling Christian because that new Christian still smokes? Who keep themselves so busy with breaking fancy cakes and pouring countless cups of coffee for the sake of Christian fellowship that they have no time left to be "broken bread and poured out wine" for the sake of bringing some desperate, sin-shackled man or woman into the fellowship of Christ?

We cannot condemn our Christian brothers when we face these facts. I must confess I did at first, so stunned was I to see how complacently the average Christian moves through his respectable and protected life, literally ignoring those outside the walls of his own particular doctrinal belief! Having been "out there" and left alone by Christians for so long, my heart broke for Jesus' sake; and being still carnal, at first I condemned in my heart. Now, my heart still breaks for Jesus' sake, but my condemnation has turned, by His grace, to intercession for those comfortable Christian brothers and sisters who have not found the fullness and the joy of complete self-expenditure for the One who "is not willing that any should perish!"

DISCOVERIES

. . . Concerning My Reason for Living

8

To Me to Live Is Not to Be Religious

Opening another line of discovery together, let us ask ourselves this question: Can I honestly and without reservation say, "To me to live is *Christ*"?

As disciples, *if* we are true disciples, this must be entirely a reality with us. And since we can delude ourselves and fool our friends quite innocently on this point, I feel we must give it careful scrutiny. Just what exactly does it mean? What does it mean to you when you read or repeat, "To me to live is Christ"? What does it *do* to you? Does it ring any bells? Does it cause your heart to race with joy? Does it make you want to look up, just for the sake of knowing that you can look up and see no shadow between you and this Christ?

Or is it just another Scripture text?

If it is that, repeating the words or reading them from the Bible will do no more than stir up that respect which we hold for the written-down revelation of God which we have between the covers of the greatest Book.

Or, perhaps it arouses no more than admiration within you for the childlike humility of St. Paul, who allowed himself to be changed from a Christ-hater to one who could say without reservation that for him to live was Christ.

This altogether startling phrase could and does bring about many reactions ranging from utter perplexity in the non-believer to the quiet ecstasy of the saint whose lips form the words with the joy and certainty that add up to "foolishness to the natural man."

We pass by these varied reactions now, however, to look at the ways in which sincere, well-meaning, devoted Christians can unconsciously misinterpret it or rephrase it. Saint Paul said: "To me to live is Christ." But how easy is it for us to say: "To me to live is to be *religious!*"

Does *this* interpretation of the immortal words ring any bells with you? With me, I am afraid if it rang anything it would be a buzzer! I do not even like the sound of the word "religious." I like it even less than I did before I surrendered my life to Christ. There are many religions. Basically they are all attempts to bridge the gap between God and man. But in only one of them, the Gospel of Christ, does God reach down for man. In the others, man reaches vainly, pathetically, anxiously toward God. And so to me, living the Christian life is not "being religious" it is belonging to a *Person* who has reached down for me. And yet, according to the lack of vitality, the lack of dynamic, the frigidity of many so-called Christian lives, this text *must* be one of the most misinterpreted texts in the entire Bible! If I say, "To me to live is to be religious," I am missing the mark entirely.

I am not only missing the mark the Lord expects me to hit, I am putting emphasis entirely in the wrong place. For example, if we say, "To me to live is to be religious," how quickly we can tread respectably and stiffly into formalism! If we say, "To me to live is to be religious," how swiftly we will mount our pedestals and attempt to serve those beneath us, without once bending our necks to look at their agony of soul and mind and body. If we say, "To me to live is to be religious," how *unlike* our Lord we will become!

For can we be like Him if we are garbed in our religious regalia high atop our pious pedestals? From that vantage point can we show the world the brotherly love of the One who stood in line with sinners to wait his turn to be baptized? Can we show the world the gentle heart of the One who always took time to heal a blind beggar and take notice of a widow's mite? Can we show the world the almighty meekness of the One who turned His blood-filled eyes to the Father to ask forgiveness for those who caused Him to shed that blood drop by precious drop? Can we, sitting on our religious pedestals, convince the world that we know He hung there for our sakes too? Can we show forth from a pedestal the nature of the One who was born so low no sinner could possibly claim a more lowly beginning? Can we sit on a religious pinnacle and convince anyone that we follow a Lord who was purposely born in a stable? Can we proclaim from atop our pious perches that we serve the One who wants to wash the feet of the world through us?

After having lived in darkness, I am much aware of the freedom and satisfaction of having the world know there is no stain or shadow in my life now; that I am forgiven by and restored to my Father. But if I say, "To me to live is to be religious or respectable or respected," I am putting the blessings of my new life in the center and not the Blesser! If I am impressed with my new purity, can I expect Jesus to be able to reach down through me and lift up a bitter atheist who quite naturally hates my purity? Only when I see my own holiness as His holiness poured into my life, only when I see my victorious living as a result of having emptied my life of my self and of having that empty space filled with His victorious Spirit, then and only then can His love flow through me to those in need, to those whom He needs as they need Him. To me to live is not to be religious. To me to live is— Christ!

Is it true with you? It can be before you turn this page.

9

To Me to Live Is Not to Serve Humanity

There are many, too many words which are consciously or unconsciously substituted for the name of Christ in the penetrating phrase of Paul: "To me to live is Christ."

We have already looked at some length into the dangers of living as though the phrase read, "To me to live is to be religious." Now let us face together another substitution which is so often made in this verse in place of His wonderful name. Do not many thousands of well-meaning Christians revise the phrase to read this way: "To me to live is to serve humanity"?

Now, on this point, I want to be clearly understood. As a new Christian, I am daily surprised and sometimes shocked at the seeming indifference to the sufferings of humanity shown by many of those who make the most effusive Christian professions. Jesus did not say we had to believe in His atonement; He simply died and made it a reality for us when we take it by faith. He did not demand that we believe in His resurrection; He simply—arose! He does not demand that we believe in His coming again; He will simply return one day in His time. In fact, Jesus did not demand that we believe very many things on a list. But He did command that we love one another. He asked us to love God with our whole being and to love our neighbors as we love ourselves!

If we remember that on our own we are the most important persons in the world to ourselves, that last is quite an order. Literally, of course, it does not only mean the person who lives next door or even in our neighborhood. It means every human being on earth. I do not believe it means that we can respond emotionally in a positive way to every creature, but it surely does mean that we must be as concerned for the welfare of others as we are for ourselves. And that is a big order! Do we fly to the defense of others as quickly as we fly to the defense of ourselves?

No comment.

Do we pity members of the church down the street or of the opposition political party when failure strikes them as we pity our precious selves?

No comment.

Why? Because we do not love and want to serve our fellow man as we love and want to serve ourselves or those to whom we happen to react favorably!

Daily I have to spend time before the humble Christ, who asked me to love everyone, to allow Him to touch and transform the tender, sore spots of self-esteem and snobbery still showing up in me. It hurts to have them touched. It makes me reel and tremble for the moment to see Him changing—actually changing one of my old precious opinions of a certain person into His opinion of that person. It knocks crutch after crutch out from under my swaying ego. But when the operation is done, how relieved I am not to have to be upset or irritated the next time that particular kind of person enters my life. How safe I feel then not to need that crutch to prop up my self-esteem any longer.

Much of the barb throwing, however, between the conservatives and the liberals of Christendom, has resulted from this very point of serving humanity. The liberals tend to rephrase Paul this way: "To me to live is to serve humanity!" One such liberal friend of mine made a pithy statement to me not long ago. She contends that the liberals need to love the Lord more and the fundamentalists need to love the people more! I agree.

A social Gospel alone, where the needs of humanity are placed uppermost, is but a half-gospel. But those of us who believe in a full Gospel must, for the sake of Christ, learn to love the whole man—not just his soul. Just as we must also want to save his soul and not merely his body and his mind.

It is easy, exceedingly easy, to become eccentric in our sincere efforts to be true disciples of Christ. And if the emphasis is put upon any one corner of the life, it tips! So, just as "To me to live is to be religious" is off center, so is "To me to live is to serve humanity" off-center. *Eccentric.*

Thousands upon thousands of men and women all over the world spend their lives pouring themselves out for humanity. This is the highest human level of life. Truly, no one could deny that this is the highest natural life. But, the true disciple of the divine Jesus Christ, God incarnate, does not need to be tied to the earth by even this highest human or natural achievement. Only the twice-born Christian has access to the *super*-human and the *super*-natural, by the power of the indwelling Holy Spirit. We are insured against heart-break this way. Since the Person of the Holy Spirit is one with God the Father and with Jesus Christ, He will not "let Himself down" as He lives His life through us! Humanity will turn its back on a man. Divinity through Jesus Christ will turn the man into His own image. Humanity will break a man's heart; Divinity, through Jesus Christ, will mend that heart.

Serving humanity is a noble aim. But it is only one of the inevitable fruits of the life of the man or woman whose every thought and word and deed shout to the world:

"To me to live is Christ!"

10

To Me to Live Is Not to Serve Christ

We will speak elsewhere in this book about the startling fact (to some) that Jesus Christ does not want our *talents*, He wants *us*. Of course, He wants our talents too, but not *without all the rest* of us thrown in. With this in mind, and with our minds wide open, let us look still more deeply into a popular rephrasing of the all-inclusive statement of St. Paul: "To me to live is Christ."

We have thought together so far upon these rephrasings of Paul's profound declaration: "To me to live is to be *religious*"; then, "To me to live is to serve *humanity*." Now we go even deeper than these two convenient interpretations. We look honestly at an interpretation of the immortal words which would at first glance seem to be synonymous with what Paul was actually saying. Consider this with me: "To me to live is to *serve* Christ!"

"To me to live is to serve Christ!" "To me to live is Christ!" Did not this Christ say, "Go ye into all the world and make disciples"? Did not this same Christ say, "The fields are white to harvest"? Yes, He did. And so, we must lift many of the top layers off the familiar testimony of Paul in order to reach the place at the heart of *his* statement which shows us the grave difference between a simple *belonging* to Christ and merely *serving* Him!

For reasons known only to Him, my Master put me almost immediately into the thick of the harvest field. One year and one week after my conversion to Jesus Christ, I stood in the control room of a large radio studio directing the only big time Christian dramatic program about lives which had been transformed as mine had been transformed by the touch of the Holy Spirit of God. The program was well named—"Unshackled." Every fiber of its writer-producer's being vibrated with the consciousness that she, too, had been "unshackled," just as surely and from just as defeated a life as any man or woman who reached the black alleys and the dusty gutters of Chicago's Skid Row! The mail count climbed, the studio audience increased, magazine writers began to call for interviews and the requests for speaking dates poured in—more each month, until there were not enough days in the week to fill them and still continue writing "Unshackled." People clasped my hand and from sincere hearts said: "Oh, how wonderfully the Lord is using you! How glorious is your great *service* for Christ!"

And my eyes filled with tears of wonder along with theirs as I moved through the glowing days with the amazement of a child suddenly set down in a toy shop a hundred miles square! Offers came for more radio programs, for TV programs, for magazine articles, for columns. And instead of feeding my previously over-sized vanity, by His grace the opposite took place! I began to understand what Paul meant when he said: "I determined not to know anything among you, save Jesus Christ, and him crucified."

The Crucified Himself overshadowed me *and* my new Christian service! I became more and more drawn toward the pursuit of a deeper personal walk with Christ, my new Lord. I was grateful for the confidence of God's people who urged me into wider and wider fields of service, and I recognized the need for it. Daily, I became more and more aware of how *much* Jesus needed disciples in whose very bodies He could walk the earth once more, ministering to his lost sheep! After having been one of those lost sheep for thirty-three years, my arms ached to take every troubled human being in the world to my heart, where I knew they would at least be close to Him who held my heart forever.

And yet, above the din of the world's need, above the definite call into a life of service, I heard the unmistakable high, clear notes of the call of His heart to mine: "Come unto me . . . Learn of me . . . Learn of me!"

I answered His call to my heart. In just three short years, I have learned to walk with Jesus, as the disciples walked with Him down the dusty roads two thousand years ago. This is no accomplishment of mine other than my willingness to seek Him before I sought greater fields of His service. It is a warm and wonderful feeling to share the fellowship of the blessed community as one after another of God's people clasps my hand in love and encouragement, but following Him into the deeper life means less of this and more hours of silence and weeping and crying out for mercy as one after another of my pet opinions and prejudices and abilities are cut into and changed and reshaped according to His intention! It is far easier to serve than to be changed. It is easier to speak from a platform than to be spoken to in the silence by the One who sees my heart laid bare. It is easier to write and direct an exciting dramatic radio program than it is to spend the cold morning hours on my knees being redirected by Him who alone knows His purpose for my life. But when I am altogether His, and walking minute by minute in His strength, He can automatically use me more because then and only then can He serve others through me. As long as I'm there, He can't get through, can He?

No, and if you have not discovered this in your own life, I beg of you to discover it now in the silence with Him, so that you too may say, "To me to live is not to serve Christ; to me to live is Christ!"

11

To Me to Live Is Not to Be Christlike

In digging into the depths of the meaning of Saint Paul's glowing testimony, "To me to live is Christ," we should seem to be able to come up with a conclusion right now and then move on to another thought. We should be able to tie it all up this way: if we say, "To me to live is to be or to do—anything," we are on the wrong track! The little infinitives should give us the key. And indeed in a general sense, they do. The very implication of the "to be" or "to do" shifts us into the place where, according to Paul, Christ must be.

And yet, there is one more "to be" which is so often used innocently when one is trying to let his or her life say, "To me to live is Christ," that I feel we must dig into this one before we move on. What is it? Just this: "To me to live is to be Christlike!"

Have you ever tripped over this one? I have many times. Those of you who, along with me, have been brought into a close, personal relationship with Christ out of another world, may have tripped over this rephrasing of Paul's famous line even more than those who have lived merely respectably even Christian lives. Nevertheless, I feel quite sure that if we face facts honestly, we can all say that at one time or another in our Christian lives we have been absorbed with our own holiness! Or, we have become so preoccupied with checking up on our own spiritual growth that we have neglected or have completely forgotten that the Lord God said, "Feed my sheep" as well as, "Be ye holy." We can become so taken up with wishful thinking concerning our own spiritual growth that without realizing it we are again in the center of our own lives and Christ and His purpose have been moved to the margins.

It is well to remember the familiar story about the little girl who kept digging up the seed she had planted to see whether or not it was growing! Disciples of Jesus Christ who become fascinated with their own potential resemblance to their Master slip dangerously near the brink of the so-called "new thought" cults. Absorption with our own holiness or our spiritual progress is *self-development*, isn't it? If Jesus did a finished work on the Cross, do we need to do more than stay in position to have His great redemption become a completed reality in our lives?

Please do not misunderstand me. I do not mean to imply that we must not "walk in the light as he is in the light," that we must not keep constant vigil over our relationship with Christ. I merely mean that those well-intentioned men and women who become impressed with their own growing resemblance to Christ *or* depressed by their growing lack of it are quite likely to put a sudden stop to the entire procedure. The Living Water will sink to a low level and stagnate. And we will wonder why when we have been giving such implicit attention to our own spiritual growth!

Did not our Master say we could not add one inch to our height by any effort of our own? Did He not say that He is the Vine and we are the branches? And did you ever hear of a branch clenching its leaves together in verdant agony as it pleaded with the vine to send down more sap? No. The branch merely stays fastened on to the vine, and *expects* the supply of life-giving sap sufficient for its growth. The lilies and the tall green corn of the fields just stay in position to receive the sunlight and the rain and the nutriment from the soil.

Mrs. Anna Mow (happily for me, a friend of mine), for years a missionary to India, and now on the faculty of Bethany Biblical Seminary in Chicago, gives this formula for one of those knotty, black days when we are inclined to put our spiritual conditions in the center of our attention. First of all, Sister Anna checks whether or not she has had enough sleep the night before. If she has had, she checks the possibility that she has hurt someone inadvertently or intentionally. If this is not true, then she goes over the resentment and bitterness and self-pity departments. If all is well there and she can simply find no reason for her spiritual indigestion, she throws back her head and laughs her contagious, characteristic laugh and says: "All right, *you* stay here, Anna Mow, I'm going on with the Lord!" I've tried it too. It works.

God did say, "Be ye holy as I am holy"; but no amount of fascination with our holiness or lack of it will *increase* our holiness. He tells us to be holy, but then He sets about making us that way *when* we yield ourselves utterly into His lovely hands!

My dear friend and companion, Ellen Riley, twinkles with good-humored laughter at herself when she tells of her first years as a Christian. She was organist at the Methodist church back in our home town of Charleston, West Virginia. And so fascinated was she with the change in her personality after her conversion to Christ that she used to sneak long, admiring glances at herself in the mirror above the console of the big pipe organ on a Sunday morning as she sighed inwardly and thought: *Oh, isn't it wonderful? I'm growing more spiritual looking every day I live!*

This story always brings a relieved laugh from any group of Christians, because we are all guilty of becoming preoccupied in greater or lesser degrees with our own purity. And any movement of our *full* attention away from the face of Christ toward even our own Christlikeness is a dangerous and a confusing thing. It is risky for us and confusing for those who depend upon us. As glorious as holiness is when we see it actually happening in our own lives, we must not say, "To me to live is to be Christlike"; we must say and mean and then our very lives will proclaim "To me to live *is* Christ!"

To Me to Live Is Christ!

We have seen that it is an easy procedure for a well-meaning follower of Jesus Christ innocently to rephrase the singing words of Saint Paul: "To me to live is Christ!" We have seen how easy it is to say, "To me to live is to be religious, to serve humanity, to serve Christ, to be Christlike!" We have also seen that any of these variations will result in sub-Christianity and an unvictorious life. Why? Because to a true disciple of Christ, his life is not a religion; it is the simple following of a living Person. And to him, this immortal testimony comes as naturally as breathing:

"To me to live is—Christ!"

Your writer would claim this testimony as her own in closing this group of discoveries. To me to live is the person of Jesus Christ. And this is true for many reasons. Among them: I was not led into a way of life when I received Jesus Christ as my own personal Saviour and Lord and Master. I have dedicated this little book to the disciple of Christ who led me so carefully and so lovingly, not into a "better way of life," but into a close, intimate walk with the person of my new Lord!

I never think on the fact that I have found a better way to live on this earth. But I think often and joyfully about the living Person who so recently drew me unto Himself—forever! I don't think, "Now, I can stay out of trouble"; but I live by the very fact of the Person who overcame my trouble on the Cross! I don't think, "Now, God will comfort me when tragedy strikes my life"; but I do rest in the tremendous knowledge that should tragedy strike, the person of the Holy Spirit will be right there to show me how to use that tragedy for His glory! I don't think, "Now that I'm a Christian, I won't drink anymore, or throw my money to the four winds and wind up deeper and deeper in debt!" This is all true, but I don't dwell on that negative aspect of the whole thing. Instead, I just let the involuntary smile play away at the corners of my mouth because now that I belong to Jesus and He belongs to me, I don't need to drink. And I've found the fulfillment and excitement in Him, on which I used to have to spend my money! I don't think, "Now that I'm a Christian I must tithe and live conservatively"; I just return every dollar to Him at the outset and let Him spend it for me! "To me to live is Christ" because I was led, not into a better way of life, but into an intimate minute by minute walk with a living Person.

I have dedicated this book of discoveries to the one who convinced me not merely of a "plan of salvation" (I wouldn't have understood that phrase at all!), but who introduced me personally to the Saviour, who did His own convincing in my heart and mind. As beautiful and as awe inspiring as is the divine plan of God for the salvation of His lost sheep, it has little or no meaning for the pagan mind. Mine was a completely pagan mind, believing in nothing higher than my own wits. And so, the most careful intellectual or Scriptural explanation of the plan of salvation would have confused me; and since my pride would not allow me to admit confusion of any sort, any theological explanation of salvation would only have served to slam the door of the kingdom in my face!

But, thanks be to Christ, He had convinced my friend of His own personal wonder. He had drawn her unto Himself out of a time of heartbreak and personal tragedy. She had found Him to be the living Lord with healing in His hands. She loved Him with all her heart when she met me, and she merely stood aside and let Him woo me unto Himself. "To me to live is Christ," because I was not merely intellectually convinced of a divine plan for the salvation of my eternal soul. I was permitted to fall in love with the Lover of my soul, Jesus Christ, the living Son of God!

This little book is humbly dedicated to the disciple of Jesus Christ, who through her consecrated life allowed Him to confront me face to face with Himself. She did not attempt to frighten me into the kingdom by threatening me with an almost superstitious wielding of the written-down revelation of God, the Holy Bible. She knew I did not believe the Bible at all. And if she had had only Scripture texts (as dynamic as they are to me now) then, she would have been fighting a losing battle. She won me to Christ, though, because she allowed the Holy Spirit full rein in her mind and imagination, and therefore guaranteed no blunders in timing. I was led gently and completely into a new life with Jesus Christ in a hotel room, and there was no one present with me but my friend, Ellen, and Jesus Christ!

After He had transformed me, then my desire for the wonder of the Holy Scriptures leaped into being; but if for some fantastic reason I should be told that the New Testament is all a mistake, I would still go right on following my living Lord! After all, the early Christians in the upper room had only the Holy Spirit Himself. If some reader decides from this paragraph that I do not believe with all my heart in the inspired Word of God as we have it in the Bible, I beg of him to reread this meditation again more thoughtfully. But to me to live is not the Bible, because the Word became flesh, not printer's ink; and as glorious as is that Spirit-inspired account of God's divine nature and plan, its light is to me the person of my Lord, Jesus Christ! Without reservation, "To me to live is Christ."

And this same Christ, available to me personally through His Holy Spirit, has proved Himself to me; so that I am not only a converted Christian, I am a totally convinced Christian, "strengthened with might by His Spirit in the inner man." Jesus Christ, the Holy Spirit and the Father have at last become One to me. And so, more than ever now, "To me to live is Christ," because all I need know of the Father is what He showed me in His Son.

DISCOVERIES
. . . Concerning a Number of Wonder-filled Things

13

Are You Free?

Are you free? I know you live in a free country, but are you really free? I have lived in a free country since my first birth on June 22, 1916, but I have only been free since my second birth, October 2, 1949, when I was invaded from above and set free of my self by the transforming touch of the Holy Spirit!

This startling fact is almost humorous when I confess that most of those thirty-three years which passed between my first birth and my second birth were spent in loud protest against any kind of restraint and even louder declarations of personal freedom. I had to be free! I wanted everyone to leave me alone to live my own life as I wanted to live it—in freedom. I was a rebel from the word "go." I hated confinement and convention. I detested being disciplined. In fact to me "discipline" was the most unpleasant word outside of "obedience" in the entire English language, until I was thirty-three years old. Although my years numbered thirty-three, I had stopped growing emotionally at about a precocious sixteen. In my thirties, at the head of my own business, I was still asserting myself like an adolescent, kicking and yelling at life: "Leave me alone . . . I'm the type who just has to be free!" All this is too sadly true of some Christians who demand to remain the type that insists, "This is the way I am!" *Can't* Jesus Christ change our natures?

But back to freedom. In spite of the kicking and yelling for freedom all my thirty-three years, only now that I am at last free of my self, am I truly free. And, hold on to your hats, I found this freedom through obedience and discipline!

If we examine the inorganic matter in the bottom of a pool, we find it to be trapped there as dead matter. But, when that dead, inorganic matter is invaded from above by the root of a water lily, drawn up and confined within the disciplinary process of giving of itself to the lily, then and only then is that once-dead matter free to grow. Indeed, for the first time it is free to—live!

Not until I was invaded from above by the Holy Spirit was I free to live. "He that hath the Son hath life; and he that hath not the Son of God hath not life." Now, drawn up into the life of the Lily of the Valley, I am free to give of my once-dead self as nourishment to others. Confined in the glorious disciplinary process of giving of myself to Jesus Christ and His sheep, I am, for the very first time, free to grow!

Take the train off its track, and how far does it advance toward its destination? Suppose the engineer decides to indulge a sudden whim of his own and make the run between Chicago and Denver without a track to confine him. Will his passengers ever reach Denver?

Only in complete holy obedience to the merest whisper of Jesus Christ do we truly find the freedom for which we were created. And I firmly believe He created that desire for freedom within us all. The Father's heart grieves when His creatures are chained to earthly habits and beliefs. He created us to be free. And in Himself, through Christ, He provides that freedom.

A missionary friend of mine, a truly radiant Christian, once told me my life now reminded him of a flight he took over India some years ago. He smiled as he recalled the trip. It seems the pilot asked my friend if he would like to fly the plane, assuring him that if he did just as the pilot instructed, all would be well. The missionary agreed to try it. When the pilot said, "Pull this lever," he pulled that lever. When the pilot said, "Push this gear," he pushed that gear and so on.

"And sure enough," my friend beamed, "as long as I obeyed that pilot's every instruction, I was free to fly!"

My brother, the missionary, is right. My life is like that now. As long as I live every moment in complete obedience to the will of Christ—I am free to fly!

What are some of the things which rob Christians of their freedom? Surely, as we mention elsewhere in this book, worry is one of our most constant jailers! I believe that during the time we are worrying, we are actually atheistic. Either we believe Jesus Christ or we do not. He said, "I have overcome the world." Did He? Or is He playing a fiendish cosmic prank upon us? I have, for a year or more, permitted myself the luxury of worry for five minutes at a time and no more. At the end of five minutes, if I am still worried, I go to the nearest mirror, look myself right in the eye and say, "This tremendous thing which worries you is beyond solution. Especially is it too hard for Jesus Christ to handle." Usually, I am restraining a laugh by that time, and when I let it go, the tears of gratitude come with the laugh, and I turn my eyes gladly back upon the face of Him who *gave* me a foolproof "worry-tree" in His Own Cross.

Worry, and fear and self-pity and bitterness and resentment and jealousy and temper and so forth and so forth and so forth can and *do* fence Christians in and prevent them from capering in the freedom Christ died to give us. He died to set the alcoholic free from the bottle, and the dope addict free from the needle, but they are in the minority, and I wonder often at those of us who go about trying to save alcoholics when we are just as shackled to our sins of the spirit in the eyes of Him who wants us to be free!

I have discovered that God's spiritual laws are equally as reliable as his physical laws. If I jump out of a fourteen story window, I don't break the law of gravity, I just illustrate it. When we disobey God's laws, we don't break those laws. They're unbreakable. We simply illustrate them, as we break ourselves over those laws. A pilot who defies the laws of aviation crashes to the earth. He is no longer free to fly. Is the analogy so difficult to apply? Can we not see the freedom in complete and total obedience to Christ? Is Jesus Christ a God of His Word, or is He trying to confuse us?

I believe Him. I believe every word He says! And Jesus Himself said: "If the Son . . . shall make you free, ye shall be free indeed." The Son made me free; free to caper safely and unrestrainedly for the first time in my life, because I am possessed by the Holy Spirit of the One who created in me that longing for freedom. The Son of God has made me free, and I am free indeed.

14

Are You in Love?

Are you in love? Has your heart been touched by the hand of Him who alone knows the deeps of your heart? And has your heart responded? Has it responded to His voice? Has it been transformed by His touch? Has your heart been laid against His heart, there to stay forever?

Are you in love with the Creator of your heart? Are you in love with the Lover of your soul? Is He your Beloved and are you His? Now, this minute . . . tomorrow morning . . . tomorrow night and forever?

I am in love, and the plan of my love is very simple. To some it could be called my theology. To me it is simply the pattern of my love. This is the pattern:

I belong to Christ and He belongs to me!

If you are not in love with Christ as you read these lines, surely you have been in love with someone in your life. And so you will know that when two are in love, the only true happiness for those two comes from being together. If we are separated from the one we love and know the time of reunion is near, don't we count the weeks, then the days, then the hours and then the minutes until we are together again? Did not Jesus pray that we would be one with Him as He is one with the Father? That is the measure of His love for us. He wants not just to be near us, but to be one with us! And by His blessed Holy Spirit, He can literally indwell me. By His Holy Spirit, He can literally indwell you. He can be your Beloved and you can be His. He wants it that way. Do you?

Jesus of Nazareth, risen from the grave, went to sit at the right hand of the Father in heaven. But, oh, my soul trembles and my heart leaps at the wonder of knowing that although Jesus no longer walks the earth as the Man-God, He can still be present in an even more intimate and deeper sense through the person of His Holy Spirit within me! Out of the chaos of a hectic day, through the tense stillness of a sleepless night, the Voice within me whispers, "Peace, be still . . . I will never leave thee, nor forsake thee." In the midst of weeping, my broken heart is touched by the hand of Him who reminds me, "Lo, I am with you always . . . Let not your heart be troubled . . ."

How little we seem to know about love. How often we confuse love with lust or affection or self-love! Our divorce courts are crowded with men and women who want to be rid of each other because the other person didn't turn out to be the kind of ego-inflater he or she had promised to be. Men and women "fall in love" with their own ideas of what the other person should be. They "fall in love" with only the facets of the loved one's personality which happen to please them. I know this is true. In my B.C. days I was very "loving" to my friends who pleased me. So many tragic times we fall in love for what we can get from the relationship.

Close, constant contact with the One who is Love shows us to our shame that love is giving and not receiving. I honestly believe I loved only one living creature unselfishly before Jesus Christ transformed me. I loved my English bulldog with as nearly an unselfish love as my unregenerate nature could muster. And her love for me? It charmed my life. It gave me, many times, a reason for waking up in the morning! I could desert her for hours, stay away from home until dawn, and instead of barking at me and taking me apart in fury when I finally came home, my doggie just about ate me up with joy because I had come back to her at last.

She taught me something about love. My mother's faith in me through the years taught me more about love. My father's loyalty to me no matter what he found out about me taught me still more about love. My brother's devotion to me in spite of the different worlds in which we lived taught me about love. But not until I met Jesus Christ face to face, did I meet Love as it was divinely created.

Divine love: there are no words to enlarge upon it. Nothing begins to describe it. It is complete in itself. It is—divine love. It has transformed my *self*-love into other-love. It has shown me the freedom of pouring myself out at the feet of Him who poured Himself out for me on the Cross! It has touched and transformed my possessiveness into a passion for being completely possessed by Christ. It has given me the freedom of not needing to love myself anymore. He loves me so much, I have no need for self-love, and this sets me free from self-pity, and self-defense, and self-assertion. If I am asked to go the second mile, I am free now to go gladly, knowing that en route, He will press even closer and bind me ever more securely to Himself in divine love.

I wonder at the men and women who follow the chilly reasoning of the cults which propagate the love principle. When a child wants its mother, it doesn't want the mother principle. It wants its mother's arms!

When my heart longs for the God for whom it was created, I do not want the God principle. I want the person of God. I want the divine Son of God, Jesus Christ, whom I may have, through my submission and response to the Third Person of the divine Trinity of God.

When I long for love, I could not be satisfied with the love principle. I want the everlasting arms of my Redeemer beneath me!

We must surrender ourselves utterly, we must yield ourselves completely. And yet, there is another word which I like even better than "yield" or "surrender." That word is "respond." It implies that He needs the response of my love to Him. It makes me feel needed. There is no sweeter emotion in all of life than to feel needed by one's beloved. My Beloved needs me and I need Him.

This same Beloved needs you, too. Does not your heart cry for Him? And will it not continue to cry out for Him until it comes to rest against His heart forever?

15

Are You Satisfied?

Are you satisfied and filled, or are you hungry and longing for more and still more of the wonder you have found in Jesus Christ? At first thought, it would seem that the victorious Christian should answer, "Yes, I am completely satisfied." And when the disciple is one with his Master, truly he is satisfied. But still he longs for more!

We will return to this aspect of satisfaction in a moment, after we have thought together about the restless kind of dissatisfaction which seems to haunt the heart at night and nip at the heels at noon. So many nervous, jittery Christians dodge through life in much the same tense manner as the non-believer, who must make a go of things by his own wits.

As we consider this tormenting dissatisfaction, let us keep it separated from the healthy hunger about which we will speak later on. If you are nervous, if your spiritual cup is dry, if it has been a long, long time since you have had anything to shout about where your Christian life is concerned, face yourself honestly under the searching eyes of Him who promised to fill the hungry with good things! If you are not filled, could it be that God has gone back on His promise to you? Did He promise to fill you with good things and then did He get busy with some other celestial undertaking and forget all about you? Did He run out of living water before He reached your empty cup? If I am cross and restless and dissatisfied, does God have too many children to bless so that I can only reason that He must not be able to get around to blessing me today?

Does the Christ who said, "If any man thirst, let him come unto me, and drink," mean to go on depriving me of water for my spiritual life? Am I to go on worrying and fretting and stewing? Are you to go on being anxious and jealous and bitter? Are we to go on feeling sorry for ourselves because all around us others are bubbling over with living water and eating the bread of life?

Now, wait a minute . . . Let's examine our side of the agreement. Assuming that we have made an eternal transaction with God on the basis of His redemption and have been reborn and given the power to become sons of God, are we keeping our side of the bargain? Are we spending enough time in the presence of God in silent adoration of Him? Are we feeding our minds and our hearts on the spiritual food in His Holy Scriptures? Are we working for God? Are we spending ourselves for Him? Are we "feeding His sheep"?

Are we?

Or, are we expecting a one-hundred percent return from a twenty-five percent investment of ourselves? Of our time? Of our energy? Of our love? Frankly, I can't think of any person on earth who must be more miserable, more restless and more dissatisfied than a part-time, twenty-five percent Christian. If a man has just a little bit of religion, he can no longer enjoy the world's pleasures. He sits in abject misery in the midst of old worldly surroundings where once he reveled and where now he squirms. He sits in church or in a group with victorious, happy Christians and also— squirms! No matter where the poor fellow goes, he is a misfit. He is neither worldly nor Christian. He is divided. He lives in perpetual conflict. He is dissatisfied. And only a complete one hundred percent yielding of his life into the hands of the living Christ can calm his conflict, can unify him into one person again—a whole person, who can move toward a goal once more powered by the Dynamo of God, a man united within himself and with his Creator, a man at peace.

If you are restless and dissatisfied, no doubt you are two people trying to live one life. And it's a losing effort, until you unite all of you with all of Christ.

But what of those of us who are not *dis*satisfied, but who seem to be perpetually *un*satisfied? Is this good? Yes, this is healthy and a sign that we can be filled. We do not really enjoy a good dinner unless we are hungry, do we? So, if you are hungry for more and more and more of Jesus Christ, rejoice! And again, I say rejoice! The pains of hunger are His doing, I believe. He alone can make us want more of Him. He alone can create the hunger within us, just as He alone can satisfy that hunger.

It is very easy for the Devil to disturb us with anxiety over our spiritual condition when those healthy, normal hunger pains begin. He tells us that they are spiritual sickness, spiritual disease. We believe him and become discouraged, and he has the time of his life laughing at us as we writhe and agonize before God, begging to be filled when all we really need is to feast on Jesus Christ, the Bread of Life.

Are you unsatisfied? Are you still hungry? Good. Our Lord does not permit a single need in His children which He Himself cannot and will not fulfill. He longs to fill us with good things. The good things of the Lord stack up on the back stairs of our souls because we simply do not take them!

Let us rejoice in our hunger, all we who are children of God, because He wants to feed His hungry children upon Himself, the eternal Bread of Life.

Isn't it wonderful to be hungry when we can feast on Jesus?

16

Are You Worried?

Are you worried? How much time do you spend each day worrying? How much time do you spend being afraid? Literally millions and millions of men and women are haunted night and day by fears, are nagged night and day by worry. For these millions life is one long desperate struggle; one long, futile search for some kind of peace of mind. Pitifully few ever find it.

The writer, a comparatively new Christian, is oftentimes shocked at the amount of fear and worry and anxiety indulged in by older Christians.

What is worry? I have found two favorite definitions:

"Worry is a cycle of inefficient thought whirling around a center of fear." Read and reread that definition, and its truth will make you stop short! First, because we all know of a certainty that worry does produce inefficiency. A worried mind is never an efficient mind. Then, the very use of the word "whirling" describes the usual behavior of one who worries. Move on in the definition now. "Whirling" around what? The wrong center. "Whirling around a center of fear."

"Fear thou not; for I am with thee . . . I will never leave thee, nor forsake thee."

Are we as Christians supposed to have Jesus Christ in the very center of our lives? Then, how is it that we, too, are guilty of "inefficient thought whirling around a center of fear?"

Another provocative definition of worry goes like this: "Worry is a chronic process of making mountains out of molehills." A Christian woman once looked a friend of mine right in the eye and said sincerely: "Well, if I don't worry, who'll hold things together?"

"Fear not; for, behold, I bring you good tidings of great joy . . . I will never leave thee, nor forsake thee."

With Jesus Christ in the center of our lives, how is it that we continue to worry?

Medical science has long since proved that literally thousands of illnesses are caused directly from worry and tension and anxiety. American Medical Association statistics tell us that well over sixty per cent of all illness is caused by emotional, mental or spiritual disturbances! We know these things, and yet we continue to worry. Even Christians continue to worry. Our churches are pathetically populated with anxious Christians. Nervous Christians clutching doggedly and grimly at their doctrines and their problems instead of becoming "as little children" and resting in the Lord they profess to follow. Why do we do this? Isn't our faith big enough to hold us? Isn't our Lord strong enough to carry our burdens? Must we continue to worry them out ourselves?

"Come unto me, all ye that labour and are heavy laden [with fears and anxieties and worries], and I will give you rest."

We ask: Is there a way out? Is there a way out of fear and anxiety and worry for the tied-up human beings in this old world?

Coming home one night on a local train, I noticed a national magazine on the newsstand in the station. On its cover were splashed these words: NEW DRUGS TO EASE FEAR AND WORRY! I bought the magazine, and found that sure enough, science is gingerly offering a new drug called mephenesin which does, in many cases, offer blessed relaxation from nervous tension. The drug has aided in the improvement of patients with high blood pressure, heart trouble, alcoholism, asthma, etc. It has subdued that demon companion of the anxious—insomnia. A God-sent drug for a certainty. But, the article had a feeble pay-off. Science freely admits that this "anxiety fighter" (mephenesin) holds but one promise: it can show the victim what real relief from tension is. It said in effect that once having experienced the incomparable feeling of complete release and relaxation, many people will be able to go on from there to achieve true peace of mind and body.

This last statement made me want to sit right down and cry. One would think that people had to be talked into wanting relief from fear and worry and anxiety! That they only had to be convinced that they should try for it! Instead of sitting down to cry, however, I decided to write about this problem.

What have we said? "Worry is a cycle of inefficient thought whirling around a *center of fear*." We have said that even Christians worry.

Now we ask some questions. Are not Christians supposed to have *Jesus Christ* in the center of their lives? And if so, how can fear be there too?

"Let not your heart be troubled . . . I am the good shepherd."

How can we as Christians worry about the fulfillment of our needs? How can we worry about financial matters? About clothes? About bank accounts? If our God is a God of His Word, how do we dare worry?

"Therefore I say unto you, Take no thought for your life, what ye shall eat, or what ye shall drink; nor yet for your body, what ye shall put on. Behold the fowls of the air; for they sow not, neither do they reap, nor gather into barns [bank accounts]; yet your heavenly Father feedeth them. Are ye not much better than they?"

Christians who worry must simply be Christians who have not yet gone the second half of the way with Jesus Christ. Christians are the only people on the face of this earth who can possibly escape worry; but only those Christians can escape who are willing to go the second half with Jesus, and say, "Yes, Lord, I have You, but more important You have me!" Those Christians have Jesus Christ standing straight and tall in the very center of their lives. Worry with them is an impossibility. A little boy doesn't worry if he's holding his father's hand, does he?

For our country and for us, the only way out of our inner turmoil of confusion and anxiety and worry and fear is the way of Jesus Christ who said: "Come unto me . . . and I will give you rest . . . I will never leave thee, nor forsake thee."

If we admit to spending even half an hour a day in worry, can't we promise our Lord we'll spend that half hour looking into His wonderful face, while standing steadfastly on His promise, "Seek ye first the kingdom of God, and his righteousness; and all these things [about which you worry] shall be added unto you"?

Jesus Christ is a God of His Word. I know. I have tried Him and have found Him faithful. I have problems, yes. Some days they seem to come thicker than snowflakes in a Chicago blizzard. But thank God, I can honestly say these problems—large and small—never turn into trouble. I don't keep them long enough. I hand them right over to Jesus, who is always standing by waiting to take them. Standing by, keeping His promise:

"I will never leave thee, nor forsake thee."

17

"Learn of Me"

If, for some fantastic reason, I were to be suddenly forever deprived of every other passage in the Bible save one, I believe I would choose the last three verses of the eleventh chapter of the Gospel of Saint Matthew:

"Come unto me, all ye that labour and are heavy laden, and I will give you rest. Take my yoke upon you, and learn of me; for I am meek and lowly in heart: and ye shall find rest unto your souls. For my yoke is easy, and my burden is light."

In the Scofield Reference Bible, these three verses are called, "The new message of Jesus: personal discipleship." And since it is this all-compelling personal discipleship which must dominate our lives, if we are to be Christian in the true sense of the word, I feel a deep desire to share a few of my own somewhat recent discoveries concerning one particular line of this wonderful message of Jesus.

The everlasting invitation, "Come unto me, all ye that labour and are heavy laden, and I will give you rest," is a heart-call which no man or woman can resist, once his or her heart has truly been opened to it. But we would look now at the next line: "Take my yoke upon you, and learn of me." A strong childhood memory of having heard that "take my yoke upon you" portion gave me the altogether backward, but unfortunately lasting, impression that the "yoke" of Jesus Christ was a burden in itself. A moment's thought will show how stupid an impression that was. Yokes are devices to lighten burdens. Jesus knew all about yokes, because He must have made them, many of them, with His own hands in His carpenter's shop. He knew they helped rather than hindered.

But leaving the "yoke," let's look squarely at the end of that sentence—"learn of me." A direct command of our Lord—"learn of me." As a new Christian, I am wide-eyed with wonder at the prospect of a lifetime . . . an eternity stretching ahead in which I will be able to learn of Him who so completely and wondrously transformed my life—top to bottom, inside and out! After thirty-three years of squeezing dry every situation and exhausting almost every person, I am overcome with adoration of a Lord whom I know I can never exhaust, and who not only says, "Learn of me," but helps me in the learning.

What is it to learn of Jesus Christ? In the beginning of my Christian experience I was convinced I knew all about Him. With a great sweeping gesture of abandon, I "sold all" and flung myself after Him, I thought! Now, I see that I didn't know Him at all. Quite suddenly He had invaded me, but I was still too blinded by my own "light" to see His face. Then, a little later on, when my own light began to die out, I was too dazzled by His light to see His face at all.

When we begin to be puzzled by Jesus Christ, I believe that is good. It is doubtful that He would ever turn out to be like our conception of Him. How could we conceive a Lord whose face is "set like a flint" and who stands like "an angel with tears in his eyes" at one and the same time? How could we conceive a Lord who "hath torn and [yet] will heal us? [Who] hath smitten, and [yet] will bind us up"? At these times of utter dismay about Jesus Christ, we feel we are being drowned in darkness. We begin to realize that there is a great distance between Jesus Christ and us. He is up ahead. We must run faster. We must pray more. We must spend more time with Him. Somehow, O God, somehow we must get closer to Jesus Christ! He is up ahead. He is up ahead. We cannot reach Him, and yet He said:

"Learn of me!"

"How can I learn of you, Lord? Where will I begin?"

"If any man will come after me, let him deny himself, take up his cross daily, and follow me."

My Lord's answer: "Deny yourself, take up your cross daily, and follow me." Hard? Yes. Without His grace and His strength it is impossible. With Him "all things are possible." And delightful and greatly to be desired.

Even a cross? Yes. Because of His Cross our cross can be a joyful thing. Can there be joy in pain and suffering? For the true disciple of Jesus Christ, yes. But only for the Christian can this be so, because only the Gospel of Christ has a direct and effective way of dealing with suffering. By the grace and because of the suffering of Jesus Christ, the Christian is enabled not just to endure suffering; he can use it.

This is one of the recent things I have learned about Jesus Christ, in my somewhat stumbling efforts to obey Him when He says insistently: "Learn of me." On the next pages we will speak more of the way out of suffering. Not by escape, not by denial, but by redemptive use of whatever blows life deals us. A way out available only to those of us who follow the One who "took our sins into His heart and smothered them to death."

18

What About Suffering?

There is nothing so wonderful to the dedicated Christian as to think about Jesus Christ. I spend most of my available free time just thinking about Jesus. Nothing shortens a long train ride like thinking about Jesus Christ. Thinking about His gentleness, His almighty meekness, His tears, His deity . . . His lordship . . . His love . . . and all these things leave me sitting happily drowned in His grace. The never-ending, inexhaustible river of His grace. Never flowing away from me. Always flowing toward me. Always toward me . . . coming on, coming on, like a mighty river of love.

Thoughts like these set fire in the hearts of those of us who are His present-day disciples. But, even though Jesus Christ is first in many lives, and even though there are those who say gladly and joyfully, "Though he slay me, yet will I trust in him," still there are more who say, "What has He to offer me when tragedy strikes my life?" Or, "I know a wonderful Christian woman whose life has been cut into by tragedy at very turn! How is Christ the way out for her?"

What of all the horrible suffering in the world?

Where is Jesus Christ in all the suffering?

What does He offer as a way out of suffering?

What of the mental anguish inside the churches themselves? What of the wars—mechanized, well-planned—and the bleeding and broken hearts they crush in their iron-hunger for spoils?

What of the tragedy in the panic-wake of an earthquake or a volcanic eruption? Or tornadoes and hurricanes and floods? What of physical sicknesses, and the mental anguish that weeps along behind the thousands of funeral processions that move across our world each day? What of the suffering from poverty? From race prejudice? From jealousy? From possessiveness? From doubt? From fear?

What does Jesus Christ have to do with all heartbreak? If He is alive, if He really came out of that tomb, what part does He have in the suffering of His creatures? Does He simply sit at the right hand of the Father and look down with remote pity on us as we cry out, "Turn thee unto me, and have mercy upon me; for I am desolate and afflicted?" Is this the role of the Son of God in the suffering of His creations? What does Jesus really have to offer when we hear our own hearts break? When we listen to the breaking in the hearts of those we love?

If we worship ourselves as god, in the time of suffering we turn to the most common form of dealing with it—self-pity. We derive pleasure from feeling sorry for ourselves. There is a touch of this in the fact that almost every man thinks his troubles and sorrows to be the greatest. Self-pity is one way to handle suffering.

Others among us turn to the ancient philosophy of Stoicism. This is the attitude of accepting suffering and inwardly steeling oneself to it. The old bloody-but-unbowed treatment. In a sense, this is admirable, but this very inward steeling turns invariably into hardness of heart. It is Stoic. Not Christian. In fact it is far, far from being Christian, and yet many Christians practice it. Many Christians smile through their tears and mutter between clenched teeth, "Well, I'll take it if it kills me! This thing won't get me down!" In such an attitude there is a touch of pathetic bravado, but not of genuine Christianity.

Buddha dealt with suffering and sin by declaring, "Existence and suffering are one. There can be no existence without suffering." And since desire causes the suffering and the sin, then the only sensible thing to do is to cut the root of desire completely! To lose one's identity in that passionless, actionless state called Nirvana is the Buddhist's way of handling suffering.

The Hindu denies the existence of all suffering and sin. He declares himself to be the divine and denies that anything whatever is wrong!

The Moslem lies submissively under the whip hand of sin and suffering and declares all of it to be God's will. This attitude is also shared by many who think themselves completely Christian. How often have you heard someone say in the face of some violent tragedy: "Well, we'll just have to accept this as God's will"? Christians say this firmly believing that they know the nature of Jesus Christ who said: "I am the good shepherd: the good shepherd giveth his life for the sheep." Would a God who said this Himself actively will for a baby to be burned to death? No. Suffering is in the world because of sin and evil. Not because it is God's will. And we as Christians must realize and proclaim loudly in our actions that Jesus Christ, our Lord, and only Jesus Christ offers a way *out* of suffering! It is a sure way out because He and He alone showed us by example how to use suffering. Can anything that happens to us be worse than what happened to Jesus? And didn't He use the Cross to save us?

All other religions deny suffering or dodge it in some manner. The religion of Jesus Christ uses it. The Holy Spirit can and will take your suffering and transform it into good.

This is not idle philosophy. This is fact. Radiant Christians step from prison camps where they have seen their own families murdered before their eyes! How is this possible? Because our Lord accepted the fact of human suffering instead of dodging it. He accepted it and made ready the one and only way of using it redemptively. "He did not bring a philosophy. He brought a fact." The fact of Himself. By the very fact of allowing His own dear body to be broken on the Cross, He took the world's greatest tragedy and turned it triumphantly into the world's greatest testimony! He did not just bear things; He used them.

This same Jesus Christ is alive today in all His resurrection power with this practical way *out* of all our human suffering. And He does not expect us to do it alone. He explains little; but if we are willing, He will change anything.

He will take your suffering and your sin into His own heart again right now, and there He will transform it into goodness and joy for you. And best of all, out of your suffering will come a new awareness and new nearness to Jesus, the Christ of God.

I know this to be true. I have discovered it for myself as He showed me how to use a personal tragedy about which I could not even speak. I am grateful that I was not permitted the luxury of sympathy. I had to turn to Him alone. Now He has turned my suffering into joy! And scarcely a day goes by that He does not use it at least in some small way.

19

Listen to What He Has to Say

If a new acquaintance asked you the question, "With whom do you live?", what would you reply? Would you say, "Oh, I live with my mother, my father and my brother"? Would you say, "I live with my husband and my three children"? Or, "I live with my wife and four kids, one dog and two canaries"?

No one else? No other Person in your home? Or is He there, but shut away in a dark closet, unable to be a part of the fun in the family, unable to share the warmth around the fireplace in winter, or the cool expectancy of a spring evening daringly spent on the front porch ahead of all the neighbors? Is Jesus Christ shut away in a closet of your home? Can't He come to dinner with you? Can't He converse with you? Is He being deprived of all the *joy* in your home? If this is true, then how can we expect to be able to remember where we've hidden Him when tragedy strikes our home?

Jesus Himself said: "Learn of me." How can we learn of someone whom we never see? With whom we never have intimate conversation? With whom we never laugh? *To* whom we never listen?

Who is this Jesus Christ who dared to say: "I am the way, the truth, and the life"? Who is this Jesus Christ whom we declare to be the only way out?

"I am the Lord . . . Look unto me, and be ye saved, all the ends of the earth: for I am God, and there is none else." A few short years ago, before my conversion to Jesus Christ, I would have argued: "But how do I know He is God? How do I know?"

"Be still, and know that I am God."

"Be still, and know that I am God . . . Learn of me." It is my observation that few Christians take time to be silent and listen to God. How can we obey Him if we do not hear His voice? The Scriptures give us a general plan for guidance, and surely we should take no step which in any way contradicts God's inspired written Word. But, what of the particular times of confusion and indecision which spring from particular circumstances in our own individual lives? The only possible way we can be sure that we are obeying God in these instances is to know Him. To know His character. To know God Himself, as He has revealed Himself through the person of our Saviour and our Lord, Jesus Christ. We can learn much about Jesus Christ personally from learning what He has done in other lives. And yet, this gives us only what the study of theology gives us—knowledge of things about Jesus. I would know Him personally. I must know Him personally. And so I obey Him when He says: "Be still, and know that I am God."

From the very first morning following my conversion to Jesus Christ, October 2, 1949, I have faithfully kept a "quiet time." I read the Bible, perhaps some devotional book other than the Bible, and then sit for at least half an hour in silence before God. I have been in the homes of ministers during the past two years where I was privileged to share the morning devotions before catching a train. The procedure went something like this: the minister or his wife read from the Scriptures, perhaps one of the children sang, perhaps we all sang (there can never be too much singing!), then usually the minister prayed. And then? Well, then he got briskly to his feet and said, "Now let's be about the business of the day!" I do not mean this in a critical spirit. I am simply puzzled. Because I could not . . . would not dare face a day without the fresh infilling of the Holy Spirit during that time of being quiet before God when it is morning.

When we go to a doctor we sit down before him and tell him what hurts us. We tell him the symptoms. We ask his advice. Then what do we do? Do we dash out the door already intent upon our next bit of business, pleading with the doctor to help us after we are well out of his sight, perhaps down on the street hailing a taxi or waiting for a bus? No, we wait quietly for the doctor's advice. We not only wait for it, we expect it. Can he cure our ailment if we don't hear his diagnosis and his remedy?

I think the analogy is apparent. I prayed earnestly for a year for the salvation of one very dear friend, and then one day God managed to get through my much talking with a divine nudge to "Be still, and know that I am God." I fell silent finally. I waited. And in a day or so I realized full well that I had many restitutions to make before that friend could possibly see Jesus Christ through me. Since I was the only plausible link between her and God, I had to set about making those painful restitutions at once.

Surely we can come to know Jesus Christ personally in no better way than being quiet before Him. Time spent in feeding our inward lives with His lovely presence will ultimately make it possible for us to carry this inner life out into the market place. Time spent in silence before God teaches us what it really means to "pray without ceasing." We come to live on two levels at once. The calm of the deep, quiet, unchanging inner level where we are Christ's and Christ is God's, where the pool of His peace is never disturbed by any tornadoes blowing from without, will begin to be felt in the bustle and turmoil of our exterior lives. Those who spend time with us will not only know that we "have been with Jesus," but that we are with Jesus. Our very lives will speak for Him, because Jesus Christ the living Lord will speak through our lives to an anguished, frightened world: "Come unto me . . . Look unto me, and be ye saved . . . I and my Father are one . . . be still, and know that I am God."

20

"I Am the Door" (I)

I find one fragment of Scripture coming again and again, and so I shall set down this fragment, and allow it to lead us down still another path of discoveries about Jesus.

"I am the door: by me if any man enter in, he shall be saved, and shall go in and out, and find pasture . . . Verily, verily, I say unto you, He that entereth not by the door into the sheepfold, but climbeth up some other way . . ."

What other ways are there? How do we dare choose another way beside the way of the One who declared and got a world to believe that "I am the way, the truth, and the life"? How do we dare go against the One who also declared: "I am the door"?

What other ways of facing life are there? Too many to list. But commonly, there is the way of resentment. There is the way of escape mechanisms. There is the way of self-defense. There is the way of materialism. There is the way of fear. There is the way of pleasure. But do these ways lead to a victorious life? No. they lead to—nothing. They are dead-end ways. They are blind alleys. And yet we, the blind, lead the blind up and down these alleys daily, refusing the one way out. Refusing even to try the Door.

The famous nerve specialist, Dr. Walter Alvarez, says: "I often tell patients that they cannot afford to carry grudges or maintain hates or resentments. Such things can make them ill and can certainly tire them out. I once saw a man kill himself, inch by inch, simply by thinking of nothing but hatred of a relative who had sued him. Within a year or two he was dead." God has fashioned us for love. Not hate. For love. Not resentment. "Love is our native air." Anything else is poison. Surely the way of resentment is a rough road with a dead-end. The only way out of resentment permanently is by the cleansing and redemption of the One who offers Himself as the Door.

Then there are the ways of escape mechanisms. Among those ways most struggled along are the winding, endless catacombs of alcoholism and sensationalism. Just as one drink usually leads to two, so one sensation tried leads to boredom and the pursuit of still another sensation. The Door out of these twisting tunnels of darkness? There is only one Way . . . one Door of release. Jesus tells us: "I am the way . . . I am the door."

There is another often-trod way with a dead-end: the way of self-defense. "I've got a right to stick up for my rights!" But Jesus said: "He that findeth his life shall lose it: and he that loseth his life for my sake shall find it." We stand our ground and scream: "I'll fight for my rights!" Christ says: "If any man will sue thee at the law, and take away thy coat, let him have thy cloke also."

Another very popular way of life is the way of materialism. We are a material-mad race of people. Build, increase, expand, pile up, hoard! More and more and more. "If we can just make enough money to—to—!" Jesus said: "Sell that ye have, and give alms; provide yourselves bags which wax not old, a treasure in the heavens that faileth not, where not thief approacheth, neither moth corrupteth."

Still another way is the shadowy way of fear. No one consciously chooses this way. But anyone can leave it behind forever. An ancient Persian saying contends: "Worry eats up the human flesh." Medical science says, "So does fear." In Mark 4:19 we see that: "The cares of this world . . . choke the word, and it becometh unfruitful." One writer declares, "Not only do care and fear and worry 'choke the word,' they choke the person too!" It is a well-known medical fact that fear-ridden patients are easily choked. They are shallow breathers. What is the way out of the way of fear? There is only one. The One who declared: "Fear not, little flock; for it is your Father's good pleasure to give you the kingdom."

There is space to consider but one more way which we, the people, insist upon trying as we refuse to try the Door. The way of pleasure. This so-called way leads perhaps more quickly and more heartbreakingly to a dead-end than any other. I know. I tried it for some fifteen years. Tried it skillfully. Carefully. Expensively. Imaginatively. Diligently. And ultimately—desparingly! The pursuit of pleasure occupies the minds and spare hours and energies of nine out of ten men, women and children in this vast land of ours. No one loves a good time more that I do. And I thank God that at last . . . at long last, I have learned the art of having a good time "in the midst of." A certain vacation trip to a particular place no longer guarantees a happy vacation for me. I will have joy and the "peace that passes all understanding" if my vacation doesn't pan out as I have planned it in any detail! Why? Because Jesus will be wherever I am . . . giving His joy minute by minute by minute . . . "in the midst of."

People shout: "We wanta' have fun our way!" Jesus says: "These things have I spoken unto you, that my joy might remain in you, and that your joy might be full."

"These things have I spoken unto you . . . I am the door . . . no man cometh to the Father but by me . . . I am the door . . . I am the way, the truth, and the life."

We who have tried to climb up some other way have found unmistakably and forever . . . that Jesus Christ meant every word He said!

21

"I Am the Door" (II)

Jesus said: "I am the door." What did He mean? Obviously He meant much more than we know about. Certainly much more than we could set down here. But think with me for a moment about doors themselves. We think of a door as an article which opens *into* something. A door leads from something to something. A doorway leads from one room to another. Jesus said: "I am the door." He also said: "I am the way." Jesus Christ, then, unless He lied, actually leads from one state to another. We can agree on this.

What, according to psychologists (and according to what we know of ourselves) do we, as human beings, fear or dread above all other phenomena? What would we avoid if we could? Here are four major "dreads" which, if man could pass through, or avoid, or be delivered from them, he would, I believe, be free from most of his fear.

First, death. We fear death for many reasons. God has planted in every living thing the desire to live. Even the tiniest bug will struggle for life when faced with death. Injured men will crawl for miles for life-saving aid, fearing, dreading death. Psychologists say, "Every man in his right mind wants life." And yet, there is nothing . . . nothing so certain, so absolutely inevitable as death! Birth may fail. Never death. But wait . . .!

". . . whosoever believeth in him should not perish, but have everlasting life."

If we are to believe Jesus Christ, if we are to believe the inspired word of God as we read it in His Word, the Holy Bible, we are faced with a startling statement: "I am the door . . . I am the way . . . [to] everlasting life"!

Did Jesus Christ mean what He said? Was it all true? *Is* it still true? If it is not, He was the most shocking deceiver who ever walked this earth. But He was not. It is true.

From my own experience, I know I have found the Door which leads from death into eternal life. I have been found by the One who said: "I am the resurrection and the life." Jesus cancels the fear of death by His life.

We look now at dread number two, failure, defeat. No one wants to be a failure. There is nothing to celebrate in failure. Celebrations go with victories. No one wants or seeks failure . . . and society as a whole does not love a man who is a failure. We fear failure. We dread defeat. The alcoholic who sits dejectedly before his half empty bottle, after having sworn off forever, knows the abject humility and pain of defeat. The mother who watches her son being led away to prison knows the heartbreak of personal failure. The schoolboy lags behind his classmates as they leave for home the last day of school; the blood is pounding in his head from the humiliation he feels because his report card reads: Failure. No one walks through life without major and minor defeats and failures. But wait . . .!

Jesus said: "I have overcome the world." And dear aging John, the disciple Jesus loved, drew on the strength of His Lord to declare: "Whosoever believeth that Jesus is the Christ is born of God . . . [and] whatsoever is born of God overcometh the world: and this is the victory that overcometh the world, even our faith!" From my own experience, I know that by my faith in Christ Jesus, I too, need never taste failure or defeat again. Surely, Jesus Christ is the Door from defeat to victory.

Dread number three is the dread of bondage. Of not being free. Our wonderful country is built upon the belief in freedom. And yet, no nation can guarantee personal freedom to its people. Personal freedom from the bondage of self and sin and the inevitable circumstances of life must come from above and be worked out within each individual life. We have seen radiant Christians chained to their wheel chairs. We have been guided by radiant Christians with sightless eyes. We have watched bed-ridden Christians "mount up with wings as eagles." Why? How? Because they have walked by faith through the Door to—freedom!

Jesus said: "If the Son . . . shall make you free, ye shall be free indeed."

Lastly, man's fear and dread of insecurity can rule and ruin his entire life. There are two ways of meeting this fear on the human level. We can lay up material security, or we can deny the need for it. Both ways are false. But the man or woman who, like Paul, has "learned both to abound and be in want" is truly free of this black dread of insecurity forever.

. . . When you have stopped reading, now, I beg you to spend several minutes in quiet contemplation before this One who dares to say: "I am the door" which leads away from defeat, bondage, insecurity and death, and "I am the way" which leads to victory, freedom, security and eternal life.

22

Where Is Jesus Christ?

Where is Jesus Christ?

Where would one find Him in your life? Where do you find Him? Do you have to travel to some particular place? Do you have to do some particular thing?

Where do you go to find Jesus? Where do you go to be sure of the presence of God? In all ages, religion has been associated with sacred places. Thousands drag their sick and weary bodies to the banks of the Ganges river, so they may die in sight of this sacred stream. A friend of mine, a missionary, once saw a Mohammedan saying his prayers on a train. The Mohammedan knelt upon his prayer mat on the floor of the train and tried to face toward Mecca. I say he tried because the train happened to be spiralling up a twisting mountain track, and the poor Mohammedan had to resort to a compass placed on the floor in front of him so that he could keep turning his body in a rather frantic effort to face the holy place of Mecca!

Does this make you smile? Does it? Well, where do you find Jesus? How do you contact God?

You may have read, as I have, of the Indians of Latin America who take long pilgrimages to a sacred shrine made in the image of Christ. But as they leave, they are heard to cry: "Adios, Christos! Adios, Christos!"—"Good-bye, Christ! Good-bye, Christ!"

They leave Christ standing there trapped in that sacred shrine, as they walk away tearfully waving good-bye to the One who died that they might be one with Him forever!

Where do you find Jesus Christ? In church you say? Yes, so do I. But what about the moment when you walk out the front door of your church and down the steps toward your home? Does Jesus go along with you, or do you leave Him behind–trapped in the stained glass window or shut until next week between the airless pages of the Psalter resting in the church pew where you sat?

Before I received Jesus Christ as my Saviour and Lord I thought of those who bothered to go to church (if indeed I thought at all about them!) as having a sacred outlook and a secular outlook. I thought of these two words, "sacred" and "secular," as being poles apart. And now, when I can look about at God's children from within the warm, safe encirclement of His everlasting arms, I am hurt and many times bewildered that so many of His followers only follow Him part of the way. The dividing line between their sacred and their secular is wide and sometimes uncrossable.

I knew the utter darkness of a life of atheism. I am completely Christ's now. I am spared the struggle of indecision, the agony of choosing and the throes of the double-walk. I simply follow Jesus and take my strength from His Holy Spirit which dwells within me. I tremble at the turmoil which rushes toward me like a black and angry monster when for just a mere instant I inadvertently step off the "holy highway" of complete obedience to Christ.

I wonder and sometimes marvel at the human fortitude of Christian believers who manage to live both a secular and a sacred life. I marvel at those who can leap back and forth across that darksome gap between trips to church from week to week. I do not speak of worldly indulgences now; I merely speak of those who leave Jesus Christ in the pews when they leave their churches.

I have found Jesus Christ to be directly interested and quite personally involved with me in every line I write in radio scripts. He helps me choose the actors who will portray various roles. The actors may think I choose them alone, but every decision is talked over with Jesus first. Each meditation in this book is written with Him. I find myself chatting aloud with Him now and then like this: "Now, Lord, was that just what we meant to say there at the end of that paragraph? Or did I jump ahead and think that up on my own hook?"

Some may think that this is not reverent. I am firmly convinced that Jesus Christ is interested in our vocation plans, our recreation time, our fun. I have a devout friend who lives in His presence from minute to minute, who once had his early morning devotions broken while on a fishing trip. A large fish nearly jerked the pole out of his hand. He landed the fish, and went on with his prayer. "There didn't seem to be a real interruption," he said later. "The Lord was interested in my fishing trip." I believe this. This man belongs to Christ completely. Why wouldn't Christ be interested in his fishing trip? Can't we take God into everything? To take Him into everything does not mean that we lower Him; it merely means that we lift our lives! To take God into our pleasures does not mean that we make Him commonplace. I believe it means that we allow Him to make our pleasure uncommon.

As I write these words I am beginning the fourth year of my walk with Jesus Christ. I have discovered many things. I have been given a completely new life. Not one of the least exciting discoveries I have made, however, is this: when I determined to take Christ into my every pleasure, I found the one sure way of finding out just what a Christian can and cannot do and still remain true to the Person whom he follows!

And so, as an extremely happy and joy-filled and delighted Christian of three years (at this writing), I want to go on record as saying that I believe no Christian has a right to take part in *anything* into which he or she cannot walk wholeheartedly with Jesus Christ. We can just toss out the two words "secular" and "sacred" from our vocabulary from now on, and rejoice as we gladly call it all—His!

23

Your Talent, Yes, But You Too!

"Jesus Christ does not want your talent. He wants you!"

I have dashed several young (and not so young) hopefuls full in the face of late with this seemingly blunt and discouraging statement. I don't enjoy seeing my words wipe smiles away and furrow brows of these would-be Christian writers, actors, musicians, singers, producers, directors, et cetera, ad infinitum. It is embarrassing, in fact, since at the moment I am serving Jesus Christ as a Christian writer, director and producer.

I cannot, however, but believe this is the truth of the question of service: "Jesus Christ does not want your talent. He wants you!" After all, upon facing the matter squarely, doesn't giving yourself entirely to Him include your talents too? Now, perhaps you are saying: "Well, what's all the fuss about then? Isn't it all the same in the final analysis?"

No, my friend, it is not the same. It is a fearful and dangerous thing, I believe, for a disciple of Christ to decide how Christ is to use his or her talents. It would seem that if one is blessed with a lovely voice that he or she should serve God as a singer. Or a writer, if he or she can write. Or as an artist, if he or she can paint. But I am forced, by my own firm conviction and by the results of my own experience, to insist that Jesus meant what He said when He said: "Come unto me!"

He didn't say, "Bring your talent unto me." He said, "*You* come yourself!" To me it makes all the difference in the world which comes first. If we bring the talent first—even if we offer it completely—we are holding onto the right to ourselves! If we say, "Lord, here is my lovely singing voice, I would use it for thee," we are, as a friend of mine says, "making a cosmic errand boy of God." We are directing Him.

But, if we come to Him first, holding out empty hands, offering ourselves and the right to ourselves, then and only then can Jesus Christ make full use of our talents to the glory of Himself.

I know this to be true. I tried it.

Some three years ago, when I surrendered my life into the hands of the living God, I thought dramatically (and quite naturally): "You have been a successful writer for ten years in the service of the enemy of God. Now you must give your years of experience and your talent to Christ, perhaps to write the great Christian novel!"

I have to smile now, remembering my spiritual blindness in those first, eager days in the kingdom of God. Jesus Christ knew about the talent. And He knew what use He might have for it—in the future! But He also knew that He had a still stubborn, still carnal, still unbroken newborn creature on His hands. She was waving her arms and saying: "I will serve Him with my talent," and He was holding her in His hand patiently awaiting the moment when she quieted down enough for Him to get a word in too.

He could not use her talent until He had her completely!

Gradually, over the strange new months of that first year, as I began to get closer and closer to the person of Jesus through greater and greater submission to His Holy Spirit, I said less and less about "the great novel." I thought less and less about "writing for God" and more and more about *knowing* Him personally. Slowly this began to dawn on my newly awakened consciousness concerning things as they *are* in the kingdom of God: my business was *not* to serve Jesus Christ. My business was to *belong* to Him utterly and completely and without one single reservation. Then, and only then, could He trust me with His service.

Is it not easy for us to decide *for* God about how we are to serve Him? Is is not easy for us to satisfy our own egos by cloaking our personal ambitions in the language of God, and arranging the spectators and the setting to suit our own ides of our own merits and capabilities?

Yes, it is more than easy. It is *natural*. But the Power with which we reckon as Christians is *supernatural*, and so it is not for us to consecrate our gifts to God. They are not ours to give! Rather, we must consecrate ourselves to Him, and that means that we simply give up entirely the *right* to ourselves.

Ours is not to decide; ours is to belong. Ours is to do the will of Him we adore. And He said: "If any man will come after me, let him deny himself, take up his cross daily, and follow me."

"Follow *me*" not a particular form of service for which we seem fitted. "Follow *me*!" And we can only follow Him according to His will by drawing ever closer to Him in our daily lives. Not closer to a religion, but closer to the altogether lovely person of Jesus Christ. We cannot please a friend completely unless we know that friend's every wish. And so, let us open our minds and wills and hearts to Him, asking Him, by the Spirit of truth, to teach us more and still more about Him*self*. Because the more we know of Jesus as He is, the less we are concerned with our own personalities except that they be caught up in the light of the personality of the One whom we serve—not for the sake of serving, but because we belong.

You say: "But if I am born with a talent, isn't it just common sense that I use it for God?" No, not necessarily. If common sense had been enough, Jesus would not have had to die.

Is that true? Yes.

If common sense had been enough, Jesus Christ would not have had to die!

24

Adventure in Holiness

I want to share with you an adventure in holiness which I experienced in the early summer of 1952.

I had, for some months, been anticipating a week-long speaking engagement in three farming towns in Illinois because I looked forward to spending some time with my friend, Mrs. Lorena Galloway, who arranged the tour. Otherwise, to all outward appearances it was to be a fairly routine engagement. But from the first hour, I felt something unusual stirring within, as the streamlined train slipped away from Chicago, across seemingly endless fields planted row on row with new green corn, past quiet towns, bright green patches of forest, and tidy little front yards where women and children looked up from their flowerbed planting to wave at us.

I expected a happy time. I knew the food would be garden-picked and prepared with love; I knew the water would be well-fresh; I knew the people would be warm and the welcome wide. And yet something unusual stirred within me and I wanted to stretch forward in my seat in an effort to help the train along its speeding way. The book I had open kept falling unnoticed to the seat beside me as my eyes were drawn, time after time, away from its pages out toward the wide, blue and white miracle of summer sky overhead. I longed for "eyes that could pierce the skies and look into the Father's eyes" as Jesus' eyes had done when He walked this earth.

I wondered vaguely if I would ever attempt to explain to anyone about this strange stirring, this anticipation beyond what would seem to be the plausible. Time after time I went back to the book, telling myself that I was indeed duller from the heavy round of speaking engagements and writing assignments than I had realized.

. . . And yet, time after time, the book slipped back down to the seat unnoticed and my eyes ached to penetrate the sky which alone remained vast and almost still as the rest of the landscape whirled by at a dizzy speed. I was moving toward something which I almost feared and yet for which undoubtedly I longed! I was being "called" as it were.

Now, I can report to you that I was hurtling across more than the seemingly endless stretches of Illinois prairie land. I was hurtling toward an adventure in holiness.

I have heard a complete walk of holy obedience to Jesus Christ described as giving the follower "the naivete which is the yonder side of sophistication." I had longed to obey Jesus literally and truly to become as a little child. I had seen evidence in the lives of the departed saints, in the transfigured faces of certain contempo rary saints that the wholly surrendered, wholly submissive, wholly listening, wholly obedient life is "astonishing in its completeness."

This I had seen. This I believed. And at times my own experi ence had proven it to me beyond the shadow of any doubt. But . . . only "at times." I would intend fully to remain wholly obedient. Wholly submissive. Wholly trusting. Then an unusually difficult bit of work would come along, or someone with a badly twisted personality would come to me for help; and before I real ized what was happening, I had once more taken the reins into my own hands and was bumping along under my own *knowledge* of Christian behavior, spilling the very Living Water out of the cup I attempted to give to the thirsty person who had come to me to drink. I was again managing my own universe!

I was once again "making God a cosmic errand boy" in my prayers and was rushing eagerly ahead of Him, tripping over my own spiritual feet as I strove to serve Him—my way!

I knew too that a Christian's only duty is to belong to Jesus Christ. I knew that. I believed it. And sometimes I lived in that realm of happy freedom, wholly dependent upon Him for days at a time. But . . . those days passed, because my heart was not fully invaded by His blessed Spirit. Perhaps the reader has another explanation for the spasmodic peace I knew. I believe I had merely been blocking the divine invasion of the person of the Holy Spirit of Jesus Christ.

. . . I rejoice to report that to the best of my knowledge now, the invasion is complete; and it was made via my *heart*, which was forever melted into submissiveness as I lived and ate and laughed and rejoiced and loved among a few of God's totally obedient children who live here and there in various stages of poverty and plenty in and around the three small farming towns of Bushnell, Smithfield and Macomb, Illinois. Words grow stubborn . . . in fact they refuse to be set down upon paper in what would inevitably be a futile attempt to explain what happened as my passionate hunger for the Bread of Life was satisfied at last as I was let into the hearts of the Galloways, Minnie Sims, the Recors, and their friends . . . to feed with them upon Jesus. With complete single-ness of eyes those people are centered down in the One who alone can perform the miracle of the transfigured face and the trans-formed life. They don't *wonder* about God. They *know* Jesus personally! They live with Him minute by minute in complete obedience. They not only possess the Holy Spirit; the Holy Spirit possesses them.

It is my prayer that the reader may open his heart now to this divine invasion! The life of holy obedience is not reserved for the few. If we would survive, it must not be limited to the few. It is for every follower of Jesus Christ to know the pure wonder of the utter simplification and rest that come inevitably when the life has been drenched in apostolic power from on high. There are many who will swarm Jesus Christ, but few who will touch Him. But let us remember that "as many as touched him were made perfectly whole."

25

The Difference Between "Life" and Life

We've all heard the expressions, "I want to live!" or "A man only lives once, so I'm going to make the most of every minute!" Your writer has not only heard both expressions; she has used them time and time again . . . before she found out what life really means. What living really means.

"I am the way, the truth, and the *life*. No man cometh unto the Father but by me . . . whosoever believeth on me, shall have everlasting life . . . he who hath the Son hath life."

Before grasping the eternity of difference between "life" and life, we have a tendency to squeeze that last drop from every experience. A good interlude, such as an absorbing book or an enjoyable concert, or a happy vacation time can make us feel that "life" is good. We hang onto each ephemeral moment of these happy times and say, "If only this could go on—this is really living!"

Well, that is living a "life." But we would find the life, and "this is life eternal, that they might know thee the only true God, and Jesus Christ whom thou hast sent." And, to know God as revealed to us in His Son, Jesus is to have eternal life! A life, which is not only for some future time, but a life which begins the very instant a man or woman turns the reins of his or her existence over to the Son of God.

At thirty-six years of age, I have finally found that under my own steam—searching about wildly as we may—we cannot live through earthly power. Nor through chemical power (including all the artificial stimuli known to mankind!). Nor can we *live* through human power: physical, intellectual, emotional or will power. The only Power by which we can find life is the Power promised by Jesus to all believers . . . that inexhaustible, dynamic enduement of Power that comes to us the moment the Holy Spirit comes in to take over in our stead!

Only one or two Christians (including the clergy) have been able to give the writer (a new Christian) a realistic definition of the Holy Spirit. Some theological explanations have stimulated the mind, but I am overjoyed to report that the Holy Spirit Himself has revealed Himself to the writer in a new and vital way. The Holy Spirit has ceased being "It" and has become He! The Spirit of truth is come . . . he will guide . . . into all truth.

The Holy Spirit is not a freak of God nor a spasm of the divine nature, nor a pocket edition of Jesus Christ. He is not a mere influence nor the inspiration of a poet or teacher. He is a divine Personality, an almighty Being who has a will, an intellect and a heart. He Himself must live in us or there is no more divine power in us than in others. He Himself must move in us or we are helpless. He Himself must speak through us or else our words will be "as the babbling of fools or the crackling of thorns under a pot."

When Pilgrim started his progress away from the City of Destruction he cried, "Life, Life, more Life!" Too much of our cry today is, "Work, work and more work." Or, "Service, service and more service." Or, "Funds, funds and more funds." Or, "Crowds, crowds and more crowds."

In my own personal life I have discovered as an irrefutable truth that unless the presence of the Holy Spirit of God goes along with my progress away from my "city of destruction," I will cry helplessly against a canvas sky . . . and hang my highest hopes on no loftier summit than the point of a cardboard moon!

The Holy Spirit manifests Himself in us in the "more abundant life." And life can only be defined as—life. We cannot analyze it, imitate it or create it. A professor at a large western university once took a common squash and put it in a steel case. On the lid of this steel case, he placed a one hundred pound weight. The squash grew and its *life* lifted the hundred pounds. He then put on a two hundred pound weight. The squash lifted the added weight. The professor then put on five hundred pounds of weight. The squash grew and up went the five hundred pounds. Then on went an anvil and a piece of railroad iron. And the life-filled squash plant broke the steel case to pieces!

If God can put that much power in a squash, what amount of power can He put into a Spirit-filled disciple of His Son, Jesus Christ? And what potent kind of *life* can we as disciples send out into all the darkened world, if we but turn completely to the life for which we were created?

Why waddle along through "life" when we can soar through *life*?

26

What Is in the Center of Your Life?

What is in the very center of your life? If we follow Jesus Christ, it would seem the answer would be obvious. We should be able to say without hesitation: "Why, Jesus Christ is in the center of my life!"

But can we say this and feel certain our statement will stand up under close investigation? As one so lately a member of the pagan world, and as one so deeply concerned that other pagans are allowed to see Christ as He really *is*, and so come into His kingdom joyfully, as I came, I beg of you to look closely at your life as we come to the closing pages of this book of discoveries about the person of Jesus Christ.

On the absolute childlike belief that He meant every word He said, I stake my eternal life on the fact that if Jesus Christ lifted up—as He really is—He will draw all men unto Himself! He said He would, and I believe Him. And with this promise of His in our hearts, let us face clearly some of the innocent, unconscious habits of thinking into which Christians fall; habits which turn away non-believers when the sincere desire of the Christian's heart is to bring them into the wonderful light.

I believe these habits can all be summed up under the heading of "too much self-effort." And this is why I say that: we get so carried away with wanting to serve Christ that we leap in and try to do His work for Him. I have spoken at some length earlier about the gentle, simple way in which I was brought into the glorious personal walk with Jesus Christ. And I want to emphasize for the sake of clarity, and for Jesus' sake, that there is *no one set way* of leading a man, woman or child to Christ! Our part is merely to "lift Him up" and let Him do His own work.

In the portion on the viewpoint of Christ, we discussed this in detail. But now, let us look at just a few of the *right* endeavors which we put in the *wrong* places in our Christian lives.

First of all, Jesus did say, "go ye into all the worlds and make disciples." And any effort on our behalf to lead another human being into a saving knowledge of Jesus Christ is one of the vital roots of a victorious Christian life. *But*, how many of us put "soul-winning" in the very center of our lives and thus go about tight-lipped and tense, hiding Jesus Christ behind our own anxious natures, instead of "lifting Him up"! Again, I ask every reader to think as he reads these lines. They can be so easily misread. No one among you thrills more to the pure joy of bringing a stray sheep home to the Shepherd than does your writer. I know how lonely and lost it feels to be out there in the world without Him. I know what a desperate feeling it is to have the universe end with the top of one's own head. But, if I allow my desire to "win others" to settle in the center of my life, Jesus Christ has to move to the margins. I become tense and nervous when the days go by without my having brought anyone to Christ, and before I know it, I am hiding Him from the world behind my own anxiety.

We must keep Christ Himself in the center!

We need only stay in position to be used. We need only to do as the lilies do. Wouldn't we pity the poor apple blossom that cried to bear an apple of its own effort? But we needn't pity the poor apple blossom, because it is wise enough to stay in position on the branch until the apple is born through it!

It is easy for well-meaning, sincere Christians to put soul-winning in the center of their lives, so that Jesus Christ is moved to the margins. But if He is in the center, dominating our thoughts, calming our fears, erasing our anxiety, balancing our lives, He will keep His words and draw others unto Himself— because of Himself?

It is also easy for well-meaning, sincere Christians to put "witnessing" in the center of their lives. We hear well-intentioned admonitions to witness daily for our Lord. And we should. But if I talked about Jesus Christ simply because I thought it was my duty to talk about Him, secretly I'd begin to resent the whole thing in no time. I am not ashamed to admit this. It is a simple fact. On the other hand, when we are so in love with Christ, so completely convinced that even if there were no eternal reward when we leave this earth, His is still the most fulfilling, the most exciting, the most joyful way of life, then we talk about Him because we just can't help it! I have asked myself this question for many months and at last I can answer it in the affirmative with no hesitation: "*If* for some reason Jesus Christ came to me and said that He had made a big mistake, that there was not eternal reward, and no heaven and no hell—would I still follow Him?"

Would you? Can you answer that right now with a quick, uncompromising "Yes"? If you can, then you do not worry about when and where you will be called upon or permitted the chance to witness! You will just talk about Him because you are so full of Him you can't help doing it! I have heard sincere Christians pray for the "opportunity" to witness. Every breath we take is that opportunity. Every cab ride, every dinner out, every bus ride, every guest who drops in, every time the front door bell or the telephone rings—we are swamped with chances to talk about Jesus. Now, I do not mean to imply that we must clench our fists and set our jaws and force a word about Him every time we brush another human being. That, in fact, is my point. If we force ourselves to witness, then we are putting our duty to witness in the center, and over into the margin of our lives must go our Lord!

Just as we can put service to Christ, to humanity, to our churches in the center, so we can put winning others and witnessing in the center. I believe all these are fruits of belonging entirely to the only One who has the right to stand forever in the very center of our lives—Jesus Christ.

27

Easter

When I was a child of about seven or eight, my mother bought a lovely straw Easter bonnet for me. Usually careful in the extreme about the fit of my garments, somehow she slipped up on the particular hat. And the first time I wore it, she asked with tender concern: "Dear, is your new hat too tight for you?"

"No, Mother," I sighed philosophically, "it's all right after my ears go to sleep!"

That incident, the memory of my mother conducting the Easter cantata at church, Irving Berlin's song, "Easter Parade," and a passing interest in which of my friends made the Sunday rotogravure on a few Easters in particular, constitute the over-all meaning of the season to me until I was thirty-three years old. Aside from a rather characteristic eccentricity of refusing to buy a new hat until well after Easter, because the hoi-polloi bought bonnets at Easter, it was just another commercial holiday which I was asked to note in whatever radio show I happened to be writing in the spring of the year.

Now . . . every morning is Easter morning to me! I found it easy to toss off the above lines of description of Easter B.C. in my life. Words become stubborn now as I struggle to combine them into some semblance of what I have discovered to be the true meaning of this glad time of the year.

First of all, when Easter morning breaks in all its light and glory upon my consciousness, it trails an unmistakable crimson cloud just lifted from the empty Cross which my Lord left behind Him in order to "come back" to indwell me. I know His actual presence with me now only because He came out of that grave on the first Easter morning. If Jesus, the risen Christ, had not gone to be with the Father, the blessed Comforter—my Lord with me now—could not be here. Could not be there with you as He is, if you have allowed Him to indwell you.

Just as Jesus must have swayed a moment on His wounded feet, as he stood in the mouth of the newly opened grave, adjusting His eyes to the sunlight of His own resurrection, so I sway in wonder at being able to share in this same resurrection today! Just as the nail prints were still in His hands and feet, so the scars of my own crucifixion with Him remind me that I am crucified with Christ! And am free because of it. The victorious life I have discovered in Him has scars on it. But they are glowing scars because He lives in me now that the grave is open and empty.

Do we as Christians live every minute of our lives as though we really believe He came out of that tomb that first Easter morning? Do we live as though Easter is a legend or a reality? Do we let the world know that the very same power that brought Jesus Christ out of the heavy-shadowed blood and spice encrusted grave that first Easter morning is operative in us today? Do we live by this same power of God unto resurrection?

The Mary who loved Him so, Mary of Magdala, occupies a high place in my heart. I might have been that Mary. I love Him enough to have been that Mary. He forgave me for so much and I love Him according to that which I have been forgiven. My heart beats near hers now and I hope to be her close friend throughout eternity as we sit together at His beloved feet . . . pouring out our love before Him forever! I love Him for coming to her ahead of the others that first Easter morning. Perhaps He did not love her more, but she was there looking for Him. And He honors those of us who are always seeking for new ways to tell Him of our love. He honors our seeking for more of Himself . . . for the sake of Himself. She did not seek a blessing from him. He was and *is* her Blessing. As He is my Blessing forever. I cannot ask for any other gift from Him. He dwarfs even His own gifts. My heart longs for more and still more of the Given Himself. And this constant seeking for more of Jesus, for some new glimpse of Him, is one reason why every morning is an Easter morning for me.

And then, too, every morning is Easter morning to me because He lives within me every day. I could not believe in the actual physical resurrection of Jesus Christ before it took place in my own life!

I know He is risen now. He is with me minute by minute. My risen Master, my Lord . . . Rabboni! And I, too, go quickly and tell!

28

I Am His and He Is Mine!

I am His and He is mine! That is my theology. It is very simple and I have discovered to my great and eternal joy that it works.

I did not become a Christian to save myself from eternal damnation. I did not become a Christian to make certain my passage to heaven. I did not think about either hell or heaven when I was being moved within by the Holy Spirit of Jesus Christ. Had I thought about them, I would not have been influenced by them because I did not believe they existed. I believe in them now, but then my attention was completely taken up mentally, emotionally and spiritually by the person of Jesus Christ. I was captivated by the One who holds "captivity captive"!

I did not pick and choose among the various churches during the time the Holy Spirit bore down upon my brittle heart. I did not think much one way or another about churches. I had not been inside one in almost eighteen years and although I love them now and believe every new Christian must unite his life and efforts with some Christian group, at that moment when the Holy Spirit pressed in upon my sin-encrusted consciousness, I did not think of churches. I thought about Christ! And the more I thought about Him, the more real He became to me; and the more real He became, the more I wanted

Him to be mine. And then my simple theology came into being. He seemed to say:

"I'll be yours if you'll be mine."

This is our last meditation together for the present time. If you have read through this book thus far, you know that my discoveries about the Christian life can be included in one sweeping over-all discovery:

I belong to Him and He belongs to me!

In the person of the Holy Spirit, my Lord is with me and in me as I work and play and laugh and weep and love on the earth. I am one of His sheep. I know His Name. I am His and He is mine.

It is His privilege and right to instruct me to do anything for His sake. I will go anywhere and do anything Jesus Christ asks me to do; and by His grace, I will do it calmly, willingly and quickly, because of who He is. He does not tell me to do something He cannot do. And therefore, I will tackle anything no matter how far beyond my capabilities it is, knowing that He stands ready to do it *through* me.

I do not plead for Him to help me. I simply try to stay in position so He can work and love and serve *through* me. This is very restful for me *and* brings me into a climate of high excitement at one and the same time, since I am allowed to "rest" as His energy pours through me into the tasks He has set to be done.

There is no need for me to wonder whether or not He will get through to me in time to make ends meet. He is here "nearer than breathing and closer than hands and feet" every instant.

If I fall ill, and there is a mountain of work to do, the very completion of this book proves that He never feels ill and He can continue to work through me, pouring His health and His strength into me as His work goes on. From actual experience, the experience of this moment through which I am living as I write this line, "I am strengthened mightily by His Spirit in my inner self!"

When the press of the crowds and the demands of people in trouble hack at my nerves, He whispers gently in my ear: "Leave them to Me, no one ever gets on My nerves!"

When I am inclined to wonder if there will be enough material supply to go around on some project which I believe to be within His will, I am reminded that if He could create, he can maintain. Again . . . I need only to stay in position. I need only to keep my hands empty of myself and my own ideas, and open to receive Him and His thinking.

I have discovered with deep relief of soul that the Father is like Jesus Christ. I must confess that for more than a year after I became a Christian, there was deep unrest in my heart as I tried to conceive a blood-thirsty Father who was so selfish that He would not take me, His creation, back without forcing His only Son to suffer on the Cross. I am not ashamed to admit that these thoughts haunted my dreams at night and blocked my flow of words from more than one platform as I spoke, until a short time ago. I believed in the sacrificial death of Jesus Christ on the Cross, but I resented God the Father for it because I loved Jesus so much!

Now, I see at last that the Cross is on the very heart of God, the Father. It is clear to me now that God Himself *was* in Christ reconciling the world unto Himself. He tries in every possible way to approach us in ways we can understand. He came to Earth and confined Himself within the feeble frame of man, in order to make Himself more approachable to us. The Israelites understood the blood sacrifice. God gave Himself in a way His people could understand. He must remain true to His own holiness. And when we, by faith, receive His Son, we receive the Spirit of the Sacrificial Lamb as well.

I am filled with joy and peace to have discovered that God, the Father, is not a bloodthirsty Power. He is one with Jesus Christ. He showed us His own loving nature by sending His Son. He said in essence: "I am like my Son." Jesus said: "I and my Father are one."

I am also overjoyed to have discovered that my Lord is a jealous God. That He wants me all to Himself. But I am relieved to find that His jealous nature is unlike ours. He is jealous for our own good. He created us, and only He knows how we will function best and find the greatest joy. He demands that we follow His laws, not because He is an ogre and a stern, relentless Being. He wants us to obey Him because only He knows our hearts and only He knows what is for our good. I am glad He is jealous and I am also glad I have discovered why He is jealous!

I am also glad I have discovered directly from my own experience with Christ that Christianity is not something foreign and strange and unnatural, which must be forced upon me if I am to live it successfully. To my happy amazement I have discovered that when I received Jesus Christ and when His work of redemption became a reality in my own life, I was transformed, restored to that relaxed, natural, childlike state when man first walked in the garden with the Father in the cool of the evening and talked with Him as a child talks lovingly with his parent! I am a "new creature," at home with her God.

Finally, and most blessedly, I have come upon the happy moment of discovery that this life hid with Christ in God is a continuous unfolding. It is not a creed to which I pledge myself and between whose rigid confines I must from thenceforth march! This new life in Christ is to me an eternal beginning. A fresh moment by moment unfolding as I walk moment by moment in the very presence of the One to whom I belong completely. I find that as long as I am aware of His presence, I am adequate for any event.

To my great, glad amazement, I have discovered that I am His and He is mine—forever!

The Burden Is Light

To

The One Who Dared to Call
His Burden Light!

Contents

Introduction

There still are some people in the world who believe the age of miracles is past. My observation is simply that these people have not met the author of this book. Her life has been one continuous miracle for almost five years, and I have watched it. In August of 1949 she was a tired, bored, radio writer with no belief in God. Six weeks later she was a relaxed, radiant child of God! The miracle in *her* life started in *my* life three years before and this is the way it began.

One day in New York City I wandered into a great church which was always open. I had hit an impasse in my life. In the face of an overwhelming circumstance my Christianity had collapsed. I was seeking to know why my Christian life seemed to fall to pieces every time I had something difficult to face. I hoped to find my answer in the silence of that great church. People came and went and I stayed on. Still groping for an answer, I walked up the long center aisle to leave the church.

A little old man with white hair and a lighted face came up another aisle. He was leaving, too, and we neared the door together. Quite suddenly he said to me:

"I beg your pardon. I am not in the habit of speaking to people I don't know, but the Lord has told me to tell you something."

We both stopped and he had the merriest eyes I have ever seen.

119

"I have a message for you, young lady. 'Seek ye first the Kingdom of God and His righteousness and all these things shall be added unto you.'" Then he repeated it and told me again that he did not make a point of stopping strangers.

Outside I was completely unaware of New York. My mind was fastened to the little man's message because I knew God had sent me a direct personal answer!

The key was in the word *first*. It made me see the root of my trouble. I was seeking a *victorious life* first but *I* was running my life. The Lord had just said to me, "Seek *Me* first. Let Me run your life."

This was completely clear to me that day, but it was several months before I was ready to put Christ first. When I did so, with no reservations, *everything* took on another meaning. I was no longer in the world to "be"—I was here to "belong." That changed everything. I began to get a deep insight into the words of Jesus: "If a man compel you to go a mile, go with him twain"; "He that saveth his life shall lose it"; "Whosoever shall smite thee on thy right cheek, turn to him the other also." I discovered that the ground is level at the foot of the Cross, and if we really follow Him we have to come along with the penitent thief who went with Him into Heaven.

The spiritual insight was the Lord's gift and it prepared me to meet Genie Price. Eighteen years had passed since we rollicked through our teens together and I hadn't seen her in all that time. But when I did see her again it was the right time because I had begun to take Jesus Christ at his word.

For a few days in the summer of 1949 we were both in our hometown of Charleston, West Virginia—she from Chicago and I from New Yrok. When she called and asked me to be her houseguest, I was glad to go. But, more than that, while we were talking on the telephone something seemed to say, "This is important."

I remembered Genie as a pretty, happy-go-lucky girl who thought she owned the world. Standing beside me in her mother's living room that day was a tense woman who was still desperately trying to *tell* herself that she owned the world. I knew that she was tired to death of the telling but she didn't dare stop. Her face looked as though she were warding off a blow. She might have called it "veneer." Magazine writers might have called it "sophistication." But the expression in her eyes was one I can never describe, and I felt somehow that she was at the end of her rope. Still, I was sure she didn't know *that* at all. A sense of urgency and destiny hit me. Although I saw tragedy on her face, at the same time I saw the possibility of a tremendous miracle, too. I knew that I was standing before "something" which from the human standpoint seemed very unlikely. Yet she was there as she was, and He was there as He is, and I knew the Shepherd had already laid down His life for the sheep.

While she was showing me over the new house her parents had built, my mind was trying to adjust itself to all the thoughts whirling there. She told me afterward that I didn't seem to notice the beautiful house very much. I was trying to admire it but my heart kept asking, "What *could* have happened to have made her this way?"

Genie will begin on the next page to tell in her own words what had happened before and what has happened since. My part in this book is simply to be witness to this amazing transformation which He has allowed me to watch these last five years. Watching for me has meant the deep joy of a rare friendship, many tears, much laughter, and a closer look at the face of Jesus Christ.

ELLEN RILEY URQUHART

Part One
B.C.

1

The First Time

I was born once and thirty-three years later I was born a second time. If this appears to be fantasy to you, read on and you will see that it is fact. And especially Reality.

This book is not being written because I was born the first time but because of the absolute *fact* of my second birth. It is after that in my life when things warrant writing a book.

Five years after I was born the first time (in Charleston, West Virginia, on June 22, 1916) I began the first grade one year ahead of time because I.Q. tests had become popular. Then excited teachers told my mother that I should "skip" grades. And Mother, being very young and also president of the Parent-Teachers Association at Elk School, said "all right."

I skipped 2-B, 4-B, and 5-A.

And in several years at three universities I never learned how to do the things in arithmetic which I had "skipped." I believe this is one of the ways I first learned the art of bluffing—which art I continued to cultivate until my second birth in 1949.

During my childhood we had very nice homes in which to live. We were completely average in that the more money my father made at his dental practice, the bigger and nicer homes we built. Mother always told me not to boast about it, but I did. I shared the basic insecurity of every American born to moderate means in a rich country. Early I caught the foolish belief that the normal thing to do is to move ahead materially. And then move ahead again.

And again.

We "built" according to this basic insecurity and felt perfectly honest when we said: "Oh, Grandmother wants to live on the river again and so we're building on the boulevard," or "The schools are so much better in this neighborhood," or "Since they widened the boulevard the traffic is unbearable."

I was rightly reminded that I sprang from good middle-class German, Scotch, and Welsh ancestors, that our new homes were just because Daddy was doing so well, and that I mustn't brag about it to the other schoolchildren.

But I did brag and was still doing it along all lines until I was born the second time when I was thirty-three years old.

Until I was *sure* for the first time in my life.

First I was born in a big white Victorian house at 1313 Bigley Avenue.

Then we "built."

The house we "built" was a large, then fashionable, brown bungalow right next door at 1311 Bigley Avenue. When I was about ten and very convinced that my father was undoubtedly the only really *good* dentist in the entire capital city of Charleston, West Virginia, we "built" again.

This time it was a big (then-fashionable) colonial house on the lot right next door to the no longer fashionable, brown bungalow.

Because I was her pet along with my father, my lunches were almost always prepared for me by my paternal grandmother, Callie Price, whom I called Gram. Gram was my mother's mother-in-law, my father's boss, and my champion. I know dear old Callie is rejoicing around Heaven as I write these lines because she did walk with God and only turned aside to storm up and down the peony bed now and then in a fit of "Stoffel temper." Gram had been a "Stoffel" before she married my well-loved country squire grandfather, Joe Price. And although Dr. E. J. Westfall preached the "complete cleansing" at Central Methodist Church, many people still did not quite believe that Christians do not *need* to lose their tempers! More accurately, that Christians *can* completely *lose* their tempers if they want to.

Grandmother Davidson was my mother's mother and we always called her Big Grandma because she was literally five by five and gentle and refined and mild and loved to put on a dark dress with a lace collar and have her picture taken.

Big Grandma and Gram got along because Big Grandma had such a sweet disposition, although she was not really converted to Christ until several years after I was born the first time. And the Sunday she received Him as her own, she really received Him as her very own and reached up with her pretty little plump hands and took off the two expensive purple plumes from her black velour hat.

This act characterized Big Grandma who married Bonnie Charlie Davidson, a self-styled psychiatrist from Scotland who admired himself very much and died and had his picture put on his tombstone when I was in 4-A. What I remember about him is that he was very handsome and didn't like the shape of various of his grandchildren's heads and predicted those children would come to no good end. He liked my head though and a few times he went on picnics with us and quoted Bobbie Burns and Keats to me while we sat under a tree and ate cold green beans, tomatoes, and corn bread—all three of which we both loved.

My country squire grandfather, whose name was Eli Edward Price but who was always called "Uncle Joe," caused one of my few childhood heartaches by dying before I was born the first time. Everything I had ever heard about him makes me long for the day when I will meet him in person when I, too, die physically. He owned the big general store and lived in a white house with a porch upstairs as well as down, in a town which spreads out along Elk River a few miles from Charleston.

"Uncle Joe" loved my pretty mother, Ann, whom Dad brought to live at the big Victorian house at 1313 Bigley after his parents moved into the city. During the days before "Uncle Joe" died, Mother spent long hours with him reading to him from the New Testament. Mother was so interested in the New Testament because she had just become a Christian shortly after she married Dad. They were converted together one night and Mother was very excited about Christ.

My father would be the first to agree that although he "went forward" with Mother and was "converted," religion was the property of Mother and Gram who didn't have too much in common with each other except religion.

I was like my Dad in almost every way and religion was definitely not in my department. I went to church because all "nice girls" did. Even though I hated being a "nice girl," as long as Mother let me wear high-topped boots with a pocketknife on the side and tomboy skirts with hip-pockets, ride my bicycle to school, and put on knickers the minute I got home, I agreed to "nice girl" dresses and suffered through Sunday school and church on Sunday mornings.

I didn't mind church too much because Mother conducted the choir; she was so pretty in her white robe with her beautiful auburn hair and her hands made such nice patterns as she led the good people through choruses and codas which should have been a little further out of their reach.

But I don't remember anything I ever heard in a sermon.

Dad and Joe and I sat and drew pictures and tried to make Mother laugh in the front row of the choir.

My brother Joe and I have to this day the kind of friendship and love that is rare because it has no strings on it. If this is a virtue on the part of either of us, it must be his because I bit his little finger and hit him on the head with a cologne bottle when he was a fat, pink infant in his crib. Mother vows I thought his finger was candy and that I was only experimenting when I hit him with the bottle. Mother and Gram always insisted that I was never in the least "jealous of the new baby."

Mother is beginning to see me now as I really am. Neither worm nor wonder, but "a bundle of possibilities in Jesus Christ." And this is setting me free in a way I was never free because Mother's approval motivated my life. And when I didn't deserve it, I found a way to get it anyway. I worshiped her and although I did exactly as I pleased when I was not with her, I would go to any lengths to keep her admiration and approval. My lovely mother was a Christian in my childhood, as deep a Christian as was likely, considering that by nature she is a very self-sufficient woman and was caught up early in the snare of "Christian service." And in an effort to "bring me up properly" she innocently added to my growing conviction that Jesus Christ was someone with a black beard who was out to spoil my fun.

The relationship that exists between my father and his only daughter is one that began in the mind of God even before little Walter Wesley Price was born to Callie and Eli Edward Price some sixty years ago. We had never had to work on our love for each other because we are as nearly alike as two people could be and still be two people.

Dad and I will never need to be reminded that we are sinners saved by Grace. We know it. And although He has captured us both now, I'm sure Dad had trouble, as I did, trying to conceive Jesus Christ. It was because of Him that Mother always had to "go to the church." He was distant and remote and yet trapped right there in the big stained glass windows. In one window He knelt beside a big rock and in the other He had a lamb in one arm and a big shepherd's crook in the other hand, and His face looked different in each window. I believe my Dad, like me, was unable to get Him to be one Person.

He was supposed to be a God of Love, and yet Gram walked hard through the upstairs hall so that things rattled when we didn't want to go to Sunday school to learn about Him. He was supposed to make people good and kind, but when I went to the church on Thursdays with Gram and played around the window seats of the Ladies' Aid Room where they quilted, I heard some of the members giving others what they called a "*good* tongue-lashing."

Once one of them got very red in the face as she shook her fist over the quilt and said she'd "never let a man inside her living room if he were smoking a cigarette even if it were the dead of winter and he were freezing to death!"

This did not seem very kind to me and I certainly did make every effort to hide my cigarettes from Gram and all her friends when I began to smoke at about fourteen.

I did not have very many close friends as I grew up because the Prices always prided themselves on being a complete family not in need of outside friends. But when I was very small a girl named Clara Alice lived next door in my grandmother's house where I was born, and we played together nearly every day. I was always told that I was calm and contained and poised, even though I bit my fingernails, and so I was simply fascinated with Clara Alice because when the doctor came to stick the little wooden paddle down *her* throat she could kick and scream and throw what was called a "tantrum." We made rose-petal "gravy" from petals we pulled off Gram's prize roses and we ate the "gravy," petals and all. I remembered doing that when years later I used to try to re-awaken my tired tastebuds by putting gardenia petals in high-balls; I ate the gardenia petals, too.

There were other chums in high school and the usual boyfriends who fed my rapidly growing ego. And then there was Irvin who played his fiddle just a shade better than I played mine and was sensitive and had pretty white teeth and wore a white linen suit in the summer and bought me Evening in Paris perfume. I was madly in love with him from thirteen to fifteen. I don't remember the details but they were deep with emotion. When I went to college, however, Irvin became "frightfully far out of my world" because he still believed in God and wanted to know Jesus Christ's will for his life.

The last time I remember seeing Irvin we went out in the country in our car to get some holly and pine branches for Mother to decorate the church—possibly the last time she ever helped decorate it because I was already a freshman in college and our church days were quickly numbered after that. Irvin tried to ask me some serious questions like what I was "getting from college" and why I had stopped believing in God. I laughed at him and told him I had grown beyond anything so infantile. I explained that in a course in Comparative Religion I had learned there were many other religions, that the church people were superstitious hillbillies.

That there was no God.

That if there was, "it" was just some kind of force or abstract power. That a God of Love would not let such horrible things happen as happen in the world.

I said my whole life was going to be spent in having a good time and building my own career. When he asked what career, I said I didn't know but it would be mine! I said this life was all I was absolutely sure about and I meant to have all I could *take* of it.

He said something about my responsibility to my fellow man and I laughed again and told him I didn't ask to be born.

We gathered the pine branches and found a little bit of holly without any berries and he drove me home.

I thought him overly emotional then. I know now why he had tears in his nice blue eyes when he drove away that day.

2

Ellen Riley

Sometime between the age of eleven and the age of thirteen I met a girl at church who had big green eyes that slanted a surprising way and naturally curly brown hair. This made me very sorry for her because I was going regularly to the beauty parlor and thoroughly enjoyed the "maturity" of the thing. Without either one of us knowing it at the time, this girl became my best friend. I imagine both of us might have said quite casually then that two other girls were our "best friends." We wouldn't remember their names now but we were strangely unaware of having begun any vital friendship with each other then. Like Topsy we just "growed" together. Her mother had died not long before I met her and this also gave her a depth which I admired very much. Somehow it made her seem older and sadness always attracted me and made me want to run and help.

My friend with the slanty eyes and naturally curly hair and the "depth" was the best pianist around. When someone asked me to play a solo on my fiddle at church I found that if she accompanied me everything always came out all right. I hated to count and so played by "inspiration" and somehow she could always manage to be "inspired" the same way, or at least she knew just when to drop out a handful of notes—usually they were the same ones I dropped out.

"My, but the girls do play well together."

People said that over and over, although they talked all the while we were playing. But they kept asking us and I certainly did always prefer to have her accompany me.

Her name was Ellen Riley and she was about the only other girl I thought as pretty as I was. I haven't asked her if she felt the same about me, but we did consider ourselves of immense importance in many ways.

We met at just the right time and felt just the right way about each other to "begin" a lot of things together. We "began" experimenting with variously advertised cosmetics together. We "began" dating at about the same time. We "began" making fun of people together. And when we played, as we did for about two or three years, for the annual revival meetings at the church, we "began" early to let everyone know that we played only because we were so sought after and we left immediately so no one could possibly think we had "gone religious." We "began" to smoke together also.

Ellen was born the first time one year before I was born the first time and that gave her an added "depth" to me. She had "skipped" the same number of grades in school and so gained still more stature in my sight because she was graduated from high school one year before me. We considered ourselves superior on every count, when we happened to pause long enough to do any type of considering. And through the years when we had completely lost track of each other I remembered "pointers" she had given me.

Pointers like this.

On Sunday mornings we would slip down with a couple of girls to what was then called Charleston Street and sit in the back booth at "Shaker Sadds," and drink Cokes and jauntily share a package of Old Golds. Soon afterward I changed my brand to Camels. But Ellen taught me on Old Golds, and in a distant world, tired and bored and trying to find it all again, many times I thought of the girl with the slanty eyes and curly hair and depth; and I remembered how she used to declare on Sunday morning in the back booth at Shaker Sadds (with all the maturity that a fifteen-year-old sophisticate could muster) that women should always hold a cigarette "up and away from their faces and never, simply *never,* flick ashes by beating on the top of the cigarette with the forefinger, but by gently touching same with a casually bent pinkie."

She does not remember these lessons. But she knows that I cannot tell a lie now.

And I remember them.

Ellen pursued a career in piano after high school and I went on to college. For no reason our paths separated, as paths do, for eighteen years. But I was *forced* to remember her now and then through the years in a way which I cannot explain but which I can simply describe, as I intend to do a bit later on.

Bridge

This is something of the way things were until I graduated from Charleston High School in 1932. My grandmother who lived with us had been giving me fur coats and hundred-dollar bills through the years vainly attempting to induce me to stop biting my fingernails. She had just begun to try in her misguided but well-meaning way to make me stop smoking et cetera and to begin to act like a nice girl, when she died one day and then for over eighteen years the Prices did not go to church at all.

Some of the pressure to go to church was gone. Mother had a serious illness and I began to pull hard away from God. Some people had some misunderstandings and after the illness we never went back to church. Somehow it was easier to stay out, although I know Mother did not mean it to be that way at all.

By that time we had "built" again because big, square, so-called "Spanish" stuccos with red tile roofs had become fashionable. Ours was at 712 Columbia Boulevard (now Kanawha Boulevard) and definitely a much better neighborhood. And on the Kanawha River.

And pleasing Mother had very nearly become my god.

4

Higher Education

In 1932 I went to college because it was the thing for Dr. Price's daughter to do. Mother thought it would be nice if I became a kindergarten teacher. I didn't because I definitely did not like children. But temporarily, until I had a chance to look around, that's what I did the first year.

As I remember I made two A's, one B, dropped two courses completely, and got one "incomplete" for cutting so many classes.

Also after the course in Comparative Religion when the professor asked in effect: "Where do Christians get off thinking theirs is the only religion where there are so many others?" I decided I was an atheist.

I did not decide this completely, however, until in Chemistry I learned how to write the formula for a sunset with certain colors. Without bothering to remember that God also created the chemicals that made up the sunset, I went back to the dormitory and cried and then it was that I became an atheist.

Also in my Freshman year I decided that I was not the sorority type, although I carefully made sure I had received bids to all the top ones before I decided. I would spend my life seeking complete freedom from any kind of confinement!

I tasted home-brew then for the first time because it was still the Prohibition Era and discovered, too, that I could write rather good sonnets.

In my Sophomore year I changed my course to straight Liberal Arts with an English major. I would write.

This was the pseudo-Bohemian year in which I gained entrance to the National Honorary Writing Society called, if I remember correctly, the Quill Club. And the piece on which I was accepted for membership was a long opus entitled "An Ode to Convention" in which I once more declared my personal *freedom*.

I finished my Sophomore year with my usual brilliant marks and "incompletes" and felt definitely that I had "grown away" from the sham and shadow of intellectualism and "art" and agreed with Mother that my skirts were too long and my hair too severe and since my eyesight was perfect, I would not insist upon horn-rimmed glasses because I no longer cared whether or not I appeared to be "gifted." Science had my attention.

The next fall, in my Junior year, I changed courses again and with my very first real purpose began digging for enough pre-dental credits to enter dental school the next year. I figured I could be really free in a lucrative career like dentistry. Free and different. My Mother and Dad had "weathered" the shock of another decided change and were "in it" all the way with me. As they always were.

I made excellent grades the next year and piled up enough needed credits and good marks to counteract some of my previous scholastic inconsistencies and surprised everyone but Mother and Dad by being the only woman to be accepted at Northwestern Dental School in Chicago for entrance the following year. I entered, made honor grades for almost three years, grew bored, quit, and dove headlong into philosophy with a brief sojourn at the University of Chicago for "atmosphere."

5

Near Reality

This period in my life from about twenty-one to twenty-four skirted very near Reality. Temporarily I seemed to step quietly out of the rollicking hedonism into which I had flung myself after I quit dental school and really wanted peace and good study and creativity and a home that was a home. This I had on Cornell Avenue in Hyde Park in Chicago in the neighborhood of the University. And even after I wandered away from the confinement of the classroom I spent long hours in deep books about literature and life and writing.

At this time *writing* became my god.

From sonnets with rhyme schemes and Edna St. Vincent Millay candor, I sought a new music and seemed to find it. I wanted to write something which was of "now." Because, as I wrote in a lengthy "preface" to a never-published collection of the poems which sprang from this time: "Now is the middle and the middle is quite different from the first." (Speaking of the century.)

In this "preface" which will either make good sense or no sense to you I also wrote: "Many people do not think that poets teach. But poets particularly are teachers." I knew I could be a poet right at that minute, but I also knew I had nothing to teach. And very little to say. I wrote also that "the poetry of today is value-lost in immediacy. It is not poetry in the true sense of now. It is poetry of immediate things and before them. And poetry of now in its truest sense is poetry of contemporary things and I beyond them." I knew these things but I did not know what lay beyond them. I seemed to want to know and yet there seemed no way of knowing.

In the very next paragraph of this "preface" I wrote something heartbreaking and empty and very true: "The one and first problem is the poet himself. He must live poetically before he can write poetry. Poetic living produces poems because of itself. It is the antecedent of all poems."

I wanted to live poetically, sanely, simply.

I longed for simplicity of life.

I wrote of it and longed for it. At twenty-three I sat long hours on the back porch on Cornell Avenue and looked at the Illinois Central tracks and my heart cried out for something certain and simple and sane. At twenty-three years of age I was sick to death of ornate living and too many adjectives per sentence!

Suddenly I broke all my Tschaikowsky and Rachmaninoff and Ravel recordings and bought quantities of Bach fugues and toccatas and albums of Beethoven string quartets and clean, relentless piano Boogie Woogie.

I longed to be geometric about things even though I had almost failed geometry twice. But in this period I was not consciously trying to be what I was.

I was in certain aspects ridiculous, and sometimes I knew it, but I had begun an honest search.

After three years of not finding, I left the South Side of Chicago with a flourish and an extra stipend from Dad and took an apartment back on my dear Near North Side where I had lived during my first years in Chicago. Philosophy and even my own poetry which did please me very much had turned to ashes in my hands and I wanted to be back where there were people but fewer children and noise that was not the Illinois Central Electric; where the bars were better and where there were old marble mantels and wood-burning fireplaces.

I wanted to be back where it was the Near North Side again. And familiar.

At home in Charleston, Mother and Dad didn't "build" again, but they did extensively remodel a Victorian mansion which had been moved up the Kanawha River on a barge at great expense to old Mrs. Dawley who built it in the Gay Nineties. *Life* magazine ran pictures of its trip up the river and the Valley watched and when Mrs. Dawley died my parents bought it.

I moved, too, in Chicago. Back to my beloved Near North Side.

6

A Little Fawn Bulldog

As soon as I was moved into my lovely sage green apartment with a warm tea-colored marble fireplace on East Superior Street Spunky arrived, even before the bed arrived.

Spunky was not the name I would have given her because she was to me a goddess and a baby and my best friend. And although she was known to be fiery when one least expected it, Spunky told practically nothing about her "wonder." But my Dad had bred her and someone who bought her for a week when she was a puppy gave her that name, and then returned her for no reason anyone ever knew about except that she was intended to be mine all the time. She had already learned to answer to the name Spunky by the time she traveled from Charleston to live on East Superior Street with me and so we had to let it go.

But "Spunky" soon turned to "Pinkle" except when I wanted her to obey me. Usually I obeyed her because she almost always knew best first. Sometimes she was called "Pud," too, and as long as I used the "voice" that belonged to her, she responded with concentrated, depthless, delighted, and very focused love.

Response was her genius.

And I needed her response very much.

She was a little, cobby, low-to-the-ground, unusually marked, fawn brindle English bulldog—a show specimen, but I cherished her freedom and respected her hatred of any but very familiar territory and so did not show her after she had "cleaned up" in the puppy class for Dad back in Charleston. I still have her little loving cup from that event. But Dad said she trembled and waited for the show to close, and it was her last and she was very glad. She and I knew how gorgeous she was anyway and we were all that really mattered very much to either of us.

Spunky and I lived together under very varying circumstances and loved each other for ten hectic, extravagant, eccentric, ambitious, periodically successful, occasionally frantic and completely Godless years.

It was in this ten-year period that I learned to write for radio and did. Daytime serials and nighttime free-lance shows and then my own production office for the last five years before I was born for the second time in 1949.

I did not daily address myself in the mirror as "one who is a sinner and living entirely for herself." I did not know that was the situation. I couldn't have known it because I had long ago decided there was no such thing as sin or God and that nothing *was* actually right or wrong. Thinking merely made it seem so. I had become so neurotic that I could not have seen the sin in my self-life had someone told me about it. I felt that my parents were fortunate to have such a talented daughter (because I didn't dare feel anything else) and kept right on writing them elaborate letters about vague shows which were always just about to make me a big success and thousands of dollars.

Mother and Dad kept on believing in me. Or if they wondered they did not let me know about it. Once when I had sent Mother a sheaf of the poems I wrote on Cornell Avenue she wrote back that I must never let anything get in the way of developing my writing talent.

I know how she meant that but I took it to cruel extremes as I did many things. Stepping on faces ceased to bother me at all. And yet I saw to it that the people whom I liked and needed thought I was generous, kind, loving, and outgoing. The others I shut out.

May I repeat, I did not tell myself these things about my selfish self in those days. Because I did not know them at all.

Spunky may have known them because she watched me so closely. She never achieved a fondness for the smell of alcohol and seemed at times to be pulling me off to bed when she thought it was time to quit. She knew about the deep longings which I had ceased to recognize and when a desperate thought lingered too long and tore at me as I mosied along the gray, lake-misted, "Gold-Coast" streets while Spunky had her dawn walk before we went to bed of a Sunday morning, she would know it. And more than once she would take her attention from little grassy spots and exposed tree roots and come and sit right down on the sidewalk and bat at me with her round fat front foot.

Once I sobbed out loud on the street at dawn and she ran back and sat down and grunted her hoarse little grunt that said, "I love you. Doesn't it matter that I love you?"

It did matter.

Other people loved me, too, but often in the press of a roomful of close friends, through the scream of our determined gaiety, would slip that longing that turned wordless and sometimes sobbed when Spunky and I took our walks together in the evening or at midnight or at dawn.

If anyone remembered to ask me I would have said and did say that I didn't believe in God or any life beyond this one. The world ended with the top of my own head. But once a year I remember I prayed a kind of prayer to some kind of God. This prayer-time always came in the spring when Spunky was finding those first ecstatic traces of "life" in the black, half-frozen earth.

I didn't address God by any name, but I prayed every spring that if He did happen to exist would He please let me keep my dog until another spring.

He let me keep her for ten years and then one night after we had played like rough children on the living room floor with some big boxes of recordings I was shipping out to radio stations the next day, Spunky looked at me and asked for help. She was too old then to jump up on my bed, and so she had begun to sleep on the floor on a big, soft alpaca blanket. I got down there beside her and held her while she cried her hoarse little cry.

I swore at the vet on the telephone when he said there was nothing we could do for her; that she was older than most bull-dogs already. I felt vaguely sorry later when I remembered that I hung up on him in a wild fury of fear.

Didn't he know she was the most important thing in the world to me? He knew it. He loved her, too. He had saved her life twice. But in a few minutes she stretched out her little back legs like a frog the way pedigreed dogs often do, slipped out her pink tongue about an inch over her lower teeth the way bulldogs do when they sleep, sighed deeply, and left me.

I touched her eyeballs and she didn't blink. I called her in "her voice." But she couldn't wiggle her little curly feather tail anymore. She was dead.

She would have responded to me if she could have but she was dead.

I sat in the house with no reason to take walks any more and felt death in me, too. I bought another fine female bulldog named "Petunia," and she was a darling, but she was not Spunky. I was just not capable of another intense friendship, and so I gave her back to the people from whom I bought her in Indianapolis. And one day I sat alone on the front steps where I used to sit with Spunky and *almost* realized that nothing really mattered in my whole life enough to bother to write it down.

I didn't have anything coming up which I had to write and it was a good thing because I had nothing whatever to say.

7

Very Heavy

I had nothing whatever to say as a writer and so I dreamed up one or two formats for sports shows which would be built around boys and girls. They were designed for quick sales to beer and/or cigarette sponsors.

I had nothing whatever to say as a writer and I was very heavy. Not only was I at least sixty pounds overweight from so much sitting around cultivating gourmet eating and drinking tastes, but there was so much added "weight" around my heart.

Layers and layers of it. "Stone" it used to be called in Victorian verse and in 1920–30 popular song lyrics which implied that the person who had a "heart of stone" just did not care. I doubted this and found that I was right. If we do not care we do not bother to weep into quick rhyme-schemes and liquids aged in wood. The stone around and in my heart was not from *lack* of feeling. But from feeling too much and from being completely locked up in it.

I was heavy. Things were heavy for me. In spite of periodic financial success the debt grew heavier and the lies to the creditors grew in proportion to the debts. Naturally I blamed life and that added a heavy load of resentment. I had what I thought I always wanted and then didn't want it enough to accept the responsibility for it. I deceived my parents and one friend in particular. And I hated myself—heavily. But saw no way to change and so eventually dodged behind the thick (heavy) wall of neuroticism and declared more loudly than ever that I loved things just as they were.

Self-deception is very, very heavy.

Fear is very, very heavy.

Worry is very, very heavy.

It is heavier even than these when you have spent your life convincing yourself and everyone else that you are a success and then have to be—or find a way out of it all. Money isn't exactly what you mean either, although you tell yourself it is.

Money bought another fine female bulldog when Spunky died, but she was not Spunky.

The heaviest thing of all is to have no beginning and no end.

No Alpha and no Omega.

No reason for waking up in the morning although so much of what you have always thought you wanted is all around you. A nice house, friends you love, your own office, your record collection, and the possibility of more of the same for all of your life. And all of your life was only about thirty-five or forty more years, so did it matter so much if you were so bored you looked at the food almost every time you sat down to eat and wondered why some palooka couldn't invent another vegetable?

Boredom is not smart. Boredom is very, very heavy.

I would never have used a word so Biblical as "burden" except in doggerel, but that was mostly because I might have cried with embarrassment or fear of facing things as they were.

And even though I would not have used the word, considering it obvious, things were—a *burden* to me.

All of life was a burden.

A very heavy burden.

8

The Burden of August, 1949

All of life was a burden and I was tired from carrying it myself. Tired and overweight and bored and afraid to admit that I was afraid. Able to convince myself for certain hours out of the twenty-four while under the influence and sway of the rhythms and madness and ecstasy of certain favorites from my fine collection of jazz music that life was like *that*. Mad and ecstatic and rhythmic. Or could be now and then and that would be enough. Along with books.

But outside of these times it was all heavy and more and more was required to stimulate or interest me. I was considered successful and I was thirty-three, but everything was heartbreakingly heavy.

Like this I went home in August of 1949. For some reason I remember that my pullman reservation was marked August twelfth. At home in the clean, newly built elegance of my parents' long, low, stone ranch house high on the top of the highest hill around Charleston, things looked better as they always did. And as always, when I came under Mother's influence I wanted to change myself. And as always I stopped drinking and went on a diet.

I didn't need to drink at home anyway. I could have and did occasionally, but we had fun at home and it was always for such a short time that I didn't have a chance to get restless. I became a child there, with no responsibility to escape.

As a result of my chaotic, self-centered inner life, I always left deep unhappiness behind me in Chicago but this time I had brought a heavy load of it home with me.

There wasn't any great catastrophe over which to gnash my teeth and dwell on in second-act-curtain finalities. There was just deep unhappiness lying there wondering at all the empty space around it.

And I sat on the patio outside Mother's kitchen door on the top of the hill and drank black, iced coffee because of the diet and smoked and tried not to think. I tried just to look at the height and depth and green of the top of the grove of ancient oak trees beneath which our home is nestled just before the grove moves down over a steep wooded ravine.

I was home again. As all the other years. It was summer. I liked myself sun-tanned and so set about getting a tan. Dad brought me suntan lotion and a couple of cartons of Camels the first night and we talked lots of baseball. I knew everyone's major league batting average then. Some of my inner unhappiness could have been caused by the Chicago Cubs and was. But "emptiness" was more to the point. Dad brought me suntan lotion and Camels and that week's issue of *Variety,* as he always did, and Mother asked me please to lose lots of weight and showed me her new bird books, and we decided the names of the birds that flocked in bright, quarreling dozens to the stone bench outside the windows where we ate breakfast. No one said anything more except how much fun it was to be home. And how glad we were that Charleston had its own Class A baseball club that year.

Mother looked at me now and then as though her heart would break and they both seemed to be trying to cheer me up.

On the diet I lost about nine pounds in five days since I always did everything extremely and then during the night of August seventeenth I had the dream again.

9

The Dream

Writers, particularly commercial writers, have many mountains that are quite high and many valleys that are quite low. Especially are there many valleys that are quite low.

Emotionally and financially.

At these "valley times" I would always go home and Mother would buy some new clothes designed to "do something" for the bulges we were continually battling, remind me of my great talent, tell me how much she loved me, how much she expected of me. Then they would give me a hundred dollars or so bonus for being their daughter and Dad would drive me to the station or the airport and then prepare to cheer Mother up after I had gone.

There was one other thing that happened at many of these low periods through the years. Over this I had no control. It was subconscious. It was a dream.

I cannot write pages of vital description because the dream was very simple. I was always the age I was while dreaming it. But the setting was an overgrown, tangled garden in which children were playing and laughing. Really laughing. Not the substitute which shrieked from the windows of my various apartments in Chicago. This was the kind of laughter I have found again when Christians are together and relax, remembering Christ is there, too.

In the midst of this laughter and play in the dream I would walk down a path at a certain time by my watch (the one I really wore) and there sitting under a happy old apple tree, would be Ellen Riley as she was when we were effervescing teen-agers. Nothing happened except Ellen always jumped to her feet (as fifteen-year-olds do) and exclaimed that she was so glad to see me back again.

I said she "always" did this because I suppose I must have had that same dream at least a dozen times in ten or fifteen years. Nothing ever stimulated me like that dream and its good effect lasted sometimes three or four hours.

It made me feel all clean inside and not a bit tired.

I didn't tell anyone about it. People in the world have one diagnosis: "Old girl, you're going at things too hard"—no matter what. So I didn't tell anyone. I would have felt silly. Having the same dream over and over. And such an innocent dream with no interesting overtones nor mysterious undertones.

Well, that was the dream I had again at home on August 17, 1949, when things were so heavy in my life everywhere I looked.

The new stone ranch house was beautiful and all the long expanse of picture windows made the oak trees come inside, but the debt on it was heavy, too. This was going to be an added burden to Dad who never complained but had stood beside his dental chair for thirty-eight years already.

Mother was a magnificent manager though and being the Prices we figured of course we'd make it.

I was annoyed that they hadn't borrowed ten thousand more dollars to put on a roof of hand-tied, wooden shingles, but the fifty-five foot combination living room and dining room definitely "did something for me" as I wandered back and forth through it during those August afternoons when Mother and Dad were downtown at the office. People had said I was really eccentric when I had the wood-paneled walls all stained a permanent, cool, forest green. For once I was right and this victory also "did something for me" as I walked up and down the fifty-five feet of glass and wood and stone and tried not to think anything in particular.

I did this for several days while I dieted and sat in the sun and then during the night of August seventeenth I had the dream about which I have just written.

10

A Telephone Call

Usually I slept until eleven both at home in Charleston and in Chicago but on the morning of August eighteenth I got up and had breakfast with Mother and Dad.

The sun was so bright I had to move to the extreme end of the long, glass-topped Italian iron table where we sat on the longer window-side of the huge kitchen. This annoyed me and made me feel all over again the heaviness I pulled out of bed with me that morning because I couldn't see the birds very well from that end of the table. And the birds lightened things.

As you know, I had had the dream before. And it had always picked me up. This time it was different. I was troubled and things felt heavier than ever. Even the coffee pot was heavy after Mother and Dad had gone to work and most of the coffee was gone. But before they left I asked Mother what ever happened to Ellen Riley.

It had been so long since I had inquired after anyone from Charleston that Mother was quite surprised but as usual didn't press me with questions. "I don't know, dear. Haven't seen her or heard of her in years. The last I did hear she won some sort of piano prize at White Sulphur Springs."

And then Mother said a most amazing thing which probably won't sound at all amazing. But considering the fact that she religiously respected my hatred of seeing anyone from home during my brief visits there over the years, it was almost amazing. I had just held my match for Dad to light his cigarette when Mother asked: "Why don't you call her today?"

I laughed first and said, "Please!" which implied, *"Please* make sense when you speak, woman. You know I don't want to dig into anything tired and gone. That was a high-school friendship and no doubt Ellen is married now and has umpteen children and is interested only in them and is tired and stoop-shouldered from picking up after her husband all these years."

I didn't say all of that but my "Please" said it for me. Mother and Dad had long since learned to fill in after that "Please!" They knew it always implied that I was somehow being imposed upon or going to be if someone didn't wake up and prevent it.

It is a frightening thing to fear boredom and unfamiliar surroundings and strangeness as I did. I didn't admit fear but it had long ago admitted me to its inner chamber and there held me captive by many chains—not one link of which I would or could recognize.

Mother suggested that I call Ellen and I poured another cup of coffee and said, "Please!" Dad and I talked about baseball for ten minutes and after they had gone to work I sat there alone feeling the weight of something I might have called "cosmic" and then I went to the telephone in my room and began trying to remember Ellen's aunt's name so I could look up the number.

I knew she used to live with her Aunt Addie on Indiana Avenue but I had to call Mother to find out her aunt's last name. Mother's voice was warm and helpful. Even more than usual. She said, "Call and then let me know what's happened to Ellen after all these years."

All these years were eighteen.

Aunt Addie answered but I just asked to speak with Ellen, please, as though I knew she'd be there still living with Aunt Addie. In a few seconds Ellen said, "Hello."

Becoming immediately brisk and sharp of diction as I always did, especially when speaking with someone from West Virginia who had not worked as I had done to lose the soft, flat vowels, I opened with:

"Hello, darling . . . this is Genie Price. Remember me?"

She said she certainly did and that she had been living in New York City for six years and that it was strange that I should call just at the time she was home on vacation.

For a minute I wanted to hang up and pretend I hadn't called at all. Then I heard myself selling Ellen on the idea of spending the weekend with me in my parents' "lovely new hilltop home."

In a quiet, definite, economical way which I have since learned to love and depend on and never question, she said: "All right. I'll come."

And she did—the next afternoon in a taxi. She wore a black linen suit which made her seem quieter than I remembered her; except for that and a suggestion of a coming-crinkling around her still slanty green eyes, she looked exactly as she looked when we were fifteen and sixteen! I exclaimed about that, of course, because I always exclaimed about everything and she seemed very charming but kind of dazed and not with me at all.

I know why now.

She has told me since that at that moment when she stepped in the side door of our home and saw Genie Price looking as I looked she was rocked to the depths of her being. I had been a "bubbler" in the old days and very happy and very delighted about things of all kinds.

And then there I stood looking as I looked in August of 1949.

And she says now it was as though the Lord put His hand on her shoulder as we stood uncomfortably and very strange together just inside our living room door that day and said: "Ellen, this I want." She replied, "Oh, no, Lord—not that!"

But she loved me as we stood there and that was His doing, too.

Finally I took her overnight bag to my room and offered her a cigarette. She said, "No thank you," and smiled. I then took her on an elaborately conducted tour through our new home and wondered why she seemed so quiet about the whole splendid thing.

We sat down in the living room after a while and I asked her what she would like to drink. That was simple courtesy to me. And I needed one by then. Diet or no diet.

She smiled again and said she didn't drink. And added that she didn't because she didn't need to anymore.

This intrigued me but I let it go. And I let my drink go, too. For the next hour I stormed the conversation with highly exaggerated accounts of my great successes as a radio writer over the years including the promise to play as many recordings of various shows which I produced out of my own office as she was teeming to hear since I had had a special transcription playback made for Mother, et cetera, et cetera, et cetera, ad nauseam.

She listened quietly and at one point when my voice was way up and bragging she broke in: "That's all very interesting. I know you've done some fine work, but you're probably the unhappiest-looking person I've ever seen, Genie. What's really the matter?"

If you have ever heard your own defense shatter, remember that sickening silence that follows the crash right now and share it with me as I sat there with an unlighted cigarette in my hand afraid to look down at the wreckage around my feet.

She was not unkind. In fact, her expression and her voice were so kind I quickly lighted the cigarette and faked a cough while I batted away the tears that were there brimming.

After that I told her things which I had not even dared admit to myself. We were very close and yet we were shouting to each other from opposite shores of the universe.

The shore on which she sat was friendly and the trees waved and things grew.

The shore on which I sat was washed and barren and there weren't any trees at all and nothing wanted to grow.

Outside my lovely family home stood the oak trees that made the lot so expensive. There were no hilltop lots nor fifty-five-foot living rooms nor big dramatic productions in Ellen's life, but on the shore where she sat the tall trees clapped their hands and beckoned to me.

The universe backed up her life.

I was breaking myself over the laws God built into the same universe when He created *it* along with Ellen and along with me. She knew He created her and she knew that as long as she lived His Way the universe which He also created would back up her life.

And so we sat there shouting at each other from the opposite shores of the universe and the more I crumbled the more clearly I could hear the longing in my heart.

Those walls, behind which I had been hiding since I stopped being the wide-eyed, happy "bubbler" Ellen had known eighteen years before, were crumbling and I wanted to scream and run before the Light broke through and showed me what I had become.

Ellen talked about what was at the center of her life. She said it hadn't always been that way. Just about three years, in fact. But she couldn't do some of the things I did because "they wouldn't fit with what is at the center of my life."

Of course, I walked right in and asked: "All right, *what is* at the center of your life?"

She said: "It isn't a 'what.' There's a Person there."

"A person?"

"Jesus Christ."

What did I reply?

"Please!"

That's what I said and laughed but I didn't feel at all like laughing. I laughed because I didn't know what else to do and certainly I didn't know what else to say.

11

The Cross

We played some Bach recordings and Ellen said she felt God in them. I laughed again and said I felt Bach in them and that was almost too terrific for me to bear at times.

Then we played some of my jazz records. Boogie, New Orleans and Kansas City. I reacted to these as lovers of true jazz react and Ellen sat and listened quietly and found one (a Julia Lee recording) whose melody was so simple and haunting she could say she loved that melody and mean it. She did and I was somehow very relieved.

I see now that she loved it because it was such a good description of all the wounds which need to be "answered by His wounds."

We talked to the family that evening and then we went to our end of the house and prepared to go to bed. Sitting on the side of my bed smoking one cigarette after another, I asked:

"What do you really believe about God?"

"I believe God came to earth in the Person of Jesus Christ to show us what He is really like. And to save us from sin."

"Sin!"

"Yes, sin is anything that separates us from God, and there isn't any way to get back to Him except by believing in Jesus Christ and what He did on the Cross for us. We just *have* to be forgiven."

I smashed out my cigarette.

"Cut that stuff about the Cross! That I won't listen to!" Then I lighted another cigarette, missed the ashtray when I threw the match at it and snapped:

"Don't insult my intelligence."

That was such a trite, obvious thing to have said that it proves my frightened confusion at that moment so that I feel I need say no more about it now.

Ellen said no more that night either. I sat there smoking for a long time and wished with all my heart that she hadn't dropped off to sleep.

A few chapters back I spoke of a group of poems I had written when I was about twenty-three and had almost found Reality. If you are one kind of person you will love these poems. And most especially if you are anything like Ellen you will understand them better than I understand them. If you are another kind of person you may not even think they are poems. That is all right. All I say is that they are mine. And that night after Ellen spoke of the Cross of Jesus Christ this one kept racing through my mind:

Time is
Hang-rope
And snares
The going-on.
I must
Walk faster
And arrive
At time
Bent-back
To meet
The going-in!

I remembered it all even though I had written it some ten years before. I *was* "walking faster" without meaning to. I clung to control. Desperately.

"Sin is anything that separates us from God, and there isn't any way to get back to Him except by believing in Jesus Christ and what He did on the Cross for us. We just have to be forgiven!"

Why do we have to be forgiven?

I had never been able to memorize my poems and yet there was another one crowding in:

Another way
I am not I.

Pardon is
The gist

And 'yes'
Instead of

'No' and
Changes

Number-know
To see and

To begin
To be.

Ellen said "We just *have* to be forgiven!" My poem said: "Another way I am not I . . . *pardon* is the gist."

Forgiveness.

The next day was Sunday and Ellen acted as though she didn't notice that no one mentioned going to church anywhere. I must admit I was not even thoughtful enough to say no one would be driving off the hill that day.

We played more records and listened to the symphony in the afternoon and God was *everywhere* I turned! I hoped to move Him to the margin at least, by dragging out Mother's yellowed copies of the poems which had dodged in and out of my mind all night long.

This was also amazing because I had long since considered it extremely poor taste to show anything one had written to anyone outside of one's intimates. Or fellow writers. As poor taste as to offer to play the piano or to mention the price of your new living room rug.

But in order to get God out of the picture for a while so I could retain *my* familiar place in the *center* of things, I dragged out the poems.

Ellen read a little short one first. Then she read two more longer ones.

"You won't like this but the thing I find in your poetry is a big, wide God-hunger!"

I laughed.

She read another one and there were tears in her eyes. There were no remarks about the fact that I left out words and made free with verbs. My poems seemed natural to her! And she seemed natural with them. But the ones which amused me made her want to cry.

I was completely in the dark as to what she was really thinking, and at times even she seemed not to know. I thought she was embarrassed some of the time, but as I usually did in those days with her, I missed the point completely. I know now what she was doing when she sat for such a long, to me, nervous time without saying anything out loud so I could hear.

Then she looked at me as though this had never been true of anyone else at all before that time:

"Love is really important to you, isn't it?"

"No."

"I don't believe that."

I laughed and said: "Well, I can lie. I'm not a Christian."

"I think love is very important to you and absolute miracles could happen the day you begin to know Divine Love!"

Missing her point again, I said I no longer believed love without self-interest was possible.

Kahlil Gibran said it was, and I meditated "profoundly" over *The Prophet* in my late teens, but it had dust on it now.

I had loved people. One or two I had loved very, very much. I loved my parents, but my behavior proved that I did not love anyone quite as much as I loved myself.

Ellen read more of my poems and I knew she understood them better than I had understood them because I did not mean to be writing about the things she read into them. One was titled "Peace By One." She said, "Peace *is* only by One." I didn't think I meant Him at all! She read them all and I just sat there trying to look only vaguely interested and said nothing. She closed the notebook and asked me a very strange question:

"Have you ever read 'The Hound of Heaven'? The poem by Francis Thompson?"

"Yes. Back when we took English from Mary B. Jefferds in high school. Why?"

"I just wondered. I like your thin, simple style much better than Thompson's, but somehow I thought of 'The Hound of Heaven' just now."

I knew the "Hound of Heaven" was Jesus Christ.

And God moved once more from the margin to the center of our conversation. I doubt if He had really moved out of it. I believe He caused me to recall the poems. I hadn't even looked at them for ten years.

12

Incident

That evening Ellen sat down at Mother's new grand piano and played a composition entitled "Malagueña" which is not exactly spiritual in character but which is very, very showy. Long-haired musicians like Ellen play it and harmonica players make records of it. Its beat is Spanish and definite and primitive in spite of the flowery right hand. You probably know it and wonder why I am devoting a paragraph to "Malagueña" when she also played Chopin and Schumann and Bach. There are two reasons. One is her extreme skill in making it sound like much better music than it is. The other is that although it is definitely not spiritual, it will come up again and again in our story and I want you to recognize it when it does.

She played "Malagueña" and even my brother Joe, who is strictly anti-longhair, said: "Say, that moves!"

Later on that same evening after Joe went back to his own home and Dad had gone to bed with the sporting news, Mother suggested that we have some iced grape juice. It was August and West Virginia and very hot.

I prepared it and brought in three glasses on a tray. Ellen, who weights exactly one hundred and two pounds, said she was still not hungry from dinner or even thristy. For some strange reason this annoyed me. Probably because I weighed quite a bit more and was both hungry and thirsty and so I held the glass of grape juice straight out and said:

"Aw, come on, little saint. Take the sinner's grape juice. You can make like you're having Communion and you'll *love* it!"

Mother said: "Why, Genie!"

Ellen winced as she took the blow from Him and that was the first time I had seen pain on her face. Although I had tried to hurt her several times, this was the first time it showed.

13

The Plane

Ellen had to go back to her job in New York City in another week. Having run my own life for so long I was annoyed that she wouldn't write her employer or call long distance and say she was ill. I even offered to call for her. But she was firm in the quiet little way that only one hundred and two pounds of indwelling can be firm and after spending another night at our house later on in the week she went back to New York.

Actually, when she was so definite about not being able to lie to her employer I suddenly didn't even want her to come back to my home for the second visit. I swore to myself because I had even asked her. I had nothing in common with a religioso! What was my trouble? She seemed to sense this and made very sure that I didn't get a chance to back out of the invitation.

She knew she *had* to come again.

And then the next morning Mother and I stood on the back balcony of our house and waited for the big, silver four-motored plan to take off for New York City. From our hilltop, looking out and across the valley and the river to the top of the hills on the other side, we can watch the big planes take off from Charleston's unique hilltop airport. Her plane left on schedule and as it circled over our house and disappeared into the hot August sky it was as though before the takeoff someone had fastened a chain around my heart and hooked the other end to the big ship. The smaller it became on the horizon, the more the pain increased in my chest.

Ellen and I had so little in common except that she understood my poems as few had understood them, and I decided that must be the reason I felt that way because most people thought I was a little crazy after they read them. I had written them and put them away and then made money doing for radio what people called "fine writing." But she hadn't even thought the poems peculiar. She said they were new and clean and fresh.

And simple and clear and young.

I didn't feel any of those things as I watched the plane disappear from sight. But I wanted to cry because someone had thought that again about the poems. Instead I smiled what I hoped was casually at Mother and said:

"Ellen's turned into a real puzzle. She's so talented *and* attractive." And then I stretched and pretended to yawn. "Isn't it too bad she's gone religious? It will all be wasted now."

14

Letters

I stayed on in Charleston another week or so and then wandered back to Chicago. But during that week I could scarcely believe it when every day in the big green mailbox on the curly iron stand by the road at the front of our house there was a letter from her in the soon-to-be familiar southpaw penmanship. Some were just little notes. They spoke often of the poems and eased me in gradually on the nature of her work in one of the big New York churches and they told me little things that happened and always they moved straight to the center of my heart. While she was visiting me, I had talked so much about "my work" she had very little chance to tell me about hers.

Her letters never spoke of God unless I did in my reply. They never quoted Scripture because she knew I was very much against it. But the one I received just before I went back to Chicago said:

> Remember I did see another "you" begin to emerge, and I don't believe
> anything can stop "her" now. This new thing isn't something that you
> have. It is something that has you. Remember that, Genie, if you get
> low—especially after you go back to Chicago. I know so well that even
> now things will look different. Something has you and most likely you
> will not be able to forget. You'll have to face things back there and you

don't know what your reaction will be, and you feel as if you don't really know yourself, I imagine. But when that happens get away by yourself and just stay there and be still and then remember the Something *which has you*. When you remember that you won't have to keep trying to "find it" as you say. I wish you could get alone every day. Do you think you could? I find myself wishing I could run ahead of you back to Chicago and protect you from the bewilderment that will come, but you are the one who has to go back and you will know that I'm with you in it. And more than that, things will work out. This may sound crazy, but I feel this is only the beginning of Something so great I can't fathom it. I'll pray as you asked me to. I am now. I shall be always.

Love,

Ellen

Just before I left for Chicago another letter read in part:

The only kind of life you have known to live so far is bound to bring one crisis after another. That isn't criticism, Genie. That is just a law of the universe. And when the next crisis comes to you, remember I'll have the answer for it. You don't need to ask me to pray for you. It is as though Someone prays through me for you every minute. I am amazed at all this. I am in awe of it. I'll write again tomorrow.

I've never done this with you, but forgive me if I quote one little verse from the Bible? "And it shall come to pass, that before they call I will answer and while they are yet speaking I will hear."

Keep up the diet. I'm pulling for you.

Love,

Ellen

When I arrived in Chicago the letter than was waiting there said:

For some reason I feel you will be in New York soon. Am I completely crazy?

I thought she was and dismissed the idea. But, of course, she wasn't and of course the crisis came almost at once and instead of drinking as I fully intended to do, I got on a train for New York and started—thinking.

A close friend of mine handed me a book just before I got on that train to New York. It had been handed to her by someone whom she did not particularly like and who did not particularly like her. She hadn't read it, but just as though she were operating under Orders, she handed it to me. It was a book about an atheist who had become a Trappist monk. I wanted to forget that I had it, but I was *forced* to read just enough of it so that by the time the train was hurtling through Pennsylvania another horizon had been smashed!

I can't find the part in the book now and maybe it wasn't even anything I read. But all of the sudden I looked out the train window at the sky and *knew* life did not end here.

15

A Very Different New York

Ellen was on the staff of Calvary House which was next door to the old Calvary Protestant-Episcopal Church where she had come into her vital walk with Christ. When she was in her early twenties back home in Central Church, Ellen was converted through Dessie Arnett, her Sunday-school teacher. But after she went away from God for a time in New York she came back to Him to find Him altogether real. And Dr. Samuel Shoemaker who was then rector of Calvary Church and his wife, Helen, were among those who showed her Christ as He is. And so when I met her again after all those years her address was Calvary House, 61 Gramercy Park. Calvary House is a big comfortable eight-storied brick building where missionaries of all denominations stop on furlough and where people of all walks of life may live at reasonable rates and learn to walk with Christ as a living person. Ellen was hostess in the dining room at Calvary House.

Hating churches as I did I refused to stay there, so I ensconced myself in a large front room at the nearby Gramercy Park Hotel and called Ellen on the telephone.

This was on Monday right at the end of September during World Series time in 1949. For the first time in years I did not listen to the World Series at all. I was very busy with God. And since it "is a fearful thing to fall into the hands of the living God," what happened from that Monday until the following Monday morning when I got on another train going back to Chicago will have to be told in impressions. I don't remember it clearly in sequence.

A few definite things are that the room service was excellent in the hotel and a big steam shovel was excavating for something right across the corner and from my windows I could see the interiors of very well-turned-out apartments. One had a beautiful dark green wall.

For years in Chicago I had affected green walls—a certain sage green and people called my home "the Green Room" and came there and talked and were "brilliant and gay" as people are supposed to be in theater "Green Rooms." This one across Gramercy Park from my hotel room was a darker green and much more elegant. I remember the walls as being partly paneled. They may not be. It also looked quiet.

I called Ellen on the telephone as soon as I had dismissed the bellboy who brought up my luggage. I still had on my new brown velvet hat with a veil when she flew into the room a few minutes later very glad to see me. And very careful with me a I look back now.

I was still walking in darkness. I had not been made a new creature yet. But I had fallen into the hand of the living God and somehow I felt sure Ellen never really stopped praying even though she chatted gaily with me and tried to make plans for us to go here and there to nice French restaurants in the neighborhood until she saw that I was not interested at all in doing that. I had done it so much before. So had she. And just when she was saying we'd talk about all that later I blurted:

"I believe there is another life after this one."

"You do, Genie?"

"It came to me on the train. God only knows why it came, but it did. And I know there is now."

"That's wonderful. " She looked as though she were listening to Someone Else.

"Is it wonderful? I think maybe I'm losing my mind!"

She had to go back at noon to handle the people in the dining room at Calvary House and I hated every brick in the place. "The devil take the people in the dining room at Calvary House!" I wanted to talk.

She was very loyal to Calvary House, though, and by the second day I was blackly jealous of all those who had to have Ellen on hand to tuck their napkins under their chins in the ever-present dining room. But I stayed on and we talked and talked and talked and talked and talked. She gave me *The Greatest Thing in the World* to read and it made me jealous of Henry Drummond and Ellen.

And then we talked through another day until it was Wednesday. I had not left my room once. I loved hotel rooms anyway and had lived in one alone and happy as a lark during the war when I worked out of New York for a while. But that was the Gladstone on Fifty-second Street near Fifth Avenue. This was sedate Gramercy Park and a very different New York.

I stayed in my room because I felt safer there. And anyway a big, puffing steam shovel made grinding noises and scattered dust outside and just down the block and across one street was "Calvary House"!

And Calvary Church.

And those people who had made Christ real to Ellen.

I was terribly nervous and smoked incessantly. And walked up and down my room *and*, when Ellen was on duty at mealtimes and after she went back to her room at night (promptly at eleven), I read the hotel Bible! I didn't plan to admit that to her at all.

At first I just lifted the front cover as it lay on the dresser there in its cheap, unattractive, black binding with the ugly insignia and thick red-edged pages. At first I just lifted the cover, flipped through a few pages, and put it in the drawer out of sight.

On Wednesday Ellen suggested casually (remembering how I had stormed at the idea that the Bible was anything more than just a great book) that I might be interested in reading the Gospels sometime. Something seemed always to stop her from pushing me—just in time.

After she left Wednesday night at eleven, I picked up the Bible and sat there holding it. She had said several times that my way of handling words and giving them new meanings in my poems reminded her of the style of writing in Ezekiel. I thought I'd look in the index and see if Ezekiel could be a book in the Bible. I had taken a course in the Bible as English literature in college and remembered that some of the books in the Bible were named after prophets. Ezekiel sounded as though he might easily have been a prophet. Lo, there he was in the index and when I turned to the Book of Ezekiel I was absolutely *charmed* by what I read! Somehow I landed in chapter forty right in the midst of the truly poetic description of the man "whose appearance was like the appearance of brass, with a line of flax in his hand and a measuring reed; and he stood at the gate."

I had no idea why he stood there or why he had to measure, but the lilt and music and simplicity of style of the chapter falling line on line into my delighted and suddenly relieved mind seemed to slip loose one knot after another within me. I read on through all his "measurings" of the "little chambers of one and six cubits" and exclaimed aloud when I came to this: "there were narrow windows to the little chambers, and to their posts within the gate round about, and likewise to the arches; and windows were round about inward; and upon each post were palm trees."

Could there be delightful things like this in THE BIBLE?

Chapter forty-one with the description of the temple intrigued me even more. I felt at home. Here was someone else who felt about words the way I did. Who was not content with giving them just one regular meaning. And he was an Old Testament prophet, of all people.

"Listen!" I said aloud, as I stood up and emoted alone there in the hotel room. "Listen to this!"

"And the side chambers were three, one over another, and thirty in order; and they entered into the wall which was of the house for the side chambers round about, that they might have hold. . . ."

(That was more extreme than anything I had ever written.)

"That they might have hold, but they had not hold in the wall of the house. . . ."

And then Ezekiel sang on with the music that charges with pure joy the soul of a writer wanting wings as I wanted them.

"And there was an enlarging, and a winding about still upward to the side chambers; for the winding about of the house went still upward round about the house; there the breadth of the house was still upward, and so increased from the lowest chamber to the highest by the midst. . . ."

I sat down and wept. Wagner and Beethoven used to hurt me blissfully with too much music piled onto too much music, but it had been so long since I had allowed myself to be blissfully hurt like this. And here was an ancient prophet neamed Ezekiel hurting me again with a beauty that I had forgotten how to contain.

Ezekiel in the Bible!

Genie Price has gone stark, raving mad!

But I knew, oh, I knew that there *was* an enlarging, and a winding still upward . . . for the winding went "*still upward*" . . . and I was caught in it! I feared it but I was glad to be caught in it. For the first time I almost understood what Ellen meant in the letter when she wrote, "This new thing isn't something you have. It is Something that *has* you."

The next morning I grabbed Ellen the minute she came in the door of my hotel room, sat her down, and hotel Bible in hand began to spout Ezekiel at her in excited tones.

I know now that what she really wanted to do was fall on her knees and say, "Thank You Lord. Oh, thank You! At last *You've* got her reading Your Word!"

But what she did, as far as I could see anyway, was to pick it all up apparently on my low level of mere excitement about the literary style and gently and without my suspecting a thing led me out of Ezekiel into first of all—Proverbs 8:22–36. I was so excited about Ezekiel I wanted to go on reading about his little chambers and cherubims and wheels but she had a way of getting my attention which she did not know at all until I told her in this book: always before she began to explain anything to me or to answer my usually difficult questions or as before she began to read from Proverbs, she—fell silent. Just for a few seconds, but it always made me feel as though she were—listening. And I wanted and always paid attention. She "listened" a moment and then began to read:

"The Lord possessed me in the beginning of his way, before his works of old. I was set up from everlasting, from the beginning, or ever the earth was. When there were no depths, I was brought forth; when there were no fountains abounding with water. Before the mountains were settled, before the hills was I brought forth; while as yet he had not made the earth, nor the fields, nor the highest part of the dust of the world. When he prepared the heavens . . ."

"Stop. Please stop. Just a minute." My heart felt squeezed.

"All right. Is anything wrong, Genie?"

"No. I—No, just makes me nervous to hear anyone else read."

"Then you finish it."

I took the Book from her and although my hands had never been one bit shaky on any morning after, I noticed particularly that they shook when I reached for the Bible.

"I was reading right there in verse twenty-seven. The beginning of verse twenty-seven . . . in the part about the heavens."

I lighted a cigarette and hoped Ellen hadn't noticed that I left one burning in the ashtray on the dresser. She did notice, of course, and in her quiet manner as though it were the least she could do for me, she walked over to the dresser and put it out.

"Verse twenty-seven, did you say?"

"Yes. That's where I stopped reading."

I always liked the way I read aloud, but my vioice sounded as though it came back from a radio echo chamber as I began verse twenty-seven:

"When he prepared the heavens, I was there: when he set a compass upon the face of the depth: when he established the clouds about: when he strenghtened the foundains of the deep: when he gave to the sea his decree, that the waters should not pass his commandment: when he appointed the foundations of the earth: Then I was by him, as one brought up with him: and I was daily his delight, rejoicing always before him; rejoicing in the habitable part of his earth; and my delights were with the sons of men."

I stopped reading. I was so short of breath. Then I looked at her and it was a moment with so much clinging to it!

"Ellen?"

"Yes?"

"Who is the 'I' in what we've been reading? No, first tell me— is the 'him' God?"

"Yes, the 'him' is God, the Father."

"Well, then who's the 'I'? Who was there when He set a compass upon the face of the depth?" I tried not to shout. "Who was there before the mountains were settled? Who's the 'I'?"

"Do you have any idea who it could be, Genie?"

"I suppose you're going to say it was Jesus Christ."

"Yes, it was."

"But in the first part of the chapter it says Wisdom is talking. I caught you that time. You're imagining things. You're on a Jesus Christ kick!"

"In the Scofield Reference Bible in a footnote on that part of Proverbs it says the Wisdom referred to is Christ."

"That's just somebody's interpretation. Mother used to have a Scofield Bible. How do you know Scofield is right?"

"He gives as his authority his own devout heart."

"His own devout heart?"

"Yes. He says quite simply that the devout mind is sure that this is Christ who was there in the beginning. There are certain things a Christian just knows. Like the Gospel of John—in the very first verse it says, 'In the beginning was the word and the word was with God and the word was God. By him were all things made and without him was not anything made that was made.'"

"Is *that* in the Bible, too?"

"Yes, in the Gospel of John."

"Brother, those old birds could really write! That's magnificent!"

"Want to read the rest of Proverbs eight?"

"No, I want luncheon. Order for you, too?"

She smiled. "No thanks. You come eat with me today in the dining room."

"Are you kidding? It would take more than a few verses of Scripture to get me to eat with a bunch of Christians, dear heart. They scare me."

I tried the casual treatment, but somehow I knew I wasn't fooling her one bit. Things couldn't have been flailing inside me as they were without making marks on my face. And when she had gone, I forgot about ordering my own luncheon and began reading the hotel Bible again.

She had quoted that gorgeous bit from the Gospel of John. I looked in the index under "gospel" and didn't find it. So I started browsing in the vicinity of the Psalms. Psalm 23 looked warm and familiar when I passed it. I experimented and discovered I still remembered it. I spoke aloud alone.

"Wonder if I learned any more of this when I was a kid?" "For God so loved the world that he gave his only begotten Son, that whosoever believeth on him should not perish but have everlasting life." That was John 3:16! No doubt the same as the Gospel of John!

I felt very, very proud and pleased and thought I'd quote it for Ellen when she came back. Something fresh and clean and new had crept in. Something not unlike the dream about the garden and the children who laughed. I dropped the Bible on the floor by the big chair in front of the window and sat watching the steam shovel at work.

"For God so loved the world that He gave his only begotten Son, that whosoever believeth on him should not perish but have everlasting life."

There was more to it than this life. That I knew. The "more" almost had to be God, didn't it? But what could God be like? If only we had a picture of Him!

"God is everywhere" they had taught us in Sunday School. But that was one of the things that made me angry. Everywhere was far too vague.

Ellen came back that afternoon and stayed only about an hour because she had to do some book work for the eternal dining room. I had been trying to reach a friend of ours from Charleston who was in New York radio and before she left I reached him and invited him to bring a friend and come up for a drink.

This, of course, was to hurt Ellen. The drink part, I mean. She loved the boy from home as much as I did. She was very close to his mother.

She left and my guests came and I ordered drinks for them but could not order for myself. Naturally, I had to explain. And what I said was, "I am either stumbling onto Reality or I'm on my way to a padded cell. It has to be one or the other."

The friend from home remarked effusively about how well I looked and didn't seem to doubt that something was happening. He seemed glad to leave in a little while.

When Ellen came back late in the afternoon, I really surprised her because I was dressed and wanted to take a walk in Gramercy Park. I had never wanted to take a walk in a park in my life before and I knew for sure then that much more than I meant to happen was happening.

But since it was my first park, it "did something for me" that she had access to the key to the big iron gate to Gramercy Park. It seems it is a very exclusive park and not really public at all unless you are park of the "public" with a key.

It was certainly unlike the New York I had known, but what was difficult for me was that for moments some of the time *this* New York seemed more familiar than the other one which I had known before.

The friend who had visited me that afternoon said he was glad to see me looking so well and seeming to be so interested in life but he hoped I wouldn't go too far with this God thing. I told Ellen this in the park and she smiled.

Ellen and his mother had been praying for us both.

That night we had dinner in my room. I did not ask how the (to me) "nebulous" Christians in the dining room at Calvary House got along without her, but she says she will always remember that dinner we had together because I asked her to "ask the blessing" for the first time. I will always remember it, too, because it wasn't one of those memorized things people grind out and anyway I hadn't even heard one of those in fifteen years.

When Ellen gave thanks she talked right to God and called Him "You" and seemed to know Him personally and said things to Him about the two of us sitting there ready to eat.

That night before Ellen left to go to her room in Calvary House, she said:

"By the way, we didn't finish that gorgeous part of Proverbs yesterday."

"The part about things before the mountains were settled?"

"Why don't you finish that chapter after I go tonight?"

"What chapter was it?"

"Eight . . . verse twenty-two to the end of the chapter."

"You're being so patient with me. I'm very grateful."

"I'm grateful, too, Genie."

"Stay and talk to me some more about—Him."

"You believe He exists now, don't you?"

"Most of the time I do, yes. Please stay longer."

"He does exist *all* of the time, and it will be much better for you to let Him talk to you without me. And for you to talk to Him."

I laughed. "Me talk to God? Why, that's praying!"

"Yes, I know it is. Good night, Genie. I'll be back in the morning as soon as I can get here."

For the first time in my life I felt glad to do as I was told. And quite obediently I opened the Bible to Proverbs 8 and read silently the first verses we had read: twenty-two through thirty-one. Then I read thirty and thirty-one again aloud:

"Then I was by him, as one brought up with him: and I was daily his delight, rejoicing always before him; rejoicing in the habitable part of his earth; and my delights were with the sons of men."

". . . my delights were with the sons of men."

If the "I" in that passage did happen to be Christ speaking, as the Old Testament Wisdom, did that mean that He loved old New York and Chicago and other "habitable" places of the earth and that "His delights" were really with the sons of men?

That would mean me, if it were true!

Why did Ellen want me to *finish* that chapter particularly?

When I finished it I found out:

"Now therefore hearken unto me, O ye children; for blessed are they that keep my ways. Hear instruction, and be wise, and *refuse it not*. Blessed is the man that heareth me, watching daily at my gates, waiting at the posts of my doors. For whoso findeth me findeth life, and shall obtain favour of the Lord. But he that sinneth against me wrongeth his own soul: *all they that hate me love death*."

After that I sat there for a long time and knew why she had asked me to finish the chapter.

". . . he that sinneth against me wrongeth his own soul . . . but whoso findeth me findeth life. . . ."

Sometime after midnight, I reached for the Bible again. It wasn't nearly so ugly as it had been. I opened it to a book called Isaiah, chapter fifty-nine. But before I read any of that I happened to see the last verse of fifty-eight.

"Then shalt thou delight thyself in the Lord; and I will cause thee to ride upon the high places of the earth. . . ."

I? Would He cause *me* to ride upon the high places of the earth?

Why? How? The beginning of the fifty-ninth chapter was next.

"Behold, the Lord's hand is not shortened, that it cannot save; neither his ear heavy, that it cannot hear."

I hated the word "saved." All the people I had ever known who went in for evangelism were always talking about saving souls. Intense, dreary people like those who stood on street corners and passed out those ugly tracts. People with inexcusable bad taste talked about being "saved." Why did Isaish have to spoil everything? The other parts of the Bible had been pure art!

But I rather liked the last part of the verse about "neither is his ear heavy, that it cannot hear." That helped. Yes, I was pathetically touchy. But that's why I was there in the hands of the living God.

I *needed* so to be there! I needed so to be—saved.

Isaish kept handing me strong, magnetic things and I took them eagerly and forgot "saved." "Their feet run to evil . . ."—yes, mine did. So what? "The way of peace they know not; and there is no judgment in their goings." Mother used to say I showed poor judgment in things. ". . . they have made them crooked paths; whosoever goeth therein shall not know peace . . . *we wait for light*, but behold obscurity; for brightness, *but we walk in darkness*."

I had to stand up. I couldn't stop reading but I couldn't bear to sit down a minute longer. And I began again to read aloud alone.

"We grope for the wall like the blind, and we grope as if we had no eyes: we stumble at noon day as in the night; we are in desolate places as dead men. . . ."

No!

Then I was on my knees by the side of the bed sobbing:
"I am in a desolate place as a dead man!"

When I looked at my watch it was just 1:00 A.M. I had friends
uptown in New York City who not only would have been hurt to
know I was there and hadn't called them, but who would come
and get me right now and take me back uptown where I belonged.
Back to Fifty-second Street where the "rich people" with silver
horns in their beautiful dark fingers made the world seem not out
there to trouble you anymore.

Would I call someone or just dress and grab a cab and go?
Perhaps to Nina's on Madison just off Seventieth? Maybe a
producer I knew. Anywhere I could feel at home and relaxed and
get away from this Thing that—followed me.

This Thing that hounded me.

The Hound of Heaven.

I dressed. And then limply I dropped my brown velvet hat
with the veil on the bed and went back to the chair beside the
window. I opened the Bible to the Psalms again. One hundred and
nineteen was a long one. And as far as I know it was the Hebrew
characters that headed each section which attracted my attention.
But my voice sounded as though I had been sick for a long time
when I began to read here and there in long Psalm 119 . . . aloud,
alone.

"Blessed are they that seek him with the whole heart . . . O that
my ways were directed to keep thy statutes!"

I hadn't noticed many exclamation points in the Bible, but
there was one and well it should be where I was concerned. With
my ways I could never keep His statutes! They were too hard. I
could never, never live the way Ellen lived.

Never!

"Blessed are thou, O Lord, teach me thy statutes! Open thou
mine eyes, that I may behold wondrous things out of thy law. *I am
a stranger in the earth:* hide not thy commandments from me! . . .

My soul breaketh . . . my soul cleaveth unto the dust: quicken thou me according to thy word. I have declared my ways, and thou heardest me: teach me thy statutes. Make me to understand the way of thy precepts: so shall I talk of thy wondrous works. My soul melteth for *heaviness:* strengthen thou me according to thy word. Remove from me the way of lying. . . ." There was not an exclamation point there but there should have been for me. ". . . remove from me the way of lying and grant me thy law graciously!"

I was on my knees again with the Bible open on the bed before me. I didn't know how to pray, but maybe God would listen if I just read to Him out of the Bible with all my heart.

"Thy hands have made me and fashioned me: give me understanding that I may learn thy commandments. Let my heart be sound in thy statutes; that I may not be ashamed. Make thy face to shine upon thy servant; and teach me thy statutes. Rivers of waters run down mine eyes, because they keep not thy law."

Rivers of waters ran down my eyes and wrinkled the pages of the hotel Bible and then I pushed it aside and tried to pray but all I could say was:

"O God . . . O God . . . O God . . . *O God!"*

About 5:00 A.M. I got up from my knees and lighted my first cigarette in almost four hours. I picked up the Bible again and read the very last verse of Psalm 119. Aloud.

"I have gone astray like a lost sheep; seek thy servant; for I do not forget thy commandments."

When I was barely four years old I stood in the pulpit of our church back home and sang *all* verses of the "Ninety and Nine." Now and then through the years when I had enough to drink to tip the inside of my heart so the truth showed, I would sing the "Ninety and Nine." At five in the morning there in the Gramercy Park Hotel before the steam shovel began to work that day, I sang what I could remember of the first verse:

There were ninety and nine that da-da-da,
In the shelter of the fold,
But one was out on the hills away,
Far off from da-da-da-da;

I remembered all of the chorus and also how hard it was for me to reach those high notes when I was four. Mother had said, "Don't strain, dear."

There was nothing *but* strain that morning . . . not of my voice, but of my soul.

Away on the mountains wild and bare,
Away from the tender Shepherd's care
Away from the tender Shepherd's care.

The strain of knowing suddenly that one is separated from God is the worst strain of all. Especially after one has lived so many years believing there is no God. To *realize Him and the space between* you at one and the same time is almost too much to bear.

It *is* too much to bear.

O God . . . O God . . . O God!

16

Another Telephone Call

"It is a fearful thing to fall into the hands of the living God." But all around the fear there brooded an almost familiar assurance that "my kindness shall not depart from thee." I hadn't read that promise in Isaiah yet, but although I knew I was going to crash, it seemed as though there would be kindness when it happened.

But the fear and the trembling and the strangeness and the heaviness must have shown black and deep on my face when Ellen arrived to spend Friday morning with me.

She looked tired, too, and I wanted to tell her how sorry I was to be causing her so much trouble but all I could say was:

"Something has happened to me."

"Do you know what it is?" She was very careful with me.

"No. But I'd give anything if I had never begun to believe in God! I'm coming apart at the seams."

The waiter brought my two big pots of black coffee and a fresh supply of cigarettes. I signed the check and he bowed out of the room and closed the door.

"Will this feeling ever go away now that I believe in Him?"

"Genie, *what* do you believe about God?"

I set the hotel coffee pot down too hard and snapped:

"How do I know *what* I believe? I just know He's—alive! That's enough to make me so miserable I'd gladly shoot myself."

I started to walk up and down the dark, maroon-patterned rug in front of the dresser.

"I can't 'keep his everlasting precepts'—I'm not put together that way!"

Ellen smiled at me. "Where did you read about precepts?"

"Last night. Statutes too. All night that Bible's been haunting me. But what happens now?"

"God will win."

"You mean I can't?"

"You can refuse to surrender to Him, but that won't mean you'll win. Everything will be harder and harder now that you've come this close to Him."

"Little Molly Sunshine just came to call."

"I'm sorry. I hate to hurt you. Or frighten you."

"Forget it. And how can you be so quiet about things? You sit there acting as though ghastly things like this happen every day. Don't you give a ———?"

She turned her face away quickly and I was so sorry.

"Forgive me, Ellen. I'm sorry. And I'm so—tired!"

"Why don't you let it all end right now, Genie? He's got your attention. He won't stop until He's got you, too. Is your life so happy and so good that you won't take a chance on God's having something better? Something more exciting? Something that will really fill that emptiness inside you? If you're tired, don't you want to—rest?"

I looked at her and laughed what didn't turn out to be a real laugh at all.

"If you knew how many times I've passed cemeteries and longed to change places with the lucky stiffs lying there with nothing to do but rest, you'd never ask such a crazy question."

"I knew that."

"Hm."

"You may think it's one *thing* or another that you hate to give up. It's really yourself."

"But my work—a radio producer can't make a living without beer commercials and violence! If God objects as you say He does to people making a living, then I'm terribly sorry, I just can't—"

"That isn't what God objects to."

"But suppose a beer sponsor wants a show and he comes to me?"

"That's a marginal issue. Lots of Christians disagree on lots of marginal issues."

"More alibis, huh?" I was accusing myself.

"More excuses for hanging on to the most important person in the world."

"Don't be nasty, dear. It isn't Christian."

"I'm not being nasty. Until I was off my own hands into the hands of the living God I *was* the most important person in the world to—Ellen Riley. And right now you're fighting God because Eugenia Price is the most important person in the world to you."

"I could never keep the Ten Commandments! I'm too old!"

"You're only thirty-three, but you couldn't keep them even if you were only twenty-three or thirteen. Neither could I."

"But you do. You're a saint."

"Righteousness is a pure *gift* of Grace."

"Don't start with that theological bosh. I don't understand it."

She "listened" a minute and then said very quietly:

"If you will just turn around and begin to follow Jesus Christ this minute, He'll see to it that you *can* keep the Ten Commandments and more. That's His part. That is (if you'll pardon the expression) Grace."

"I don't want to talk about Jesus Christ."

"He's God's revelation of Himself."

"I can't swallow that."

"You mean you don't want to."

"Who knows what I mean, you or I?" She didn't answer me. But she looked so concerned and I felt so ashamed. More than I had the other times when I snapped at her or used Jesus Christ's name to punctuate my railings at God and at life. I made frequent use of Christ's name. And that seemed to hurt Ellen more than anything I said to her. No matter how unkind. This annoyed me and I thought she was being sanctimonious. Practically everybody used His name when they swore. Didn't they?

Of course I knew she wasn't being sanctimonious because she always tried not to let me see that expression at all. We drank coffee for a few minutes in silence and then I said:

"Maybe if I called Mother and told her I had discovered God that would hold my nose to the fire and I'd just have to surrender to Him!"

She told me later that she wanted so much to be sure I realized first that the *only* Way to the Father was through the Son, Jesus Christ. But Something kept her silent. She just seemed to sit there and yearn for my peace of heart and mind. I wanted desperately for her to say something.

"Do you think that would make me do it if I called Mother?"

"I know how much she has influenced you always. She's been your god in a way. What do you think she would say?"

"Oh, Mother's religious. She's been saying I should go to church. She's watched me fall apart these last two years and all the poor woman dared to say was 'find a nice church and start going, dear.'"

"I know your mother wants only the best for you, Genie."

"What do you think? No, never mind what you think! I'm going to send her a telegram right now and tell her I'll be calling her tonight long distance with the most important telephone call of my life!"

"Well, what will you tell her when you call?"

I almost ran my coffee cup over. "I don't know what I'll tell her but maybe just the fact that after I send the wire I'll have to call and say *something* will force me to——do *it* between now and eleven o'clock tonight."

"Why eleven o'clock?"

"Oh, no reason. Mother and I just always have called each other at eleven o'clock. There are some telegraph blanks here in the desk.

I'm going to send it fast and then it will be too late to back down."

Ellen looked at me with endless love as I scribbled the message on the yellow blank. "You really *want* to belong to Him, don't you, Genie?"

"Something's got to happen. I can't stand much more of this."

"You couldn't prove your intentions more than sending that wire to your mother."

I finished writing the message and reached for the telephone to get a bellboy. The old Genie Price was dying hard. *She* raised an eyebrow and remarked:

"Of course, I can always lie when I call her tonight. Very plausible that I'm in New York on 'business.' The 'important telephone call' could very nicely be a big new show. Mother and Dad wouldn't be surprised or even pay much attention by now. I've been making 'the most important telephone call of my life' to them for years. Poor darlings. I'm certainly glad I'm *their* daughter and not mine."

The telegram saying that I would call them for the most important telephone call of my life went winging to Charleston. Collect, of course. And between that afternoon and eleven o'clock that night, only the Grace Ellen talked about kept me from flying into a million tiny pieces.

At exactly five minutes to eleven that evening Ellen walked out the door of my room. I was both relieved and dismayed that she did not wait to be sure I told Mother the truth. But she left and somehow the very fact that she did made me all the more certain that she was right when she said she was leaving me there with Him. I knew He would be listening.

I addressed myself as sixteen different varieties of fool for having gotten into this call-to-Mother business in the first place. And sitting on the bed by the telephone stand I lighted a cigarette in preparation for the ordeal, smoked about a third of it, put it out, and lighted another one, also in preparation for the ordeal.

Ordeal? Calling Mother hadn't been that before.

But this time was this time and very, very different from any other time in my whole life. The operator said that Genie Price was calling from New York collect and, as always, before the operator finished her speech, Mother said, "Yes, indeed, we certainly will accept the charges."

This split second while Mother greeted me in her special cheerful long-distance telephone voice I loved so much was my last chance to fabricate a "reason" for having called. I was adept at fabrication and a split second had been ample time for years, but instead I blurted:

"Mother, I think I've discovered what God is all about!"

During that long, God-watched moment when we both just breathed on our separate ends of the wire, it hit me that I *had* only gone *that* far and no further. I had *not surrendered to God*. I had only fallen into His hands and was still fighting Him with all my wits. Wanting Him with my heart but fighting Him with my wits.

"Have you made a decision, dear?"

I hadn't heard Mother mention a "decision" since I was fourteen and playing for the revival meetings at church. It sounded strange and unlike Mother and very very much like Mother, too.

"A decision?" My laugh was nervous. "No. Not yet. But I thought maybe if I called you I'd somehow have to do it! I want to, Mother. I really want to live for God. Do you think I'm crazy? Will Dad and Joe think I'm crazy?"

Mother had begun to cry. "Are you in New York City with Ellen, dear? At the place where she lives?"

"No. I'm scared of that place. It's full of Christians, but I'm with her. I mean I've been spending a lot of time with her. She's so doggone peaceful, Mother. And I'm tired of trying to be something I'm not!"

"How's your money, dear?" The most familiar question of all.

"Low as usual. I'm going home tomorrow. Back to Chicago."

"No. Daddy will wire you a hundred dollars. I want you to stay there and be exposed to Ellen over the weekend. Daddy will want you to stay, too."

The money came the next morning and I stayed over. On Saturday afternoon further proof came that something *was* happening in me.

I went the last place I ever dreamed I'd go. To Calvary House to see Ellen's room and write Mother a note on one of the office typewriters. Ellen promised not to introduce me to anyone if she could avoid it, and I went. It was like a big college dormitory, only it had an elevator. I said it was gloomy and must be convenient for people with very little money. That's what I said, but I felt a movement and a Life there that was brand new to me.

And attractive.

I didn't feel one bit at home, but I wanted to.

We may have used the private key and walked again in the little locked-up Gramercy Park but neither of us remembers whether we did or not. I simply remember a kind of lull in things and a waiting and a restlessness that had tears in it. But I remember how sweet the air seemed and Ellen was even kinder than usual and very, very careful with me.

It was as though we both knew something tender and eternal was about to happen.

In fact, I began to wish I knew exactly what to do about it but Ellen just seemed to be "listening" and I felt somehow the way young girls must feel when they are about to be married.

I had not confessed that Jesus Christ is Lord, but the Holy One of Israel had my attention. My full attention. So much so that, even before Ellen asked me, I said I wanted to go to church with her the next morning, which was Sunday.

She said I would have to wear a hat, which I hated to do, but for some reason I had brought one with me and so I said I'd wear it. She was supposed to come to the hotel to get me at about ten o'clock so we would have time to talk a little and get there early.

She wanted me to be there before the eleven o'clock service started, she said, because there was one old window she wanted me to see. There were elegant new ones, too, but this old one was the one she wanted me to see.

It was beautiful and misty green and small and up in a high, vaulted corner, as I remember it. A big square Cross was tipped sideways in its design of heavy clouds. Light came from the Cross in rays as it burst through the clouds. Rays that had the help of the Sunday morning sun outside.

I looked and looked and looked at that window.

And particularly at the Cross in it. And the heavy clouds.

This was the apparent reason she wanted us to be there early but also she knew *He* could get "at me" there in the silence of the old Calvary Church sanctuary. Could get "at me" off my own familiar territory.

I was very quiet and kept looking also at Ellen's hands while she sat in silent prayer. I knew they hadn't always looked so peaceful. But they did now. And my heart longed for that peace. My hands were restless without a cigarette.

This was the first church service I had attended in eighteen years. I went to my Grandmother Price's funeral but that was all. Dr. Shoemaker spoke simply and with beautiful diction and deep humility about the Grace of Jesus Christ.

There it was again. The *Grace of Jesus Christ!*

I couldn't tell Dr. Shoemaker to stop talking about Christ as I had told Ellen. And anyway I didn't want him to stop. He said Grace was a gift. That we only had to be empty to receive it. That Jesus had sacrificed Himself on the Cross of Calvary not only to atone for our sins once and for all, but to release Grace that was all-sufficient for anything. And that we only had to *receive* the Atonement *and* the Grace. At least this is what I remember of his sermon.

I wanted it to be true but whether I believed it or not I cannot say. All I can say is that when he had finished talking about Christ,

Dr. Shoemaker, with a heavenly light on his face, prayed in his beautiful diction and when he talked to God in the name of Jesus Christ I longed to be able to do it, too. He was on very close terms with God. So was Ellen. They were at peace. Dr. Shoemaker obviously was an extremely intelligent, highly educated man. And yet he lived his life following the Carpenter of Nazareth. He said he was indwelt with God's Holy Spirit. He said anyone could be who belonged to Christ.

I don't know how much I believed but I know I longed to belong, too. And when it was time for Communion I thought:

"Ellen has been so kind and so patient with me, maybe if I go up there and kneel down and take Communion beside her it will help make up for all the trouble I've been. And also for that nasty crack I made about the grape juice when we first met in August."

Something was said about baptism, but I wasn't listening and I figured no one would know who I was anyway. So I got up and started to follow Ellen down the gently sloping center aisle toward the altar.

She avoided looking at me.

I felt as though I were going to faint and then I was jerked to a dead stop. No one had touched me. But I couldn't move a step nearer that altar where the Communion cup and the wafers waited to be shared by those who followed Christ.

"His Blood which was shed for thee."

"His Body which was broken for thee."

I turned and ran from the church and headed for the bar of the Gramercy Park Hotel! It was closed until 1:00 P.M. on Sunday! Ellen had to work at the church until 2:30 P.M. I had time with nothing to do. And so, while I waited for the bar to open, I walked round and round the block past Calvary Church and watched the people come out after the Communion service. A few noticed a nervous woman in a brown suit and a brown velvet hat standing across the street smoking one cigarette after another. A few noticed but New Yorkers and Chicagoans don't notice anyone for long.

So these were Christians. Did I want to be one? Ellen had said there were varying degrees of Christians. Many didn't go all the way with Christ. Many just came to church because it was the respectable thing to do. I thought that was revolting. If I were a Christian I'd want to be a—disciple.

"I'd want to kiss His feet with the nail prints in them!"

Did I say that?

Yes, I did. Aloud on the sidewalk across the street from the Church where the people were coming out to go home after Communion.

But I went back to my hotel and waited in the attractive lounge for the bar to open. About thirty-five minutes I waited. Hotels like this one were so much more attractive than gloomy places like churches.

"I belong here in this atmosphere. Not over there in that dingy place."

Then I remembered the little window with the Cross high in the vaulted corner of the old sanctuary and I thought about Grace. What a strange word for a minister to use. For the Bible to use for that matter. Grace to me had always meant to be graceful. I began turning the word *graceful* around in my mind as I waited.

"To be graceful meant to be filled with grace."

Dr. Shoemaker had said Grace was a gift. Released to us because Christ died for us on the Cross.

Christ.

Three minutes to one and I was waiting to walk in when the waiter who had given me room service opened the doors of the Gramercy Park cocktail lounge.

17

The Second Time

I sat there in the bar until almost two and then went to my room and ordered a large, expensive meal sent up. I asked the waiter to wait while I poured into a water glass the two double Scotch old-fashioneds I had ordered. I wanted him to take the old-fashioned glasses back with him so Ellen wouldn't see them when she came in after her own noon meal was over.

The water glass which contained the two drinks had been washed in very hot water and stood innocently empty on my room-service table when she knocked at my door a few minutes later. She looked apprehensive and was so sorry she couldn't get there sooner. I knew she would be wondering about me because she had seen me run from the church.

She was very, very, very careful with me. I recognized that careful treatment by then and because I had stopped off down-stairs I was prone to express myself freely. And too glibly. And very like a phony. Which in part I still was.

"Your church service was very impressive, darling. Shoemaker could have gone far in the theater. The entire thing was good drama."

She just looked at me.

"In fact, I'm quite excited about this whole Christian business."

"Are you?" She sounded far away. On that opposite shore, the way she had sounded the first day we talked in August.

I beat the top of my cigarette with my forefinger.

"I'm not doing a very good job of this, am I?"

"No." I was suddenly afraid again for the first time since I "dropped in" downstairs. I knew she knew I had "dropped in," too. "No, you're not doing a very good job." She seemed quietly pleased that I wasn't.

"Ellen . . ."

"What is it?"

"What does God look like to you? What do you think of when you think of God?"

"I've told you. I think of Jesus Christ."

I began to walk up and down and it was very frustrating because my loaded room-service table was in the way. Suddenly I grabbed up the old cocky manner and raised my left eyebrow which I always did when I wanted to appear poised:

"Maybe you're right about Jesus Christ. Maybe He *is* God. Maybe they're one and the same."

"Genie!"

"Maybe that's true. And in church today I realized when I heard your minister speak that Christians don't need to be dull people as I thought. I think Jesus Christ is the most attractive Person I've ever known about. In fact, He's just what we've all been hunting for back in Chicago all these years. I and all my friends back there. We're all bored to death and He's tremendously exciting! *But*—I think *you're* far too radical about it. You say I'll have to give myself up entirely and I think that's emotionalism on your part. Or dramatics."

She stood up and was very tall for a moment.

"I didn't say that. Christ said it. It isn't my idea to give your-self up entirely. It's His."

"Well, then your interpretation is wrong. Extreme. Radical. Jesus Christ is just what we've all been hunting for back in Chicago, only it's ridiculous to say a man or a woman can't worship God and still be human. Certainly God can adapt Himself more easily than I can adapt myself!"

"Jesus Christ will *change* you, Genie, if you are willing. It's not a matter of adaptation! Have you missed the point completely?"

"No! On the contrary. And I can't wait to get back to tell my friends what I've discovered about God!"

Ellen walked toward me.

"Are you going back to Chicago and tell those people that twisted, distorted spiel about God adapting Himself to *your* way of life?"

I stepped back from her and stuck my chin out and laughed.

"I most certainly am. I think it's a fascinating idea! Christ should brighten things up for us considerably!"

She looked at me for a moment and then reached for her coat. It was a yellow tweed topper. Something pushed hard against my heart. I gripped my cigarette so tightly it broke and I had to put it out. Even that was gone for this walled-off moment before my last defense cracked. . . .

She wouldn't dare leave me now!

Ellen had her coat on and was at the door.

She had been so patient and long-suffering she couldn't go. But she was going and I knew that if she left me then I'd be without God forever.

God!

"Oh, God, don't let her go!" I didn't say this aloud. It screamed through my tightened heart. She hadn't turned the doorknob yet, and suddenly she walked back toward me across the room.

"It won't work any other way except His way, Genie. Jesus says He is the way and the truth and the life. He says no man cometh to the Father but by Him. Jesus Christ said that. And He's either telling the truth or He's the biggest phony who ever walked the face of the earth! He also says if we try to save our lives we'll lose them. But if we lose them for His sake we'll find them. We find life in Christ, Genie!"

". . . whoso findeth me findeth life!"

I remembered that from the end of the only part of Proverbs I know.

". . . whoso findeth *me* findeth life!"

The earth slipped a little beneath me as I stood there clutching the edge of the dresser until my finger with the bitten nail hurt. Ellen didn't smile at all.

"Genie, you'll make such a terrific Christian!"

I twisted around and fell into the big chair by the window and sobbed: "Oh, God, I wish I were dead!"

Ellen didn't come over and put her arm around me the way you would think at a time like that. Instead she said very calmly and with absolute authority:

"Genie, it would be wonderful if you *would* die!"

"What?"

"It would be the most wonderful thing that ever happened to you if the old Genie Price would die right now—this minute, so the new one can be born."

I stopped sobbing, I think.

We don't remember.

And after a few long seconds, Ellen says I looked up at her. The darkness dropped away and I whispered:

"Okay, I guess you're right."

Then light.

Ellen has wondered many times since then if what she did was right. Rather what she did not do. We didn't pray. I was so touchy and Ellen had never led anyone to Christ before. And anyway I had been praying out of Isaiah and the Psalms and wordless cryings of my own all week long. This was just the step into freedom and neither of us did anything after it. We just sat there that autumn afternoon in the peace and the quiet of His Presence and let Him be all around us. That I was truly born again from above no one has ever doubted.

The rest of the book is about a new child of God who had absolutely *everything* to learn. Everything, that is, except that Jesus Christ did come out of that tomb.

I knew that.

And I was so grateful that I knew it.

Ellen says she knew it in a new way at that moment, too. He couldn't still be in the tomb. He was there with us!

Part Two
"UNSHACKLED!"

18

Train on Wings

I was born the first time on June 22, 1916, and then I was born the second time on October 2, 1949. And if this sounds like fantasy still to you, *this* is the part of the book which proves that the second birth is fact. And especially Reality.

On Monday morning, October 3, 1949, Ellen went to New York's Grand Central Station with me and put me on a train for Chicago and her faith in Christ leaped up. It had to. There would be no one to "feed the new babe" when she got there! A letter she wrote to me later that same morning said:

"I went back to my room at Calvary House and got on my knees to pray, but instead I just cried and cried and cried. And then He was bigger than He had ever been to me."

She cried in part from exhaustion, I'm sure. But she also knew what *could* happen to me without Christian "fellowship." (A word she knew better than to use, by the way, because my touchiness was far from gone.) She wept from weariness and concern and from the impact of that sudden up-leap of faith within her.

Ellen cried, but I sat up on the train in the coach all the way and scarcely knew it because to me the train had wings! As a first "birthday" gift, Ellen had handed me Thomas Kelly's *Testament of Devotion*, and she did it on direct orders from the Holy Spirit, because I don't think I put it down all the way back to Chicago except to look up at the stars now and then and say to God over and over, "You *are* real and now You're mine and now I'm Yours!" Thomas Kelly's writing and thinking had been influenced by Alfred North Whitehead and so had mine when I was in my early twenties and writing the poetry. Arid with the single-simplicity and light in each line of *Testament of Devotion* I felt more and more at home. I didn't understand much of it yet, but I knew Thomas Kelly was my brother in Christ and, even though he had died physically a few years before, one day further along in this "Eternal Now" we could sit down and have good talk together. I had only believed in eternal life for a very few days, and I relaxed to know that Thomas Kelly who felt exactly as I did about both Christ *and* words would be there when I got there. Thomas Kelly and Ellen and Dr. Shoemaker did much to "redeem" Christians for me.

As the crack streamliner moved through the night toward Chicago, my heart leaped up with joy. The joy He promised His disciples. Was I a disciple of Jesus Christ? Yes! O Holy One of Israel . . . O Wonderful, O Wonderful, O Wonderful . . . Thou art only and art all! Thou art mine and I am Thine!

Thomas Kelly wrote of Holy Obedience. My soul called back: "Yes, I, too, want to be wholly obedient!"

I wanted to obey someone for the very first time in my entire life.

I had no idea what Holy Obedience would mean, but at that point the Holy One kept me mercifully blind to that. He knew I could not bear to see yet. He simply *filled* my soul with hunger to *belong to Him*. A hunger so deep and so wide that only He could fill it. I would follow Him anywhere. Anywhere. If only He is up ahead, I will follow.

"Where He leads me, I will follow . . . where He leads me, I will follow . . . Where He leads me, I will follow . . . I'll go with Him, with Him . . . all the way!"

For the first time in eighteen years I remembered that old song, and I longed to be able to run and tell someone I remembered it. There on the train I began to experience the pangs of longing for the companionship of other Christians who were also excited about Jesus Christ.

My eyes filled with quick tears for just a moment when it struck me for the first time that Ellen would be living in New York and I'd be in Chicago! Why had I waited all week long to become a Christian when we could have been talking about Jesus instead of me?

People in Chicago would think I'd taken leave of my sanity. And they would have every reason to think that.

"I wonder what my friends *will* say?"

While I made the changeover from the old life to the new, I had arranged to spend a few days in the home of three friends who were devout Catholics. Surely they would understand what had happened to me. They believed in God. I wondered what they believed *about* Him? I didn't know much of what I believed, but I knew I was excited about Him and that we belonged to each other. I knew so many people, but it had been years since I had discussed God from a religious standpoint with anyone. I knew these friends at whose home I would stay went to Mass every Sunday morning. They would be excited when I burst in their front door and announced, "I have just discovered God! I'm a new creature in Christ Jesus. It says so in the Bible! I'm all new and never going to be the old Gene Price again!"

Yes, it was good to be going to their house for several days. I had so much studying and thinking and planning to do. And so much reading! I didn't own a Bible but I knew they would have one. I could scarcely wait to get there to begin reading it.

In the old days I probably would have helped myself to the hotel Bible as one did hotel towels and laundry bags. But that was out of the question now. I was a Christian! After all, hadn't I stood five minutes before I checked out waiting for the hotel cashier to find the slip I'd signed for four packages of Camels? I was a Christian! I couldn't cheat the Gramercy Park Hotel tobacco counter out of money. As I rode along the train, I remembered what I said to Ellen that morning as we stood waiting for the cigarette check at the cashier's window.

"You see, my new religion is costing me money already!"

I went back to Thomas Kelly and the train went on to Chicago.

19

"Go Quickly and Tell!"

Two things I had promised Ellen before I left New York. Number one: I would never begin a single day without at least half an hour of "quiet time" each morning with Him.

"Read something in the Bible first to cleanse and fill your mind and then just sit with Him in the silence."

This sounded like little enough to do, and the first time I managed to "sit with Him in the silence" for four entire minutes.

But I have kept that promise faithfully and now an hour and a half in God's Word, in prayer and listening is swift.

Promise number two: "Tell people what has happened to you."

I began keeping the second promise the minute I burst in the front door of my friends' house early the morning of October 4, 1949. They were receptive and wondering and very kind to me. One said she thought I must have received some special Holy "revelation."

They let me read their mother's well-worn old Douay Version of the Bible and I did little else for three or four days except to write long, excited, "spiritual" letters to Ellen. I was discovering things Eternal so fast I ate only to be polite and for the first time in fifteen years looked forward to waking up in the mornings. This I did at a frightfully early (to me) eight o'clock without an alarm!

I read and read and read the four Gospels. John at once became my favorite and still is. Perhaps because more than anything I, too, wanted to be Jesus' "beloved disciple." His love held me completely captive.

Little I knew in my own life of the meaning of "cruciform and blood-stained" but the thought of my Beloved hanging on a Cross made me weep and want to hang there with Him.

I went to church with my friends once and the Stations of the Cross hurt me and held me and I wept because He had to die for me. And yet I knew *life* had *found me!* Glorious, sun-filled, Son-blinded life that would never let me go. This was not masochistic torment into which I walked with chin held high, determined to serve my Beloved, even if I had to stifle my own desires and shut out the call of a dark-melodied world. This was not a walk of self-effacement and ecstatic torment. This was a command to return to childhood!

This was a call back to the Natural.

This was my Creator calling me into the joy of Oneness with Him! This was "from the beginning, or ever the earth was" and this was new.

This was a completely *new* life. Just created *in* me. I had not learned to walk in it yet. But it was mine as eternity was mine. And for the first time in many years, those short crisp lines as in my early poetry began to move to the surface of my mind.

Joyfully!

I search
The secret
Silence
Of my soul
For some
New way
To say:
I love.

An outward
Turn back
To the old
Is not
Nor will
It ever be,
For now
Is *Now.*

So spring
I inward
Where the
Light is
Ever held at
Springing
And Eternity
And Love
And All
Are mine
At last.

For the first three days after I came back to Chicago I just read the Bible, prayed, walked in the falling autumn leaves and wrote and wrote and wrote.

There I was back on the South Side of Chicago again, not far from where I had found "Near Reality" ten years before on Cornell Avenue. My friends lived not many blocks from my old apartment. The South Side smelled the same in autumn because there are trees out there and people actually burn leaves in the gutters the way people who write sonnets love for them to do. I loved the burning leaves, too, and I loved not minding admitting to something I considered suitable material only for poets who rhymed things.

Slowly the high walls of having to be one certain way or *smother* began to vanish. I had smothered and was free. I found myself talking with people on the streets again. I hadn't dreamed of ever getting into another sidewalk discussion now that Spunky was gone. I didn't like them then but I couldn't resist because people admired her so much and I was so proud of her. But there I was ambling along the sunny, leaf-smoked Hyde Park streets smiling at people and talking to them at the slightest opportunity.

Did I really love them?

Yes, I did.

Oh, yes, I really did!

October 7, 1949

Ellen, dear . . .

You know it's the most amazing thing the way I love people now! I don't have to work on it either. It's just in my heart.

October 8, 1949

Dear Genie,

I was wondering last night if you have told any of your other old friends about your conversion to Christ. If so, what did they say?

After the first three days I began to *tell* it. It wasn't that I meant to wait even that long. I just needed that time to grasp some of it myself. And then I began the rounds of my old friends and the heads of the various radio networks and advertising agencies where I had professional contacts.

They all listened attentively with reactions which ranged from misty eyes to raised eyebrows—Jews, Catholics, pagans, occasional churchgoers, skeptics, agnostics. My "audience" varied more each day it seemed and the more I told about it, the more I knew it was true.

Witnessing for Jesus Christ is supposed to be very difficult, but I didn't know that, and so I found it all extremely stimulating and exciting and not one bit difficult as it is supposed to be. I knew none of the stock phrases then, and so must have startled everyone considerably as I breezed in and out one agency waiting room after another network lobby, beaming and declaring:

"I've fallen in love with God!"

"You what?"

"I have a new Romance! This one begins with a capital R."

"Yeah?"

"Yes! I'm in love with Jesus Christ. And look, I want you to watch me from now on. I don't understand it either, but according to the Bible I'm a new creature and I won't be doing the things I used to do because I belong to Christ now and He belongs to me!"

"Don't worry, old girl. You'll be watched. Like a hawk."

I was. And nothing is more conducive to spiritual growth than the knowledge that skeptical people who don't know Him are watching your every move.

Early, very early, I was made aware that everywhere I went I had the reputation of Jesus Christ in my hands.

And within two weeks I had turned down a high-salaried TV dramatic show and closed Eugenia Price Productions, because I could not write murder stories for children to watch nor talk adults into doing what I could no longer do and follow my new Lord. Not and belong to Him as I had to belong. Came and departed the week of swift tie-breaking. And by October twentieth I was free of every professional tie except a large indebtedness to an elderly lady who had graciously loaned me money when I first opened the office.

Did I say free? Yes, free and broke and far, far in debt. But I was beginning to remember what I read in my Bible, and Ellen reminded me in at least every other letter that if I would seek Him and His Kingdom first "all these things" would be added unto me.

Did I take that literally?

Completely.

And for another week all I seemed able to do was sit out on the black and white sun porch of my kind friends' home and read the Word of God.

What would I do next? I had no idea.

How would I earn a living? I had no ideas whatever.

Could I continue in radio and still be a Christian? I didn't know and that week I seemed unable to concentrate on it. I had so much to learn about Him. He was my Saviour and my Lord and my Beloved and I knew so little about Him. Over and over and over I read things He had said.

"If any man would be my disciple, let him deny himself, take up his cross daily and follow me."

Only God would dare say that! What a relief that He *is* God.

"Come unto me all ye that labour and are heavy laden and I will give you rest."

Only God *could give* rest.

"Take my yoke upon you, and learn of me; for I am meek and lowly in heart: and ye shall find rest unto your souls. For my yoke is easy and my burden is light."

"*. . . my yoke is easy, and my burden is light*"!

Early I was able to believe that because He said it.

If He said it, it just had to be true because of who He is.

Jesus said His yoke is easy and His burden is light. So, even though for the first time I *wanted* a clean slate financially, I knew I must not fret and stew if I had no job and no idea of how I would pay my debts. I knew I must wait on God, then obey Him.

As I look back over almost five years, this takes my breath away. Figuring angles had been my life. And yet there I sat reading the Gospel of Matthew as carefree as a child in her father's house.

The *one* thing I did for which I can take credit was to *believe* that I had become a child in my Father's house. I believed it and I saw no reason not to *act* like it.

A carton of cigarettes began to last a very long time. My daily average dropped from a frequent three packs to less than one. It hadn't occurred to me at all that He might want me to stop smoking. Practically everyone I knew smoked except Mother, who didn't like the taste of tobacco, and two of the friends with whom I was staying. But one night while I was still their guest, I lay in bed praying and at the same time smoking a last cigarette for the night. Prayer was so new to me I had formed a habit of picturing a railroad track from Heaven to Earth and on that "track" which was my faith, He was able to send down the answer. Suddenly the "track" seemed all smoke-filled and hazy and cut off. And aloud I said, "Lord, could it be that You don't want me to smoke?"

To me cigarettes were like my breath and next to it in importance. I loved them. I began smoking when I was fourteen and almost twenty years had passed since then. They were a great emotional satisfaction as they are to everyone who smokes habitually. I do not say the use of tobacco will make "void" your passage to Heaven. I am simply telling you what happened to me.

I had to stop. And I did, the first of several times, that night— with that cigarette which I was smoking as I prayed. I put it out and said, "All right, Lord," and He drew closer.

Then I got right out of bed and went into the kitchen and told my friends what I had done. They wondered and admired me and for the first time in my life I didn't want to be admired at all. My only part had been to obey. But I did learn that our part is to be *willing* to go right through suffering *with* Him. There is a great Glory in the fellowship of His sufferings. It brings Oneness with Him. And the more Oneness, the more Glory and the more Glory, the more Oneness. But His heart longs for us to have fellowship with His *Resurrection* Life! And it is well for us to learn, more completely than I learned then, that even He did not have to hang on the Cross after He died.

Every time I gave up something for Him, I loved Him more. And as He walked with me through those stumbling, blundering first days in which He was testing my sincerity, He *kept* me aware

211

of His actual presence. I believe He did this because He knew how unaccustomed I was to considering God at all.

Certainly He, most of all, knew how tricky I had always been. He could not move forward with His Plan for my life until He had given me a few preliminary trials. And even though He knew I had not yet given up the "right" to myself, He did know that I had confessed Him as my Lord and Saviour . . . that I had stopped smoking and, of course, I had stopped drinking . . . that I had stopped believing worry necessary to daily life . . . that I longed to be with other people who loved Him as I did . . . that my chief happiness was reading things He said . . . that I didn't understand it at all, but that I knew I had been *made new.*

He knew I was waiting for Him now.

And He moved.

A letter came from Ellen written in a high excitement. But so definite and certain. One thing had happened and then right after it another thing had changed in her work and when a third thing happened right after the second, she knew what to do. In this letter I learned for the first time how strong her compelling to come to Chicago to "look after me" had been. And now she was at peace about it. Providential circumstances had cut her ties in New York and she was coming to Chicago to be with me!

It was October, but I sang "Joy to the World!" I didn't know many Christian songs at that point, but I knew "Joy to the World." And I sang it as loudly as I could sing it and kissed all three of my hostesses and kissed my pocket-picture of Jesus over and over and over and over.

Now I'd be able to find out all the wonderful things Ellen knew about Him! I'd rush right out and rent an apartment and we'd read the Bible and talk about Jesus Christ twenty-four hours a day the rest of our earthly lives!

I still lived under the sign of an exclamation point and overdid everything, but every exaggerated intention was toward Him and, as you will see, He blessed and transformed and *used* my every blunder.

He knew he had reached down and saved an immature, "spoiledbrat" extremist. But He knew He had saved her and now He would begin to make her like Himself.

We didn't know it, but He knew all along that the first thing He had to do, of course, was to send Ellen to Chicago so He could continue the process through her, which He had so breathtakingly begun.

20

Blunder to Transform

There is one mansion-lined, shady street on the Near North Side of Chicago which is considered by everyone to be the most elegant street on the entire North Side. Particularly is it considered to be the most elegant by those who live up and down it in mahogany-paneled "brownstones," balconied "smooth stones," large glass front "moderns" and old ivy-covered "red bricks."

In answer to an ad which read "English basement, ——— Street, nothing comparable," I went to look with a friend who had many misgivings, but knew how hard apartments were to find in Chicago in 1949. The building was one of the loveliest brownstones. Light brownstones, in fact, newly sandblasted. And inside in the owner's apartment, my heart sang, "Thank You Lord!" It was beautiful. But my friend had *seen* the one for rent which was "comparable to nothing," according to the ad in the paper. And as the owner (an altogether amazing blond lady in riding breeches) gestured sweepingly for us to follow her "downstairs," I saw at once that only the upstairs had been given the remodeling touch that makes a run-down mansion an elegant home.

Downstairs there *was* "nothing comparable."

The blond, jodhpured owner was doing an admirable job of keeping my mind occupied with herself. But in spite of her high ability, I did see the "apartment." I should be ashamed to admit that I saw it because I signed a year's lease to rent it at one hundred and twenty-five dollars per month. But I do admit I saw it and immediately leaped wildly and innocently to a completely *wrong* spiritual conclusion.

"This," I breathed to myself (remembering Thomas Kelly's thought about the Inward Light in which everything appears in an entirely new relationship), "is no doubt God's idea for me! I've been so high and mighty all my life, most likely He wants me to learn to live in peasant surroundings like this!"

I feel positive God never wills for any of His children to go head over heels in debt for something which is sheer madness in the first place. But following my wrong "guidance" all the way, with childlike abandon of the few practical maturities I had inadvertently gathered through the years, I made a profound statement about the Lord taking care of His own, misquoted the Scripture about Seek ye first the Kingdom and signed the lease with a flourish almost "comparable" to the owner's own.

With that flourish I sentenced Ellen and myself to one year in a literal dungeon. There was one pipe-paneled, pipe-ceilinged room about ten by fifteen feet, of dark, pocketbook brown with green and yellow candelabra (*with* flames) *painted* on one wall and a purple rooster on the other. Also around the crooked doorway which led to the adjoining bathroom were *painted* green ivy vines. Along one end, just following the refrigerator which one always bumped upon entering, ran the sink and stove or "the lovely modern kitchenette," as the owner called it with a half-sweep of one hand and a full sweep of the other. At the end of the things that made up the kitchen there was one window which did not open at all. It was sealed shut.

"For your protection," she said, completely discounting air.

Adjoining the sealed window was a door. This did open to the outside on a "patio with definite possibilities." And there *were* "possibilities" of calling a junkman to haul off a ton of stuff and then there were other "possibilities" of shoveling and sweeping for a matter of hours. Over these "possibilities" our only air would move into our little nest.

Through the doorway to the "bath" around which "hung" the painted ivy, one looked up into a pipe-laden ceiling and down at a stained wash-basin ("very expensive at one time and still there because of the war" in 1949), and then if one would see down into the "tub" one first mounted the "throne" which stood easily a foot above the floor level. Seeing down into the tub was better left undone because the tub (also "a war casualty and the complete fault of the government") sloped toward the back instead of toward the drain and in order to empty it completely one had to *push* the water forward for minutes, while straining to keep one's balance from the "throne level," yet still stooping sufficiently to avoid contact with the hot pipes overhead. We eventually knelt while "bailing" the tub.

Passing through the bath to the second "room," the owner scraped her knuckles as she swooped through the rough brick entrance and struck gesture 2B, exclaiming throatily as she swooped:

"Look, isn't this quaint? Genuine brick walls!"

The "old" Gene Price would have let her have it and departed.

The "new" one, sincerely following her wrong "guidance," smiled warmly at the woman, felt genuinely sorry that anyone had to carry on like that, remembered when *she* was almost as obvious, made her Christian witness and said:

"I'll take it. My friend comes in from New York next week. We'll want to move right in."

The "second" room (my office) was a semiconverted coal bin exactly six feet wide and thirteen feet long. Along one end was a closet from whose ceiling a mysterious white powder fell throughout the year. A door that opened out onto the musty, airless, basement hallway had to be locked permanently because there was no room for my big desk otherwise. But even though the owner had developed some type of metaphysical theory that there was no such thing as fresh air, she did consent to have one panel of the door opened onto the old hallway and to install a ventilating fan which pulled nice fresh fuel air in to me from the furnace room next door to my "office."

Now, if you have gone all around the "apartment" with me and found no windows to the outside, you are correct. The health department would never have stood for this, but I was a Christian and Jesus said to turn the other cheek and I did—for Ellen, too, before she had a chance to advance an opinion.

Being a completely impractical extremist and a very, very green Christian, I had absolutely nothing right except my intentions. So, when Ellen arrived she could only do one thing: grow in that Grace she talked about.

This she did. And it was a long, long time before she even let me know how far her heart sank when I first took her gleefully to our "beloved catacombs" where for one year everything financial centered around scraping together one hundred and twenty-five dollars per month for rent.

Considering the way I had lived, and had this been a normal, two-roomed English basement, the rent seemed low enough the day I signed the lease. But I had not reckoned on things being changed quite as much as God had planned to change them.

We moved into the "elegant dungeon" on the first of November, and my first year with Christ began as He began, from the very first crate we unpacked, to transform my first big blunder. Mother had sent us a few lovely things, never dreaming what their setting would be. And although I'm sure she wanted to cry when she realized what was facing her shut up in that dark, airless pocket with a still very carnal and completely unpredictable Christian baby, Ellen laughed and set herself for the *moment* only as she watched Him make transformation number one:

The legs on a lovely walnut chest I was uncrating had been broken in transit.

I *almost* swore as I would have done, drowning the entire laboring class in a torrent of self-satisfied capitalistic phraseology and blaming Roosevelt for everything! Instead, I snapped my fingers, looked up from the broken chest I had just uncrated, and smiled at her.

"Honey, let's get the Lord's picture up on the wall before we call the transit company about this broken leg. They'll send an inspector and I want everybody who comes in our little house to know He lives here with us!"

We hung a copy of Signe Larson's powerful pen drawing of Jesus, read my first chapter of dear old Hannah Smith's *The Christian's Secret of a Happy Life,* had some powdered coffee, beat the dust out of the studio bed our landlady had generously contributed, and on our knees in the midst of crates of books and packing boxes, with the purple rooster watching from the wall above the Lord's picture, we talked to Him for a while and then we went to bed.

No decorating was furnished but if we'd get the paint from the hardware store and put it on, the "duchess" would let us deduct the cost of the paint from the rent, and I was so caught up in the wonder of my new life that it all seemed very fair to me. I loved the "duchess" and I loved Ellen and oh, how I loved Christ!

Before I drifted off to sleep that night I had a vague, happy feeling that soon I could like me again, too. At least I felt off my own hands and into His. And in spite of the insane apartment, with my production office gone and no job, I still felt like the daughter of the King, and for the first time in my entire life I knew I was free.

21

Upstairs and Down

It is easier and certainly simpler for an extremist to embark upon a life of Kingdom living. One cannot get along comfortably following Christ unless one is completely willing to be a fool for Him. An extremist is always "completely." In everything.

From having depended upon the Union Club Motor Livery's long, black limousines to deliver me or the merest package for years, I suddenly seemed to forget that even hardware stores deliver. Of course, I owed Union Livery so much money they wouldn't come for me anyway by that time, but had they been willing to go beyond the call of "creditor duty," I had stepped over into another kind of life.

I was free of having to *be* somebody now. I was His child and it was enough. And it was fun to go to the hardware store and carry home paint cans. Somehow it seemed as though I did it for Him. And armed with two new paintbrushes and wearing the whole armor of God, we began to splash white paint upon our pocketbook-brown walls. This was to be just the base coat to blot out some of the dingy brown and to liquidate the rooster and put out the painted yellow candelabra with flames. We cared not one whit whether the brush strokes were even or not, and so we drew big hearts with His name inside them, printed Scripture on the walls and I think for two days the whole thing was fun even for Ellen who is not an extremist.

Her loyal heart and her one hundred pounds labored right along with me and the Everlasting Arms were underneath. And, for two "ten- or eleven-hour" painting days, it *was* fun. But on the third day, when drenched in prayer, I mounted the wobbly ladder to tackle the battery of nine pipes which traversed the entire length of the low cobwebby ceiling, I began to think profoundly upon the chapter in Thomas Kelly called "Entrance Into Suffering."

The muscles in my arms had done no more than support my fingers on the typewriter keys since my dog stopped needing a leash ten years before, and that third day they began to scream in a most Calvinistic fashion! Judging by their behavior the muscles in my forearms were still property of the "old nature," and it must have been alive because they were.

The pipes were three-inch furnace pipes and very hot by eleven in the morning. The fumes made the tears flow and every time my brush rubbed the top of a pipe, flakes of rust fell in my eyes causing more tears to flow.

But, the Lord can *use* everything and he has used the memory of this next moment "at the pipes" to turn desperation to humor a dozen times for me during the past four years. After almost three hours on the ladder in the heat and fumes and falling flakes of rust, the "duchess" descended the stairs from her first-floor luxury, and assuming pose number twenty-six in the doorway of our little dungeon, she swept the ceiling with an outward fling of her plaited leather riding crop and literally *ejaculated:*

"My, but you girls are fortunate! That's the best material available in those lovely pipes. And—isn't it simply marvelous that they all run in the same symmetrical direction?"

For just a moment the ladder wobbled dangerously. Like you, when you read her speech just now, I thought I must be wrong. But that's what she said and Ellen stood there balancing her paint bucket on the corner of a packing box and heard it, too. We were just learning about our friend "upstairs." In fact, we were still learning about her the day we moved. And we were still amazed, although the learning had led to a real fondness by then.

There will be other things to tell you which will be very hard to believe, but this book is definitely not fiction. It is all true. And I am going to be careful not to over-batter your ability to believe. But while we're on the subject of the "duchess" and the pipes, I feel tempted to add that she suggested also, just before she ascended the stairs again that day, that we might hang artificial Spanish moss over the already dust-caked pipes for an unusual "touch of decor."

I had truly been born again. I was tremendously excited about my new Christian life. I had no intention whatever of going back. But had Spanish moss somehow found its way into that "whited sepulchre," things might have been very different for us both today.

What did we do after she left besides pat and soothe our screaming, twitching muscles?

We did what we have done for four years and more now.

We looked at Him and laughed.

The "duchess" and her pipes "of the very best material, all running the same symmetrical direction" did more than any other single thing to throw us safely over into the Holy hilarity of God where His really happy saints live and laugh.

Our friend, whom we nicknamed the "duchess" because "Mrs." was so inadequate, was as kind as her wealth would allow her to be. She liked us and we really liked her. In her magnificent living room "upstairs" sat a "magnificent" Mason-Hamlin grand piano with a tone like the music Bach must have heard when he wrote. And our friend the landlady offered to allow Ellen to practice on it every day while she was off riding one of her three horses, which she did every morning at ten-thirty.

We thanked Him from the depths of our hearts for this because it seemed so wrong for Ellen to be far from a piano for long. She and the Mason-Hamlin sat right over my head when I sat in my converted coal-bin "office," but since I was converted, too, I trained myself to write and concentrate under varying rhythms and pedal thumpings.

And during these times when Ellen was "upstairs" He was very close to me. So was His enemy some days, and one morning I remember sharply. The desire to feel the dark "escape" of a North Side bar at midmorning rushed over me as I sat "penned" in the space behind my desk in my "office" with the ventilating fan to the furnace room and the "genuine brick walls." I got up to fly out the basement front door by the garbage cans, "our entrance," before Ellen came back "downstairs." But as I stood up Ellen began to play my special song upstairs. Like the Lord's Own Tears, the gentle, minor-key music came floating "downstairs" to haunt and hold me to His side.

Into the woods my Master went,
Clean, forspent, forspent;
Into the woods my Master came,
Forspent with love and shame.

But the olives they were not blind to Him,
The little gray leaves were kind to Him,
The thorn-tree had a mind to Him,
When into the woods He came.

Sidney Lanier's "little gray leaves" being kind to Him always melted me. And when Ellen began to play it through again, more strongly this time, I fell on my knees by my damask-cushioned vanity stool where I prayed alone, and wept and wept and wept at what I had almost done. This was not the last time I wept for the same or similar reasons. And the elegant damask stool looked less and less out of place with the tear stains marking the ever-filtering coal dust in my converted "office" with its genuine brick walls and the Presence in the midst.

22

No Room for Dramatics!

The most I had to contribute to our establishment in a material way Mother and Dad had given me—the first month's rent, the moving bill, and some of our furniture. Having closed my office abruptly, I walked out of it loaded with debts. They didn't seem so bad to me because I had had them around for a long time, but I could see Ellen steady herself when I looked up from a pile of past due bills and said:

"Oh, yeah . . . here's another one I'd forgotten. One hundred and forty dollars to Union Livery for my June, July and August service."

"What's that one that fell on the floor, Genie?"

"Oh, let me see. Oh, yeah—Adolph? This is one I thought I wouldn't bring up right away."

"Liquor bill?"

"Some drugs, too, and magazines and he used to cash my checks so I could pay Marie, my maid, every Friday. I probably 'charged' a few of those checks, too."

"How much is it all together?" She was very careful with me at times like this.

"How much is it? Really want to know?" I smiled what was definitely not a saintly smile because I didn't yet know how to handle things entirely without tricks. "Really want to know?"

"Yes. We'll have to begin to pay it."

"Oh—uh, yeah. Sure. Well, it's four hundred and fifty-six dollars and ninety-three cents."

At that moment our "front" door buzzer sounded off and I nearly went with it. It hadn't rung before and I had a return of my old panic at doorbells with no one to protect me from collectors and people I didn't want to see.

"What do you think that could mean?" My chest hurt. "Could we just let it ring?"

"Christians don't have any right to let their doorbells ring. Maybe it's someone in trouble."

"Oh, I forgot. I'm sorry. I'll go myself."

On the way to the door I asked the Lord to forgive me for wanting to let it ring. But when I saw who it was, I knocked over the "duchess" dress form standing guard over some old furniture in the basement hall in my flight back to Ellen and safety.

"What'll I do? It's the news agency from my old place. They've found me. I owe them money."

"Well, first of all, we'll let him in, and then we'll give him ten dollars on account and tell him things are going to be different from now on."

"Ten dollars! He wouldn't accept such a little bit, would he?"

"Let's tell him about you and see what happens."

I told him about me and he took the ten dollars and was very polite about taking all the rest in two- and five-dollar payments over a period of months. And down the long list of creditors we went. Some I called by telephone, some I visited in person. To others I wrote letters. But to each one I told the complete truth. I had become a Christian. They would get the money.

"If you trusted me when I was drinking all that Scotch," I said to my friend at the drugstore on Chicago Avenue, "then it seems a good idea to trust me now because Jesus Christ is handling my checkbook as well as me from now on."

Month after month two-dollar payments went out on my top-heavy debts. Two dollars. Two dollars. Two dollars. And much later, after every creditor had graciously accepted the appallingly small but very regular payments, I found out that two dollars is the minimum amount which a creditor can accept and not sue.

I didn't know that, but the Holy Spirit did.

Now, periodically in my life, I had made excellent money. Continually, I expected to. Winter 1949 was no different in my expectation department, although I wasn't too sure how to go about it. Having had my own production office for five years I was out of things contact-wise on the free-lance writer's market. I had been the top writer in the Chicago files of the Music Corporation of America, the country's biggest talent agency, and so thought naturally I would be able to write my own ticket when I decided to go out looking for a writing job again. The thing that puzzled me was that I was not the slightest bit interested in radio anymore!

"I still have a little money left, Genie, let's be sure what He wants you to do. Don't rush ahead of the Holy Spirit."

I meant to spin around like an executive in my swivel chair before my desk in my "converted office" and bumped my knee sharply on the corner of a drawer instead. We both laughed. My impatience and my oversupply of dramatics were taking a redemptive beating.

Instead of spinning like an executive, I just shoved back and crawled out. There was literally *no room* for melodramatics in my life now. When I wanted to pace, it had to be up and down because of the six feet of width.

"The Lord seems to be telling me *not* to ask Mother and Dad for a cent."

"Oh, that's wonderful. You're making real progress now."

"I am?" Nothing pleased me at all anymore except for someone to see that I was growing a little as a Christian.

"Yes, you are. Do you know why He's telling you not to ask them?"

"I think so. Because I've always depended on them in the tight places. He wants me to depend solely upon Him now. Also He wants Mother and Dad to see that I'm depending on God and not on them as I've always done. They've grown away from Him because of me. He wants them back, too. I've got to let them see He's really changed me." We both smiled before I said this: "And nothing would prove to Mother and Dad that I'm a *new creature* like no collect telegrams for money!"

Ellen reached for *The Christian's Secret of a Happy Life*.

"This is today. We're both willing to do exactly what He wants us to do. Right now it's time we began to read. Be too cold in here even for you to sit up after a while!"

She handed the book to me and jumped into bed to keep warm. We had the furnace itself practically in our laps, but the heat went "upstairs." It was chilly going but not once did it occur to us to neglect our times with Him. Quite without our planning it, the days seemed to divide themselves into almost regular "sessions."

Morning Bible reading and prayer. And then quiet before Him, during which time I was gradually able to sit still and actually think about Christ for five to ten minutes at a time.

After that more good reading . . . Thomas à Kempis, F. B. Meyer, Henry Drummond, Andrew Murray, Brother Lawrence, C. S. Lewis, the pungencies of Oswald Chambers, and many other saints of God who shared their wonder with us in our little "whited sepulchre" as we read aloud hour after hour from the books they had written.

Prayer, Bible study, reading the saints, silence, intercession in the afternoon, and then the one Light-filled night when, on our knees side by side we made a permanent and complete surrender of every right to ourselves into the hands of the living Christ.

We stepped forever—as far as we can see—into His glorious captivity. Into freedom. Without the load of our "rights." Indeed, the Burden *was* Light.

And every winter Sunday morning we dressed up in our good suits which did not match our dungeon, and with Ellen wearing a borrowed mink coat on *top* of her own inadequate winter coat, we stepped joyfully around the corner to church with the very elite.

I now wanted to go to church. And wisely Ellen agreed to let me choose. My main qualification was a church where I'd be left alone. Where no one would try to shake my hand and make me feel "welcome." For some reason I loved people everywhere except in church!

Oswald Chambers says "individuality is all elbows." It is. I should know. But I was still elbowing my way through some of the time. And church with our elite and weary neighbors right around the elegant corner suited me exactly. They were not interested in me and I was not interested in them. This was not altogether Christian but it was the case.

Everyone seemed so interested in himself that only Ellen and I knew her mink coat was borrowed and much too long, and we thought at least that we were the only ones who knew we could afford no more than ten cents apiece in the collection plate. Of course we knew He knew, but He also knew this was really what we had to drop in. Ellen's reserve was running low.

And once a week we needed thirteen cents each for bus fare to get to a prayer group where I experienced my first informal Christian fellowship and found it increasingly attractive.

A few people came to call on us. Only four ever came back the second time and two were drinking. And our Holy hilarity increased each time some unsuspecting person dropped by or responded innocently to an invitation from us, because waiting for the looks on their faces when first they glimpsed our "whited sepulchre" came to be our favorite amusement.

And it was so inexpensive.

We asked the three women who had befriended me right after my conversion to have tea one afternoon. They came very properly and very promptly with flowers. And they endeared themselves to us permanently because they actually sat balancing Mother's lovely Chinese Seasons teacups and discussed further decoration of our basement abode! These three ladies are real ladies. And all their careful home-training showed that day. No one laughed until I couldn't endure not laughing one more minute. And this happened when I was standing on my bed elaborately demonstrating where we would hang the equally elaborate, carved gold sconces poor unsuspecting Mother had just sent!

We all knew they'd never be hung in the "sepulchre"—neither the sconces nor the walnut Chippendale mirror nor the Italian miniatures. The lovely china Victorian lamp with the yellow roses and silk shade looked ridiculous enough against the streaked white walls. And we had long since decided one coat on the "duchess'" walls more than took care of the "second mile." Also with the "second mile" in mind we reported nothing to the OPA. In fact, we rejoiced because our wealthy landlady kept us well exercised on the "second mile" and pink of cheek with the perpetual turning of the other.

We left the walls with the chalky base coat and this, too, had its spiritual advantages. Because on the wall over Ellen's daybed stood a white brushstroke named Paul and over my bed another (a bit less stem) whose name came to be John. There were also milk bottles, two quarts and one pint, on three snow-covered back steps along the wall where the rooster had been, and on the wall behind the record player a plump lady in a ballet skirt stood the entire year on one toe. The ballet lady had spiritual significance, too, because she made us remember the wonderful line from Henry Drummond which describes the Christian who pirouettes through life on a single text!

We enjoyed our "whited" figures on the walls of our cheerful dungeon and they gave us a reason to rejoice at no windows. If we had had windows and less wall we might not have had the ballet lady, or John or Paul or the milk bottles on the back steps.

And even when we used our last ten dollars to get an old friend of mine out of a jam, we rejoiced because He had long since proven to us beyond the shadow of any doubt that He meant it literally when He said, "My burden is light."

23

Kingdom Work

We did use our last ten dollars to help a friend of mine who was not a Christian. To keep me solvent, we had put Ellen's savings in my account and the balance showed twelve in the bank. I wrote a check for ten, leaving the required two to keep the account open. My old friend, already convinced I was insane, seemed impressed when the next morning's mail brought the ten dollars back in a letter filled with love from the Greenlees back home. They are relatives who interested me not one bit through the years because they remained Christians and prayed for the Prices. Of course, at my conversion these dear, gentle people and my cousin Pearl, a blond saint, who married a minister, were the first I wanted to see. In spite of the way I had treated all of them, they were happy to see me and opened their arms and I saw that their hearts had never been closed to me as mine had been to them.

The Greenlees taught me the great spiritual lesson of being able to receive when they began sending us ten-dollar checks out of their tithe money.

Ellen tried valiantly to get a job.

I made the rounds of the advertising agencies and networks. A few years before, some of the men I visited had offered me good fees just to write audition material. I wrote some sample scripts for a show I wouldn't have touched out of my own office and I worked hard on them. But they were flatly rejected!

There was no reason given. The agency just couldn't use them.

Ellen's money was gone one day. I hadn't had any for several weeks, but we had our guidance clear about not asking our families for help. In fact, that never crossed our minds. We were not remotely worried, we were just waiting. And the closed doors were messages from Him to wait a little longer.

Neither of us was trained for practical earning. Ellen's training was advanced, but it was in classical piano. All I could do was write and direct radio scripts. No one seemed to need anything played or written for money. And yet we knew He meant every word He said when He said that we were to seek the Kingdom first and all we needed would be added unto us.

The Lord had walked right up to Ellen in the person of the strange little old man in the New York church almost five years before and told her that we were to depend directly upon His promise. Our part was to seek the Kingdom first.

And we had been doing that.

And one late afternoon when the "duchess'" third janitor in ten days had departed in a rage, an idea hit me. Ellen was out following up a not too likely ad in the paper and I could scarcely wait for her to come home. And when I heard our buzzer vibrating the building with her customary "three shorts," I was halfway down the low-ceilinged hallway before she got the key unstuck in the lock of our basement "front door."

"Hey, I've a terrific idea!"

"I didn't get the job."

"Good. Now listen!"

I began to whisper so our friend "upstairs" wouldn't hear. After all, there was no insulation on our ceiling. Just those splendid pipes of the best material all running the same way, and then her floor boards were there.

I explained that janitor number three had just departed in a cloud of invectives and justifiable fury. We knew it was *humanly impossible* to satisfy the poor woman but I figured it be super-humanly *possible.*

"So, let's you and I apply for the jobs! She's lost her maid, too. Between us we can be maid and janitor and grow spiritually, keep both cheeks pink from taming and I'll lose weight while we're both going the sixty-second mile! It'll be a wonderful chance to prove our Christianity is working, and she should give us at least half, if not two-thirds, off on our rent! Maybe she'd even allow a hundred dollars for the services of two people. That would only leave twenty-five a month and I can knock out *something somebody* will buy eventually!"

I knew her answer long before I finished my excited tirade. Ellen was remembering the tight-mouthed, cynical, proud, boasting woman who regaled her just a few months before with rave notices about Eugenia Price Productions.

Here was the same girl excited about the possibility of emptying garbage and scrubbing floors!

Ellen didn't rave. I am the raver. She just stood there with her slanty eyes brimming with happy tears and said:

"Behold I make all things new!"

"Who said that?"

"Jesus."

"Isn't He wonderful? Let's go ask her!"

This was almost too much for the strange woman "upstairs." She paced up and down the long, long living room in her riding habit for several moments and then whirled upon us with:

"But you're both ladies! You can't do servants' work!"

"Jesus Christ did." I said that.

She said nothing for a moment.

"We want to do this for you. We know you're in a spot and so are we. We haven't any money to continue paying this rent every month. Two months ago we pooled our Christmas money from our families to pay you. Last month I sold a coat Mother had just given me. This month we'll work for you if you'll let us. It won't bother us. It really won't. We're free."

She turned away so neither of us could see the effect my words had on her, but in a moment she whirled back:

"All right, it sounds like a gay lark! If you'll look at it as a lark and a favor to me, and not as though I'm hiring you as my servants, I'll agree."

We thanked Him silently and rejoiced as we rubbed one cheek. Then she graciously added:

"I'll knock off *thirty* dollars a month from your rent, too!"

A moment later, descending the stairs to our cheerful dungeon, we each rubbed the other cheek and rejoiced some more. For two hours a day, six days a week, I would carry garbage and scrub halls and porch and sweep the sidewalk and keep the yard clean and planted. For two hours a day, six days a week, Ellen would work in the "duchess'" apartment. And we would each be making the equivalent of fifteen dollars per month!

We still had ninety-five dollars a month rent to raise, but we had the Lord and He had us and that night as we read the chapter on "Growth" in dear Hannah Whitall Smith's *The Christian's Secret of a Happy Life,* we could actually feel ourselves grow.

Ellen's job changed abruptly after the first day. She was fired as a domestic in no uncertain terms! Not for any inadequacy on her part, but because our landlady couldn't stand to *watch* a lady work. I was outside in the halls and yard so she didn't have to *see* me.

"It's more than I can bear, Ellen! You'll just have to stop."

"But we need to make this money, and your apartment is so beautiful I don't mind at all. Everything in here is like dusting a museum piece!"

"Nevertheless *I* can't bear it another day. From now on you will accompany me while I sing!"

As a Christian I can say no more than that the woman no doubt could sing once, but there had been an accident. And so Ellen's work was *really* difficult after that. The voice and the knowledge of singing had been there once. The knowledge of singing was still there. But even though almost every day the eccentric, lonely, and strangely lovable woman would call "downstairs":

"Girls! My voice is coming through—listen!"—it never really came.

But Ellen went on accompanying. Day after day, if my garbage chores were finished, I'd sit "downstairs" in my converted coal bin and pray as they struggled through "Vienna Life" and the "Kashmiri Love Song."

And then *"it"* would begin. And if you will turn back mentally or literally to Part One of this book, to the page on "Malagueña," the flowery Spanish number which Ellen made sound like marvelous music, you will know what I mean by "it."

"Malagueña" struck the "duchess'" fancy; day after day after the songs were ended, the "creative exercises" began as she thumped and stretched and beat the floor in rhythm to the beat of "Malagueña." It was not dancing. It was as nearly as I could see from having been called up to watch several times, just what she called it—"creative exercises." And after "Malagueña" while Ellen ate cottage cheese and fruit with her, or brushed the "duchess'" hair, depending upon her mood, they talked about God. Her conception of God was her own. And it somewhat described a liberal Baptist coming out of a Hindu temple with a rosary around her neck and a copy of Mary Baker Eddy under her arm.

An "advanced form of metaphysics" she called it.

And each day we grew to love the woman more and although she didn't say so, we believe she came to see that Jesus Christ hung on a very real Cross for her sins as well as ours. She said there was no "material" at all. This did not include our monthly check, however. But one day she swept across her thick living room oriental (with a gesture, of course) and declared:

"Now, that rug means nothing to me. It is just the *idea* of the rug that I love!"

Ellen moved right in and said: *"I think you love that rug."*

The "duchess" laughed loudly and forgot her diction for a moment.

"You're doggone right. I do!"

No regular job for which we were qualified ever turned up during the first six months of the lease. "My father worketh hitherto and I work." My Father was working "to will and to do of his good pleasure." He had tried Ellen in New York and now was taking her deeper. Obviously He was trying me.

We both longed to "dwell deep." And deeper.

"Every time we obey Him on the tiniest thing, Genie, He transforms us on that point and it becomes a permanent part of our personalities. You'll be free of ever minding being a servant for the rest of your life. So will I. But I'm so really proud of you, dear heart, because you're going all the way with Him and you're such a baby in Christ. Matter of fact, it keeps me hopping to stay up with you!"

Where was He taking us?

We didn't bother to wonder. After all, Jesus Himself said that we should "take no thought for the morrow: for the morrow shall take thought for the things of itself."

I have always taken Him very literally. Everything He said.

And day by day the burden grew lighter and lighter. I never felt the Presence of Jesus Christ more definitely than in the dark alcove under the front steps when I stooped to spread rat poison on pieces of stale bread to discourage a sudden pilgrimage of fat gray friends as they sought to inhabit the big oil drums where I daily dumped the "upstairs" people's waste and garbage. Christ knelt there in the shadows with me and one day I had to remain very quiet because five large rats, one following the other, came up right above my head as I stooped to pick up a couple of empty brandy bottles and a bread wrapper I had dropped. And then they all went down the side of the wall in silent procession. I am not a squeamish female, but neither am I attracted to rats. But He was there and I was His and my heart didn't even pick up speed.

"Lo, I am with you always," even in the shadows by the garbage cans.

24

The Glop-Era Begins to End

If you are interested in "glop" I am sure Ellen will send you her recipe. Then you take it from there because that's what we did night after night. It begins with rice *and* . . . And on it goes. On our "glop" went until one Friday it found itself consisting of noodles and canned beef and a touch of rice and bacon with a suggestion of tomato after it had begun on Monday with rice and bacon and a whole can of tomatoes. Two bay leaves added on Wednesday did something for it and for us.

Looking back on these lean but starchy days of pure paradox we could both have shouted then and will shout now:

"The more 'glop' the more Glory and the more Glory the more 'glop'!"

We would have meant it then and we mean it now.

Month after month for six of them we got by gloriously and gracefully. We were fully supplied with both Glory and Grace and just enough money came in dribbles as we took care of a couple of sick friends along with other odd jobs to supplement our janitor service and Ellen's accompanying. Of course, when her maid-service career ended in one day, Ellen joined me with the vacuum in the long halls and up and down the wide-carpeted "upstairs" stairways, with the broom and hose on the sidewalks, the rake and hoe in the yards front and back. I also did some typing for an old friend who had her own business. She used to borrow money from me in the old days and never in her wildest moments expected Gene Price to be "her girl" as she spoke of me on the telephone with her business associates. I loved it, though, and I loved her more than I had ever loved her and we had been good friends for a long, long time. Ellen answered her telephone for a regular number of hours a day, too, for a while and we both thank her so much for everything now.

Especially for the elegant steak dinners and the expensive and delectable delicatessen spreads she and another friend laid before us on occasion.

The three friends who entertained me after my conversion until I could find an apartment also had us out to their home on the south side often in those dear "glop-days." We sang all the way out on the "L" and all the way back because we knew they were terrific cooks and always made up a surprise box for us to bring home. Having known me in my other life, they all hesitated to hand us a five-dollar bill. They thought they were making it easier to do it by invitations and in boxes. We love them all for it all and now that we can have steaks or rare rib roasts for dinner, we don't enjoy any of it as we did the "dinner" we prepared out of one of these gift boxes from our friends. The menu that night consisted of cake mix baked in a muffin pan, with bacon, and a hot dish of canned carrots on the side. And we thanked Him. Oh, how we thanked Him.

And as I write this, I realize with shame that our thanks for our abundance now does not come from as deep in our hearts as it did in the entirely Blessed Glop-Era.

During this first six-month period, Ellen had another compelling as strong as the one that sent her to Chicago to be with me. This one was to teach herself to type. Naturally, she couldn't go to school to learn and so being as she is, she simply called the Smith-Corona people and asked them to send her a book.

They did and sometimes to my annoyance she pecked away at my old Corona hour after hour until she became what she is now, a good typist and of course, very accurate. Later on, you will see where this "compelling" followed the plan.

Day continued to follow day and on one of them I had lunch with Shep Chartoc, who was my agent when MCA owned me five years before. Shep was a wonderful agent and an even better friend, and he was thrilled when I told him about what Jesus Christ had done in my life. I told him how the doors to work which we both knew would have opened a few months before had closed now. I also told him that more and more I was beginning to think God was calling me into some kind of work for Him. But there was just nothing for an experienced writer of radio drama in Gospel broadcasting. I told him what Ellen had said about this and he smiled with me. You see, when I remarked to her one day that I'd never be able to use my daytime serial experience for Christ because sponsors are afraid of the mention of the Cross, she said:

"Christ knows a lot more about radio even than you know, Genie." She had jumped into deep water so often by then, she could almost swim in it.

We both thought her naive about the "business."

Shep and I talked some more and when I rummaged through my purse for a pencil to make a note of something as we were ready to leave, I came suddenly upon a tiny, quite forgotten yellow envelope which I had carried for over a year.

It contained enough sleeping pills to take my own life. Shep and I crumbled them all up in the ashtray on the table and in a few minutes he was able to laugh about it too. He had known me and had seen me often during that year and this was quite a surprise to him.

The next day the program director of a new Catholic FM station called and asked me to take over an hour and a half record show, five days a week, beamed at shut-ins. It seems my dear friend Shep had convinced him that I had "religion" now and would work for the very nominal FM religious station salary. Ellen and I put it in the Lord's hands and I went for the interview. I had never been before a microphone myself in my life. My spot was always behind the control room window. This didn't seem to matter to them and without any doubt whatever, Ellen and I felt I should take the job.

The "duchess" had FM on her radio and she and Ellen listened every morning from nine to ten-thirty to "A Visit with Genie." And for the same basic reason she had fired Ellen as her maid, she fired me as her janitor.

"I just can't tolerate the embarrassment of having her come home from the radio station as she does each day and begin to carry garbage! What would my neighbors think anyway?"

I felt a little disappointed when I received my dismissal. I really didn't mind the garbage routine at all by then but she agreed to continue to give us the apartment for the "moderate" ninety-dollar figure. Instead of singing "My God and I" as I squirted the hose on her dusty sidewalks, I sang it as He and I stepped happily along the same sidewalks to work at the radio station every morning at eight-fifteen.

For the first week I sounded like "Kawliga" the wooden Indian, but gradually I discarded my carefully written out scripts and began to have a marvelous time adlibbing about everything from Persian pottery to birthstones and played music from Bach to "barber shop," but carefully checking it all with the Lord first in the record library every morning in prayer. More than once He prompted me to replace a recording I had selected because it was not on His level. And this close intimacy with Him among the records each morning intrigued my listeners and helped lessen the agony of soul I endured some nights as I knelt by my bed to pray. In the back basement apartment (all completely finished!) lived the jazz music critic of one of the big magazines. The music he loved had been like my blood for years and some nights the pull back was painful and I could only kneel there and let it beat on me and know Christ knelt with me with healing in His hand.

He "worked" through my record show each morning with me and each time He would tell me not to use a record I'd report to my fanatically loyal listeners that our guest of honor had made the suggestion that I change a record. My fan mail came flowing in and soon surpassed all the other programs combined. My listeners loved my personal relationship with Christ.

I was not a Catholic, and several times innocently programmed what turned out to be Protestant hymns until someone who knew the difference happened to hear. The recordings were all about Jesus Christ and the mistake was unintentional. I apologized and one of the women on the regular staff who was a Catholic kindly offered to monitor me from that time on.

Everyone was gracious to me and I believe I made some enduring friendships there. Friendships that will go right on through eternity. Within three or four months it was suggested that I should begin an afternoon "Visit with Genie." I used to tape record my afternoon quarter hour while a twenty-minute classical recording whirled away for the pleasure of my shut-in listeners on the morning "Visit with Genie."

Ellen did my research and by the middle of September, 1950, I was restless for more work to do. The station had raised my salary once and another raise was volunteered, but I wanted to write again. The first month after my conversion I talked constantly of the "great Christian novel" I would write. Ellen, through the Holy Spirit, knew I was *not* ready spiritually. And it was then I learned that He wanted *me* first, and my talent just went along with me the way my hands and my feet went. Not necessarily first.

But in September of 1950 I felt that old stirring within. I hadn't written anything but letters for over a year. I felt I had something to say and I tossed in the night under the influence of strong,

241

rhythmic phrases and brilliant descriptive passages which I lost completely upon waking.

I wanted so much to write *something* again.

But what? I prayed for guidance.

"Are you willing *not* to write at all—ever again, if that's the plan, Genie?"

"You know I am. But I love you for pinning me down. I'm really not cooking anything up this time, Ellen. Somehow this *seems* different." I laughed. "Of course, that could be wishful thinking."

It could have been. But it so happened this time it was not. It was prayer about to be answered. Prayers from two sources. Ours and one other. And once the answer was set in motion it really moved. Sometime during the third week in September an advertising man named John Camp called me on the telephone. He said he owned the J. M. Camp advertising agency with headquarters in Fort Wayne, Indiana, and he asked if I would meet him in the lobby of a Loop hotel that afternoon on an urgent matter.

I met him and for the first time in my life I heard of the Pacific Garden Mission. For four years, Mr. Harry Saulnier, Superintendent of the old Skid Row Mission and his board of Christian businessmen, had been praying for guidance concerning a possible half-hour dramatic program telling true stories of the lives which had been transformed by Jesus Christ at the Pacific Garden Mission. They had the stories, they had purchased the time on radio station WGN, but there was a missing piece in the picture. They needed a writer-producer with both professional and Christian experience.

My writer-heart leaped with delight, but I didn't trust the "writer" in me and Mr. Camp agreed to give me a day in which to seek the Lord's Will for *me* in the unique radio venture. We prayed and waited for His answer. It came with full assurance. And on the first Saturday night in October, 1950, I directed my first broadcast of the now world-famous radio program "Unshackled!"

The first three scripts were written in my converted coal bin as the Blessed Glop-Era in the dungeon ended. As though to mark it well, a thunderstorm flooded Chicago and our inadequate plumbing proved itself most inadequate. In fact, there was "nothing comparable" to the feeling we shared as we sat one night discussing an "Unshackled" script when lo, the rains came inside and spread an inch of water over the dungeon floor.

There was a tinge of kindly retribution, because that night *we* slept "upstairs"! On the third floor in the most beautiful apartment of all, on the "duchess'" orchid sheets!

The next day and for the entire week thereafter, large eager water bugs moved in, but we had had those orchid sheets and had slept "upstairs" one night and our time had come to go anyway.

On October fifteenth we left our "whited sepulchre" to the bugs and our love and our gratitude with our friend "upstairs."

The gratitude we left with her is deeper and more and different from that which anyone casual might suspect. And from our hearts we hope the year lightened her life a bit. It was certainly used of God to sharpen our souls *and* our humors.

And it deepened our hearts.

I had skimmed in scampering across the surface of my new life. After Ellen had gone with the movers, I swept out the little dungeon for the last time "dwelling deep" in the riches in Glory.

25

Across Cornell Avenue

It is interesting to me that the apartment which the Lord had waiting for us not only filled our needs for a combined home and office, fitted our income and had the added glory of a wood-burning fireplace, but its location made silent witness to what the Lord *knew* He had accomplished in my life already. Out of the "catacombs" He set me back down just across Cornell Avenue from where I had lived ten years before when I found "near Reality." I believe He kept me "Near North" until I met the hedonism of my old life in the Power of my new life, and then back He sent me to Cornell Avenue where I had a chance to meet the old intellectual retreatism with the infinitely Higher Call of the new.

There were times when *I* was not at all sure, but I didn't need to be sure, because *God* knew He had spoiled everything unlike Himself for me by then. He knew the call of the extravagant life of excess went headfirst into the big oil drums along with the upstairs garbage during the first year in the Kingdom School. He knew I would never again deceive nor depend upon my parents instead of Him. The easier-to-break, obvious ties and habits were broken. Writing had been completely surrendered and ambition swept into the gutter as surely as though I had pushed it there with my big janitor's broom.

The would-be "little big-shot" now *wanted* only to be His.

And on Cornell Avenue the second time, with Ellen all changed over from the A & P to the Jewel Food Store, He began to probe us both more deeply; at the same time daring to trust Himself to carry on His work on "Unshackled" through this thirteen-month-old Kingdom beginner. The year of the Glop-Era in the "beloved catacombs" may seem to have been wasted. My old friends certainly considered it pathetic. But the hour after hour during day after day we spent in study and reading from the Word of God had carved deeply into my very being. And although the writing of a true story ending with a conversion scene each week is a script assignment from which anyone in his right mind would run, I confess I was not afraid of it. Just before it came my way, Ellen and I had spent time in the fifteenth chapter of the Gospel of John, and I was absolutely convinced that as long as I stayed hooked onto the Vine, the scripts would be *poured through me like sap.*

He was a God of His Word, wasn't He?

The only condition involved in His constant supply to His branches is staying in contact with Him. But this requires faith. Faith holds us to the Vine, and after I had written "Unshackled" for a month or so, one day a fear came, my faith trembled and the typewriter stopped clicking.

Ellen heard the silence for half an hour or so, and then I heard her footsteps in the long hall connecting her "living-room office and bedroom" with my room.

She sat down on the big old wooden rocker in which my Grandmother Price had rocked both my Dad and me when we were babies.

"Want to talk about it?"

"Yes. What really happened to me when I was born again?"

"Do you doubt that something *did* happen, Genie?"

I got up impatiently.

"No! No, that's not the point. I know something happened! I wouldn't be sitting here writing a big half-hour radio show for a

Skid Row Mission if something hadn't happened! But what I want to know is how in the name of common sense am I going to explain it every week on 'Unshackled'? Do you realize I have to write a conversion scene every week on this thing? I think the windup is the most important part of the show and I'm the one who's stuck with explaining it! To pagans and atheists and agnostics and skeptics and Buddhists and—how in the name of common sense am I going to do it?"

She looked as helpless as I felt.

"I'm sure I don't know, but I don't think you can do it 'in the name of common sense.' It's too hard! Remember what we said yesterday? 'If common sense had been enough, Christ would not have needed to die.'"

"I know you're right. I don't mean to be complaining. I'm just scared! I don't want to use a lot of theological-sounding phrases because I want people who are just as ignorant of the Bible and redemption as I was to understand what I'm saying!"

"You've written five conversion scenes. They were wonderful."

"But this thing might go on for a long, long time! And so far the people whose stories I'm telling remember everything except their conversion scene. They're no help at all."

"I wish I could remember more about mine."

"I know, I know. It isn't a matter of the mind. It's a matter of the spirit. Our spirit and His Spirit." Then an idea hit me. "Hey, let's pretend we have someone here listening who doesn't understand a thing about it. Someone who sits there and raises an eyebrow at me and says: "So what? You say you're a Christian, you say you were converted in a hotel room in New York City, but that doesn't tell me a thing about myself and Christ. What are you really saying? How did He really *get you?* What really happened?"

Ellen looked out the window at the ugly "second" bricks on the side of the apartment building just across a four-foot areaway. And then she said:

"Well, first of all, you had to recognize that life does not end here. That there is a God, that Jesus Christ is God's one revelation of Himself . . . that God came to earth in the Person of Jesus of Nazareth."

"That 'God was in Christ reconciling the world unto Himself.'"

I beamed with delight as I always did and still do when I am able to quote a verse exactly.

Ellen went on. "That God Himself hung on the Cross in the person of Jesus and shed His own blood. God's own heart broke open on the Cross and His Love poured out. And somehow, by a mystery we can't understand, we are justified with the Father, the minute we *believe* what Christ did for us on that Cross! Believe what He did and *receive* Him as our Saviour."

"Now, wait a minute, hold it. That's all true. But that word *justified* is too theological. Could I just say, when we believe Christ died for us on the Cross, we are automatically given a clean slate with the Father? We're made one with Him because Christ stretched Himself over the gap between us and the Father?"

"Certainly. Same thing. And it's much clearer to me that way. What He did I guess was smother our sin in His own heart."

"That's what gives the peace, isn't it? 'The peace that passeth all understanding.' But there's so much more. That's what gets me tied up in knots when I try to write it down. There isn't time to tell it all every week."

"I suppose you'll just have to put the emphasis on the particular point which caused the trouble in that person's life. And I believe the Holy Spirit will give you a fresh way to explain everyone's *need* for conversion each week."

"And if He does that, He'll have to give me the right verses and words to explain how it's done, won't He? Actually, it's the simplest transaction in the world, isn't it? In that hotel room a year ago I just began to agree with God! I began to—believe that what the Bible said is right, after all. And that meant being willing to turn away from my old life to follow Christ into a brand new life."

"If everyone who turns would make as definite and as complete a break with the old life as you did, Genie, you'd never run out of stories."

"That's really all we have to do, isn't it? Turn and begin to follow Him. He had been following me all those years. Now I'm following Him. I changed places with God. He's God in my life now. I resigned. What a relief to agree with God. 'Believe on the Lord Jesus Christ and thou shalt be saved.'" I smiled. "I think that word *saved* is overused and limited, but I like it now. I *was* saved, when I believed, wasn't I?"

"I think you should make it clear always on 'Unshackled' that *believe* means to commit. Not just intellectual belief that Jesus Christ is the Son of God. We can believe it and still not be willing to let Him change us one bit. That was my trouble for so many years."

I was writing Ben Engstrom's story on "Unshackled" that day. Ben, who is now one of my favorite people and a very dear friend, was a man embarked on a restless search. He lost his excellent positions at the big steel mills near Chicago because his search took him, ultimately, to the bottle. On Skid Row, through Superintendent Harry Saulnier in a street meeting, Christ reached down and ended dear Ben's long years of searching. Ben tried baseball, show business, success in his work, and the bottle. Nothing fit the empty space in his life except the Person of Jesus Christ. Ben took Jesus Christ literally. He became as a little child and believed. He depends on nothing and no one outside of the Person of his Lord. No wonder Ben and I are fast friends. Our search is over. We have been found.

My fear and nervousness over the long weeks of conversion scenes that stretched ahead vanished, too. I felt ashamed when I remembered what Jesus Himself had said: "Lo, I am with you alway."

He said it again to me that day. "Lo, I am with you alway . . . and I will be even unto the end of 'Unshackled.'"

"Unshackled" has been on the air for three and one half years, summer and winter, as I write these lines and I am more than "absolutely convinced" that Jesus was telling the truth about the things that happen Vine-wise and branch-wise. Not once has this "branch" had to plead with the Vine to send down more sap! On a commercial program of the nature of "Unshackled," there would be at least two and perhaps three writers, a director and a producer. Someone asked me not long ago about the size of my "staff."

I replied: "There are four. The Trinity and Genie Price."

I should have said five, because if Ellen forgot even for one day to take care of *everything* else, including me, I'd never make the regular deadlines of scripts, books and speaking dates.

Her "compelling" to teach herself to type, was of course, a direct "leading" as the Quakers say. Because by winter of 1951, the correspondence required to arrange my speaking dates and to answer my personal "Unshackled" mail was a fulltime job for one person. But there again was a staff of four. The Trinity and Ellen.

26

Given and Taken Away and Given

I was still on the air twice a day with my morning and afternoon "Visits with Genie" and with the combined salaries from "Unshackled" and the "Visits," we expected to fare quite evenly and be able to cut down my debts some each month. Be it remembered that Christian salaries are Christian salaries and we needed them both to make ends meet after the move.

We actually felt flushed enough to invest the staggering sum of seventy-five dollars in an amazingly tall, rebuilt upright piano. A monster designed in the era when piano manufacturers hated piano movers. It must have been lined with granite; surely it was striped oak and a monster, but it was ours and we were going to love paying the fifteen dollars per month installments. More than anything since, my heart rejoiced at the purchase of that old piano. Ellen had done so much for me. I was pleased as a child and would have brought it as a gift in outstretched hands, except for the fact of its heart of solid stone. We had the perspiring movers place it along the wall nearest the door (after three flights up!) because we couldn't watch them suffer anymore, and although we stayed in that apartment two years, we never dusted underneath our "instrument." We felt Christians just could not afford the luxury of having the piano movers in each time we cleaned the living

room. But you will see a bit later on that Jesus used that old dust-catcher to bring His music back into my heart, and one time in particular it might have been directly responsible for the fact that you heard "Unshackled" on a certain Saturday evening in 1952.

One other important thing besides the piano was "given" during that first month after we moved out of our "whited sepulchre" and into our nice, unexciting, normal South Side apartment. And the thing that was "given" was truly given.

For several weeks before we moved, I had been in correspondence with a commercial artist who listened as she worked each day to "Visit with Genie" in her Michigan Avenue studio.

"If Jesus Christ is as exciting as you make Him sound, I'm interested," she wrote.

And during the first month on Cornell Avenue, the time came for His "giving." Her name is Alice Crossland and she came out to eat spaghetti dinner with us. But before we did that we three knelt by my studio bed in the back room where I wrote and slept and He gave her the gift of Eternal Life, at the same moment He gave *us* her friendship, which we thank God is eternal, too!

The thing that was "taken away" was also a gift as we see it now. In the Kingdom, each seeming tragedy is so closely followed by a special joy that the telling at times is a task for colors and not for words. One morning while my microphone was cut off during the playing of a long recording on a "Visit with Genie," the station manager called me into his office. I expected the promised raise and I went in thanking God ahead of time.

"I know you don't have time to sit down, Genie, because technically you're still on the air, but I have bad news. We're having to retrench on expenses. Your program is outpulling all the others, but . . ." He stopped, embarrassed.

"You mean you're cancelling the afternoon 'Visit with Genie' and my raise?" He looked so sad I smiled. "That's all right. I take God literally. He promised to take care of me. Don't feel bad about it."

"You don't quite understand, Genie. We're cancelling your work with us altogether. This is Wednesday. You'll have to wind things up by Friday of this week. Of course, we'll give you two weeks severance pay."

The poor fellow lighted a cigarette nervously. "Say, you'd better get back to your show. That record's almost ended."

Two things happened in me.

One, I remembered those little wooden toys with round bottoms my brother Joe and I had when we were kids. Mine was a clown and when I hit him, he rocked way over to one side and then he came right back up again.

I thought of him and then I thought how heartbreaking it would be to have been the poor man who had to fire me! For me this was not only a completely unusual reaction, but it warmed me inside in a strange and tender way and I felt tears on my cheeks as I hurried back to my studio to say good-bye to my loyal, loyal listeners for that day. Of course, I couldn't tell them what had happened. But I felt so near them all during those last eight or nine minutes when I adlibbed an even more affectionate than usual good-bye.

"Unshackled" was big and showy and exciting and strictly a pioneer venture, but my heart was in my informal "Visits" with the dear people I would never see, and "Unshackled" didn't help absorb the shock at all. Except to realize that He had that set and going before He allowed me to lose my other job. Neither did "right thinking" nor my courage absorb the shock. The Everlasting Arms absorbed it and lifted me up rejoicing and strangely excited about everything.

I was supposed to take the South Shore Electric out to Michigan City, Indiana, that day to interview a woman who worked in a big hospital there. She had been converted at the Pacific Garden Mission many years before and I had scheduled her story for two weeks from that date.

There was nothing to do but go right on to Michigan City after I got off the air that morning. Everything in me wanted to call

Ellen and say, "Hey, St. Paul is right! I'm rejoicing even though I've just been fired!"

There was just time to make the train, though, and at the hospital in Michigan City, I met a dear little lady with pretty gray curly hair in two pink bows and a story that turned out to be one of the strongest and most loved stories which we have ever done on "Unshackled"! Her name is Hattie Matthews and even though our worlds are far apart, we are sisters in Christ. And I am always so happy when Hattie comes slipping timidly into the big, brightly lighted "Unshackled" studio at WGN; this she still does every few months to visit her friend, Genie Price, whom she loves.

Genie Price really loves Hattie Matthews, too. When she was young and desperate, the Lord caught Hattie in His arms just before she jumped into Lake Michigan. The same arms held me that warm fall evening when I walked into our apartment just as Ellen was setting the table for dinner. I brought a big bunch of heather in a roll of green paper, and Ellen didn't even stop unwrapping it when I said:

"I've got news for you. I was fired today."

I loved the job and we needed the money but He knew all these things and it was all right with us both. Our inner climate remained the same. The heather looked lovely in a big copper urn I had salvaged from my old life and it lasted until we moved almost two years later.

"Seek ye first the Kingdom of Heaven . . ." and the burden will be light!

27

A New Un-Daily Life

It was exactly right, as the Lord knew, for me to have had a set schedule of two broadcasts daily because I had always loathed routine and insisted upon working at night simply because people with dull and regulated lives worked during the day. Since "individuality *is* all elbows," I kept the skin knocked off mine and the Lord began putting an end to my "individuality" with the regular "Visit with Genie" broadcasts. One day I actually found myself feeling cozy and glad to be one of the same people every morning on the bus. Nothing more was demanded of me than was demanded of them and I just got off and on and was glad not to have to bother about being noticed or special.

And so, from this one standpoint it was certainly all right for me to be back on "my own time" during the day again. We don't need the crutches of certain hours and certain occupations in order to bring out our "best" if the Holy Spirit has *remade* our weaknesses and faults into His own personality traits. He felt He could trust me with making my own disciplines by then and He was right. I wanted a schedule. And as soon as He saw He could trust me with following it, He began to cause things to intrude upon it. This was to prevent my growing inelastic and becoming as "fastened onto" my schedule as moss is limited by the rock to which it clings. The Lord wanted His child to be free because of

His Father-Heart and His need of her, and so after He taught me to love scheduling things, He then taught me not to mind to have the schedule knocked off schedule.

"Unshackled" was attracting the attention of the Christian world in the Middle West and invitations for me to speak to groups of all kinds began with one or two and increased to ten or fifteen a week.

"Isn't it amazing that they want *me?* Oh, I know I'm the writer of 'Unshackled' but I've been so unpleasant about Christians for so many years, I think they're wonderful to want me at all!"

Ellen reminded me about Paul and I knew it was because of what Jesus had done for me that they wanted me, but I was still so grateful and tried a very foolish and immature thing. I took four and five dates a week and still continued to interview, write, direct, and produce "Unshackled." In May, 1952, I spoke at a different Mother and Daughter Banquet *every night* in the month except Saturday and Sunday! My determination to lose weight until my body is a fit temple for the Holy Spirit, got me out of most of the eating, but in elegant restaurant after restaurant and church basement after basement, I slipped in night after night to tell the well-banqueted mothers and daughters how much Christ had done for Genie Price and her mother. I told them the very suit I wore was one Ellen had remodeled from Mother's oversupply still hanging in her closets at home. And that year they all were. Mother and I had allowed many things, including well-cut suits, to occupy the center of our lives. But now He is there, and we are using up the suits as He restores the years the cankerworm ate away. Mothers and daughters wiped their eyes and some were friends again when they left because I didn't mind telling them that now that Christ had His arms around us both, Mother and I were closer than ever before. And that we expected to love each other more and more as we each came to belong more completely to the One we had crowded out so long.

One night in a church in a nearby Illinois city, I stood behind the coatrack in the church parlor downstairs and prayed with my one arm around a mother and the other arm around her daughter. They had been strangers for a long time but they left holding hands. The mother had let the wall between them crumble. The girl said good night to me with a radiant, much prettier face, because she no longer had to carry around the weight of her double life with Mother. She had my sympathy and I wish I had known Jesus Christ could do things like that when I first started to deceive.

I might have been called Miss CTA of 1951 and 1952 because the once-elegant, would-be successful career woman who had to call Union Club Motor Livery for a limousine to take her six blocks south to the Wrigley Building for a recording session twice a week suddenly found herself raffling around Chicago and suburbs on the once-despised elevated and subway trains, whizzing up and down the lakefront on the South Shore and I.C., packing in and falling out of streetcars and buses and loving every minute of it. Someone now and then came out of his or her own troubled world long enough to look at me as though I might be dangerous because I sat there in the crowded cars and smiled. They didn't know I was thinking about my Beloved. I wish they had known. Because they all needed to smile, and without Him there's no point nor reason for it.

My new "un-daily life" rocked merrily and busily along. Ellen's work equaled and some days was more than mine because the telephone and the mail deliveries continued to call more and more of her attention to themselves. On the days when she was swamped, I muddled happily around the house, putting up rods and cleaning paint off the windows. And in the spring we planted morning glories in two wicker ferneries some dear friends gave us. These we set on our five-by-eight front porch over which hung a little elm tree which God had planted there at just the right time enough years before so that it nodded and waved at us in 1951 and 1952.

Soon after we moved to Cornell Avenue, I spoke to a Writer's Conference sponsored by a Christian publishing house in Chicago. A lady named Charlotte Quilty came to hear me and walked quietly and forever into my heart—into Ellen's, too, as soon as they met. And one day Charlotte arrived at our house with visible proof of His promise to "add all these things." Under her arm she carried a large bolt of lovely rose-colored material, and following her up the three flights of steps came her little niece, Corine, smiling too, her brother, Donald, with a big sack of groceries and her dear friend, Florence Heller with her portable Singer in her hand. Charlotte, like me, couldn't sew, but Florence could and soon we all loved each other and laughed and praised the Lord while Don put up curtain rods and Florence sewed her fine seams. About the middle of the afternoon, Charlotte cooked the food she had brought along, Florence fitted the brand-new spread on Ellen's studio bed, Don hung the brand-new draperies. And in a day of fun and real Christian fellowship, the Lord, through dear Charlotte Quilty, had transformed our bare living room into one that looked like a home. We thank them all from our hearts for the draperies and the bedspread, but most of all we thank them for being available when He needed them to help His Cornell Avenue "charges."

Many letters came from many people; some of them were on plain paper and some on cards with orchids in the corner and Scripture verses at the bottom. Very many came with large red roses taking up most of the first page. But one came on the loveliest Chinese paper with a thin bamboo design. The note was routine—an invitation to speak at a Pioneer Girls' "something" at a church in Rockford, Illinois. And it was signed, as so many letters from Rockford, Illinois, are signed, with the name of Carlson—Mrs. Don Carlson. It so happened that I could take the date and I went. After I spoke I met Mrs. Don Carlson. But before I did I asked about the woman with the peace in her eyes and the certainty of God in the way she was about everything. "Who is that lady over there?" I asked someone.

"That's Marguerite Carlson. She and her husband and son were prisoners of the Japanese during the war. They're missionaries to the Chinese."

I wasn't surprised. I learned that night that one doesn't need to proclaim loudly that one has been through deep waters and furnaces with lots of fire in them and that one has found God to be ever-present. It's good to tell, but one doesn't have to shout, one just has to have depended upon Him as Marguerite had been forced to do the day they took her beloved husband, Don, away in a Japanese truckload of other prisoners. She was left there with her son, Bruce, and she took Bruce's little hand and walked right through her fear and her self-pity into the arms of Jesus Christ. And it shows on her face. Later on you will see how He planned to use the Don Carlsons in our lives.

It was then that almost everybody began to be Swedish. Swedish and generous and lovable and kind. And if God has a nationality, through which He "covenanted" to look after these two girls, the Swedish people could call themselves "God's chosen." This is no doubt the coincidence of the proximity of Chicago to Rockford and Minneapolis, but *we* insist upon at least a capital C if *you* insist upon the word "coincidence" in connection with the relief from near tragedy which struck us just before the New Year of 1952.

Ellen awoke one morning with violent pains in her left forefinger, and being lefthanded except when using scissors, it bothered her all day. By nightfall it was red and swollen and the inflammation showed in her hand, too. The pain increased and neither of us wanted to admit what we feared in our hearts. And even when the doctor told her the next day that it was "acute inflammatory arthritis" and added quite humbly that he could do nothing beyond giving her penicillin shots which at best were only temporary, we still tried not to talk about it and I was touched and impressed with her courage.

I took over the dishwashing and laundry entirely, also with no comment, and was careful to appear to pay no attention to the outstanding fact that she couldn't type or play the songs about Jesus we loved of an evening after dinner. No more songs about Him, no more Bach, no more music at all. Also no more coffee and the alarm set every four hours all night long to give her the kind of "test" pills the sincerely helpless doctor prescribed. We knew much arthritis is emotional in origin, and this was a temptation to spiritual depression which sharpened the awareness of the pain and the helplessness she felt because suddenly I had to do more than my share of the work.

Once I caught her standing at the kitchen sink washing dishes with one hand and I saw tears on her cheeks because of the occasional touch of hot water on her red and swollen hand.

And then God had a Swedish gentleman call our number. The kindly man of seventy years who one night had walked smiling into studio 6B where we used to do "Unshackled" and after looking us over to see if we were "as good as our product," handed me a check for one hundred dollars in support of the program. Later he sent similar offerings to the Mission itself and a warm bond of Christian friendship sprang up between this dignified gentleman and ourselves. More than once he took needy people to a Loop department store and outfitted them top to toe. We knew he was a heavy supporter of the famous Lutheran Hour and we thanked God that Brother John had turned over his plenty to God to use as He wanted to use it. And so, when he called our house this night in January of 1952, Ellen was glad it was Brother John because although we had only seen him once for a few minutes, he had become a friend. He was fatherly and kind and Ellen was alone and in so much pain. They talked a long time about the program and about the church where I was speaking that night and then Brother John asked: "How are *you*, Ellen?"

Up to this point she had told very, very few people about her hand—just those whose prayers we valued most; and so she was surprised to hear herself reply: "Oh, I'm in a lot of pain with arthritis in my hand!"

When I walked in the front door that night, I knew something wonderful had happened.

"There's been an answer to prayer, Genie! Brother John is sending me to a Mr. Polson who has a health food store and has a combination of natural foods and vitamins which are curing arthritis. I'm going to call Mr. Polson on the telephone tomorrow!"

I am the daughter of a dentist and that means I grew up in the school of "medicine" and at that point anything *not* suggested by a practicing M.D. drew a raised eyebrow from me.

"Health foods? Doesn't that seem kind of—remote?"

"I know what you're thinking, but I believe the Lord has sent this. Brother John says Mr. Polson is a Christian and opens his shop every day with prayer and I'm sure it will work! I'm just sure of it. And another wonderful thing, Brother John is having the bills for the vitamins and stuff sent to him. He buys quantities of this food every month for people who need it but can't pay for it!"

Brother John must have slept sweetly and soundly that night. Surely he had heard the Lord's Voice and he had obeyed. Ellen went to see Mr. Polson and whether it was his prayers or his pills, or the combination of both, her hand was completely well within one month! It has been well ever since. And it rests even more quietly in the Lord's hand now than ever before.

It was certainly all right with us that about this time so many people began to be Swedish. And they did—except for the Scotch Covenanters who, blessedly for me, came into my new life during the second year of it when one afternoon I met Dr. A. J. McFarland, Field Secretary of the Christian Amendment Movement, in the lobby of the Pacific Garden Mission Servicemen's Center. This gentle-looking, quiet-mannered man waited patiently for over an hour while I interviewed someone for "Unshackled." This is a drain on me because of the close identification with the suffering in the person's life, and I felt quiet, too, when I walked over to Dr. McFarland. He said very little except that he represented a group of people who wanted to recognize Jesus Christ in our National Constitution. Until that moment I hadn't realized that there is no mention whatever of God in the key document of our great country. I felt a strange compelling to take this man's suggestion seriously. Time after time I had gotten the red light from the Holy Spirit when certain well-meaning Christians called with absolute guidance for me to take on their TV or radio programs. Somehow this was different. Having used the high-pressure methods of the world for so many years, I was peacefully aware that "A. J." did not use them. He just told me that they wanted me to write a half-hour drama setting forth the purposes of the Christian Amendment Movement.

I prayed about it and wrote and produced it and it has been broadcast on hundreds of radio stations across the country. I began at once to write a column for their official publication and I called the column "The Way Out." As you will see later on, this must have been guided, because these "columns" came together in a ministry which reached far beyond the circulation of the little paper.

The Scotch Covenanters sing only Psalms in their churches, but they *live* the resurrection life of the Christ whom they would honor in our National Constitution. And they own forever an inner-room in my heart.

When this half-hour dramatic broadcast, "The Way Out," began to move about the country, so did I. "Unshackled" rated an entire page in *Broadcasting,* the bible of radio, and then *it* began to move about the country; and each week new stations were added as out-and-out commercial operations, began to write for permission to broadcast this Gospel program without cost to the Mission. No one was more amazed than its writer, who continues to underestimate the Holy Spirit.

But "Unshackled" grew and kept growing like eternal life from "inside," as we purposely avoided the more sensational methods of promotion. I felt separated from the program's growing fame because I, of all, knew He wrote it through me. Week after week the scripts kept pouring out and life was good and creative and busy and my heart sang. People came up to me after speaking dates and asked how I got that singing way. In those days I always had a glib answer.

"We can all be this way providing we belong to Him—all the way!"

I took no credit. I felt I deserved none. But my answer was glib and immature, although it *was* true. But not of me, as I thought. What I had was in part head-knowledge of the marvelous workability of the "life hid with Christ in God." But I believed with all my heart that He did have all of me and so naturally I rattled off the answers.

Everything increased, including my salary on "Unshackled." The speaking date fees moved from five dollars and/or "thank you so much, you have blessed our hearts" to love offerings and what the letters called "suitable honorariums." And life was good and my heart sang a clear song and I couldn't imagine that *anything* could ever go wrong for me again. Each week Jimmy McGree (the potentially legendary Pacific Garden convert who played the "part" of the Skid Row drunk who broke a bottle over the hero's head in their film called "Out of the Night"), made regular pilgrimages out to our apartment to pick up the freshly written scripts and take them "indispensably" to the continuity department of WGN. Jimmy puffed up the three flights of stairs, caught us up on the Mission gossip, made an immortal observation or two about life in general, reported how many letters the show was pulling and life was good for us. It even had Jimmy McGree in it and darkness was remote and agony of soul "impossible."

I would have laughed if anyone had told me they were both about to come.

28

"How Great Is That Darkness!"

On Christmas day in 1951, we shared our home and the baked ham my family sent us with six people who, along with us, might have posed for an artist painting a picture called "Redemption." He could have placed us all at the foot of the Cross and we would have been excellent subjects. Around our table that day, singing Christmas carols at the top of our voices because we *understood* about "God and sinners being reconciled," were an ex-gambler, an ex-carnival man, an ex-alcoholic whose home was still broken up, another ex-alcoholic who is a headwaiter, an ex-small-time gangster, an ex-bigtime gangster's girl friend, and Ellen and me.

Neither of us will ever forget this day. His Redemption was so real we could feel it all around us. We knew beyond the shadow of the merest doubt that "the Lord had come" and that the ground *is* very level at the foot of His Cross.

Deeper in me dwelt the Christ of manger and the Cross and the open tomb when that day ended and I dwelt more deeply in Him. And yet, after that, in the spring the darkness came. And agony of soul and mind and spirit that made me want to strip the little sticky red buds off the trees and stamp them into the still frozen earth! This was not what the saints call the "dark night of the soul," when God seems to withdraw His Presence. God's

263

Presence haunted me, and the "footsteps followed, followed after" no matter where I ran. And I did run. And I stumbled and was bruised and I wept and then I ran some more because it was all such a surprise to me that the darkness had come at all and especially that it had come to me.

I pushed myself doggedly through one "Unshackled" script after another. I stood before hundreds of people telling them what Christ had done in my life, but night after night I forced myself to stand in pulpit after pulpit when I wanted to break and run for the nearest bar. Not because I craved a drink, but because I was so afraid of the new darkness.

And the darkness came when I was trying to turn on the Light!

The darkness came when I *was trying to turn on the Light—myself.*

And this is the way it came.

One day, when all seemed so well, as I sat writing at my desk my telephone rang and on the other end of the wire, a most interesting voice said:

"I'm not calling to ask you to save my soul, I simply want to tell you that I think 'Unshackled' is a writing masterpiece! On top of that, the production is out of this world, but that's *all* I want to talk about. I am definitely *not* interested in salvation!"

In a few days, as a result of that call, I ignorantly and glibly and excitedly led this person into—not a true walk with the living Christ but into a sort of subjective fascination with *my* conception of Him.

And out of this the darkness came.

Only a shadow at first, when I became intrigued with the way I talked about Him to other people . . . then a kind of thick twilight began to settle when I observed with pride the effect of my words of persuasion and even though I used the "right words" and quoted the "right Scriptures" and had the person pray what was a "more attractive" version of the publican's prayer—"God be merciful to me a sinner"—it all turned back upon me and when I saw what I had done, I threw open the door of desperation and all the darkness of Hell rushed in upon me.

But He stood in it showing me that I had "converted" not only this person, but two or three others to *my* Christian "self." They were clinging to me and therefore they had nothing to which to cling.

Sequence is not clear to me now. But it began to take ten and twelve hours to write "Unshackled" instead of five or six. The words seemed to pull themselves up to the edge of my typewriter carriage and peer at me and some of them piled up on top of each other and others slipped back down inside the machine and refused to be used at all. My voice snapped when I answered the telephone and Ellen annoyed me when she rattled things in the kitchen while she prepared our meals. The actors were slow taking cues on Saturday nights and suddenly no one seemed to understand what I wanted out of a certain line in a script, or from a particular scene. I knew what I wanted wasn't there and I was irritated that the cast didn't get it out anyway. My desk drawers stuck and my galoshes wouldn't slip over the heels of my shoes and I was so nervous I sat after dinner each night drumming the top of the table, with every cell of every fiber of every nerve center in my body crying out for a cigarette!

All at once, I began to notice the music on the neighbor's radio across the four-foot areaway outside my study and the beat of it pulled me back and back and back. I remembered old faces and instead of praying for them I longed to go back to them and shout, "I'm back! I was only kidding. I didn't mean to go away. Christ isn't real—but we are, and I love you, all of you. Will you take me back?"

Christ isn't real! *Will you take me back?*

One night I cried and stormed and shouted the more loudly when Ellen tried to remind me of the girls in the back apartment.

"If Christ *is* real and if something has *really* happened to me— if I'm converted or saved or whatever you want to call it, why do I feel like this? If I've 'seen the light'—if I'm *in* the light, why is everything so doggone dark?"

And then I cried and cried and cried.

And after the whole night I slept an hour and went to speak at an 8:00 A.M. chapel service to the staff of a Christian publishing house in the Loop. My eyes were red-rimmed and swollen but on the train going uptown, something happened. I knew I'd be sunk without Him when I faced all those Christians who admired "Unshackled" and so for my hour of need, at least, I turned my face back to His face. And miracles followed the speaking date that morning. Miracles and one very amusing incident. Even though I confessed my night-long battle, I spoke of the joy that had come in the morning on the train. And afterwards, two old sisters discussed me in the ladies lounge.

"I don't think she's saved at all, do you?"

"No, I don't. She's too happy!"

I didn't hear about this conversation until much later, after even more darkness had come and long after the uneven, hectic days had been replaced by the "peace that passeth all understanding." During these tense days in March and April, I watched dark circles under Ellen's eyes grow and she slept very little even on the nights when I didn't batter her with questions and throw scenes and shoes and books. And the day she told me she had known for three weeks that in spiritual pride I had started to run my own life again, I really jerked the reins out of His hands! My own twisting guilt turned back on her and she stood taking the blows for Him until she who had been patient and long-suffering and quiet for almost two years, stamped her foot one 5:00 A.M. and screamed:

"Don't ask *me* why you feel like this! Ask Him! If the Christian life doesn't add up, don't ask *me* why it doesn't! Ask Him! You've made me an answer-box long enough. Too long! I'm sick of it and there are about five million questions I'd like to have answered, too!"

"Well, why don't you ask *Him!*" My voice had the same old edge it had before my conversion when I was trying to knock her off her spiritual pedestal.

She opened the closet door and began putting on her coat. This had always been my trick and she had no right to use it.

"I'm *going* outside to go ask Him. Right now."

"But He's *everywhere*, don't forget. That means He's here! The catechism says so."

"I know He is, Genie. But *you're* not where I'm going and I've just got to get away from you for a while. I'm sorry. But I don't know what to say to you next. I'm at the end of my rope. I want to help you, but this time I can't. I've walked into some of the darkness you yell about, too! And I'm going over by the lake and ask Him what to do." She began to cry. "He must have something to say to me . . . about *something!*"

After I heard the front door close downstairs I fell across my bed and tried to pretend I had never been converted, had never told anyone I had become a Christian, that I was *not* the writer of "Unshackled," that Ellen Riley was back again in childhood under that apple tree playing the piano and I was back on the Near North Side just waking up out of a mixed-up dream, and that it must be time to take Spunky for a nice long walk. I needed my head cleared and I needed to be *myself* again.

About six, when the sun had decided to shine all over for that day, I heard the front door downstairs and I knew Ellen was coming home. I counted her up the three flights of stairs through the quiet early morning in the building and then I opened the door to our apartment for her.

"Well?"

"I sat by the lake for a while."

"Did He have anything to say?"

"Oh, yes."

"What did He say?"

She hung up her coat and looked at me with the same old kindness, and then she said, not looking at me at all:

"I sat there and the waves just kept coming in. Always toward me. Never away from me. They just kept coming in . . . *toward* me.

All I had to do was sit there, and let them keep coming toward me."

He shouted to *me,* too, through her from the lakeside that bright April morning, and even though I didn't want to hear, I heard.

I went to bed about ten in the morning and Ellen sat down at our big, striped oak upright and began to play softly. She had been taking a harmony class one day a week, and the new chords she was learning to form brushed back and forth across her weary, crowded mind that morning and came out in the beginnings of a haunting, simple melody that reached me where I was, behind my wall of self-pity in the back room. It was like a lovely folksong about God.

I was so tired. I was so lonely for Christ. I had formed more of a habit than I realized of praying about small things. Of "lifting up" people with unhappy faces as I passed them on the street, and of thanking Him for funny little things mentionable only to God. I missed Jesus so much I knew He *had* to be alive and I knew He had to be God. I knew He was there, too, in the room and waiting just outside the self-pity, waiting for me to come back to Him.

In my subconscious depths, up to that moment, I still owned the *right* to take the reins back into my own hands. I had given up the right to myself *consciously.* Now, He dared to show me what still lay in my subconscious and because He trusted Himself *in* me, He let the "darkness" come. But He continued to work.

I threw open both windows and fanned the door to clear the air and up the hall went the "darkness," too.

On my knees by the bed I realized Ellen was really playing that haunting melody. She had smoothed it out by then and it said to Him what I needed to say.

I had no words and no tears for a long time. But after that time, still kneeling by my bed, words came to the melody Ellen had just composed. . . .

Silent now I wait before Thee,
Trembling in the silence here . . .
Cruciform and still before Thee,
Waiting for Your healing Tear!

His healing came as it always does. Then my tears of relief and joy. The darkness was gone, and *He* filled our house and our hearts and kept the telephone quiet so that we both slept until after four that afternoon.

". . . the light of knowledge of the Glory of God was *still* in the Face of Jesus Christ."

The "darkness" was past, and the true Light shone in a way I hadn't been able to bear before.

29

Change

When I paid the rent on our Cornell Avenue apartment for the last month of our second year's lease, I felt suddenly and unmistakably that it was time for us to move. We had a happy relationship with our landlord and his family, but he did have a family—a charming wife and a small son and daughter—and up and down the three flights of stairs from the first floor past their apartment there had staggered a not too infrequent "lost sheep" plowing up to our apartment at odd hours for help. The most refined people, when "lost" in the bottle for several days, do not look refined, and although they were almost all sincerely coming for help, our landlord didn't understand exactly what we could do for them. To save him embarrassment, we gave our notice that we would move. The landlord had said absolutely nothing. And he may read this and be surprised, but we felt such a *deep* compelling that we had to go that neither of us could refuse it. Where would we move? Didn't we know apartments were still almost impossible to find? Especially on such short notice? Yes, we knew it, but we figured the Lord knew it, too. And so we told people we were moving and made our plans to go.

For several months we had been playing at the idea of someday living in the suburbs where we'd have more time to live like average people. We talked of building a tiny pink cement-block ranch house. Maybe even of buying a car, although neither of us could drive and neither of us wanted to learn. And, of course, we had no money. But when the days were tumbled so full of complaining, troubleridden people who said: "Well, here I am. I'm sad and lonely and tempted and troubled and sorry for myself. What are you two going to do about me?"—when the Saturday night broadcast seemed to come around faster each week, when the speaking dates meant more and more travel, and when the people still kept calling and coming and being sorry for themselves, we thought happily and longingly of our little pink cement-block house way, way out in a suburb where it was quiet and clean and where you could open a window without having to dust within the hour, and where telephone calls were toll calls.

When we knew He wanted us to make some kind of change, when we literally felt Him breaking up our "nest" on Cornell Avenue, we both thought of the peace and quiet of the suburbs, but what we did was tell two friends who were real estate brokers on the Near North Side that we were apartment hunting back there again.

It is even dirtier Near North than in Hyde Park where Cornell Avenue is, but it is centrally located and the people who were afraid to ride trains could get to us there. We knew He needed us in the city.

We longed for the peace and quiet of the country. Any writer in her right mind longs for a few hours of uninterrupted writing time. And Ellen's main relationship with her piano by then was to look at it standing tall and silent where the movers had put it, while she sat at her extension phone and listened and listened and listened and talked a little and then listened and listened and listened.

We thought about a clean, little new house in the country. But we knew He wanted us in the heart of the city where people could get at us even more easily! We had no right to run away from them. We believed we had no rights to ourselves whatever.

"Lovest thou me?"

"Yes, Lord, we love You!"

"Then feed my sheep."

Thus we made our plans to move back to the Near North Side where the "sheep" would know our voice and where we spoke their language and where they needed the Shepherd so much. We had no idea at all where we would move, but we got all ready to go and told people we'd have a new address Near North by November first.

30

When the Lord Moves

When the Lord moves, He is not easily tracked down a printed page. And depending upon your intimacy with Him, you are going to be variously surprised and amazed at the deft strokes of His hand and the swiftness of His workings once the start was made.

As soon as He looked into our hearts and found we were willing *never* to live in the suburbs if He wanted us in the city; as soon as He saw that we would *really* be "broken bread and poured out wine" for *anyone* who didn't belong to Jesus Christ; when He saw we were *really waiting* for Him to make the next move—He made it.

And followed it with one after another, each swifter and more awesome to us than the one before. As He worked, we alternately clapped our hands with joy and stood by in silent wonder at what God will do for two people such as we, when we will only belong to Him literally.

We belonged and waited and acted according to what we could grasp of His workings.

We did nothing more.

But there was motion everywhere at once and swiftly!

An old friend of mine named Jane, one of the two real estate brokers, called us sometime during the first week in September.

When Ellen heard Jane's voice she felt sure she had found an apartment for us.

"No, apartments at the rent you gals can pay are hard to find. But I've got a *little building* you could buy!"

Ellen was talking to her. I was out speaking somewhere and when I came home late that night, tired as I was, I thoroughly enjoyed the ridiculous suggestion.

Buy a house?

Jane knew I had closed Eugenia Price Productions at a loss. She knew Christian salaries did not permit large down payments on houses. Even if this required a small down payment, which it did, as down payments go, it was madness for us to think of buying a house.

"I'm not sure I want to be saddled with a house anyway," I said, feeling suddenly nervous, as one feels when the Holy Spirit is working in the deeps, and there is rebellion.

"Christians are not supposed to stack up worldly goods!"

This didn't ring true either. It was a deliberate twisting of a text, and I knew it. There was nothing resembling "stacking up" in the purchase of a house.

"All the money we have is sacrificial money, Genie." Ellen was stunned, too, but still she said: "Perhaps the Lord wants us to stop paying out rent for something that isn't going to end up belonging to Him."

"You mean if we used rent money to make monthly payments on a house of our own, the money would stay in Kingdom work. It would still be His."

"Wouldn't it? Wherever we live, He lives. We just live *with* Him."

"That's much better than having Him live with us, isn't it?" I smiled and so did she. We were catching the light He threw faster and more frequently than we did before. And there were active charges in the light we "caught" that night, because down deep inside us began to stir a real desire to *see* Jane's "little building." Maybe the Lord wanted to buy a house!

Jane came to the "Unshackled" broadcast the next night, and we talked afterwards over supper at London House. In the afternoon, September 7, 1952, we met Jane and went to look at her "little building." It was on a short North Side street called Germania Place, because the big old Germania Club stands on one corner. I remembered the street because the Red Star Inn, a famous German eating place, is on the other Clark Street corner. Otherwise no one pays much attention to Germania Place because it is only one block long, and up and down it from Clark west to LaSalle, for its entire unmajestic length stands one garage and exactly five old houses, one of them just fifteen feet wide including the lot. This "one" is very dear and typical of things right after the Chicago fire when it was built. Its freshly painted red-brick front looked clean and unlike the rest of the unpainted street as we approached it that first afternoon, and from under little high arched white eyebrows over its upstairs casement windows it kept an eye on an old "character" with a bushy gray beard snoozing on its wooden front steps. His head was propped against the quaint black iron railing which (unlike some) matched the little iron fence thrown protectively around the front lawn. The "lawn" rambled west for a good eight feet and north and south for the distance it took the wooden steps to climb up to the front door, and in it most serenely stood the Lord's answer to our suburban longing for green growing things.

For "green" things anyway, because although I am fairly sure it has not grown any for twenty years, looking to us like an exotic oriental tree of life, there swayed gracefully in the front "lawn" a tired lilac bush which had all turned to top and had forgotten it even intended to bloom.

That was outside.

And we were reasonably charmed by it.

Inside was a different thing. Different from anything we had ever seen. Dark and dingy and poorly remodeled and above our heels cracking and sticking on the ugly linoleum covered floors was the lingering sound of the weariness that was too heavy for the recently departed roomers to take along when they all moved out. A German family named Wilson owned it once and there was happiness in it then. The people who owned it that day when we saw it had meant to remodel it for their own home. But someone rented it and then subrented it instead, and the pictures on the walls and the faded silk cords tied to the switches of the glaring ceiling lights hung long and dejected and made us want to pray for the people who had so recently tried to "live" here. It was not dirty, just dreary and very empty and very shadowy with heartache that day as we walked through the long narrow Victorian front parlor through a crooked doorway to the "back parlor" and into the kitchen with falling plaster and a knockkneed sink and down the back stairs into the "studio room" as advertised. This was a single wall of uninsulated bricks built up to a broken skylight all covering what had once been the backyard.

Downstairs in the basement was a very "roughed-in" bath, but the second floor showed possibilities of recapturing some of its old charm. We could rent the upstairs in order to make the payments, Jane said, and we talked some more and left—both of us shuddering.

What did the Lord mean? What was He saying in this? Was He saying *anything* or had we gotten way off-center?

"Christians can do that!" Ellen reminded me. "A lot of people say God is telling them to do something just because it's what they want to do."

Did we *want* to take on a remodeling job like that?

Even more insane than the idea of remodeling was the idea of a down payment! It required a six-thousand-dollar down payment. We had between us more money than we had ever had in our entire three years. But it was just about enough to move us north and pay one month's rent on a hundred-dollar apartment.

The thing we simply could not fathom was why we had gone to see the "little building" in the first place. We loved Jane, but she didn't have time to show buildings just for love's sake.

We talked of little else that Sunday evening after we went home. Already we felt "moved." The Cornell apartment was simply a place to stay until we found our new "home." It had been ours and we had loved living there. Now it was strange and we were really gone.

"We'd better look for an apartment in the classified section. After all, we do have to move now. We've given notice."

We found nothing and our thoughts flew back to Germania Place.

From a mutual shudder at the gloominess and ugliness of the "little building's" interior, we began to make tender jokes about it. Then we began to say tender things about it that were not jokes at all.

Then we began to feel tenderly toward the "little building."

Then Ellen said: "Poor little thing, it's just standing up there all alone doing the best it can! Like 'Little Toot,' the tugboat. Remember the song about Little Toot you used to play on 'Visit with Genie'?" And we laughed and we don't recall which one weakened first and admitted that either we were losing our minds or the Holy Spirit was *putting* a love for the "little building" *into* our hearts.

We had long ago found out that He can and does do this when something is in His will. And judging from what followed swiftly after, He did just that with our hearts and Little Toot.

But *what about the six-thousand-dollar down payment?*

I thought of my parents but remembered their indebtedness on the new house they had built and anyway that would be "figuring an angle."

And we wanted this to be entirely the Lord's doing. We knew we'd be sunk otherwise. Ellen remembered that Brother John had said we should call on him for help anytime we needed it, and certainly the Lord had sent him. So, the next day, Ellen called him and the biggest miracle to date outside of our redemption took place when Brother John said:

"No, I can't let you girls *borrow* six thousand dollars! And anyway, I think you'd made a mistake to buy an old piece of property in the city when you could be out in the suburbs where people would leave you alone. But the Lord told me quite a while ago to *give* you girls a down payment on a house. I've just been biding my time, waiting for His time to do it. I'd like to see you in the suburbs but if you think Little Toot's the house, go ahead and sign the papers. The Lord's check will be in the mail tomorrow. And it's *not* a loan!"

We "closed the deal" with Jane and the nice owners, in Jane's lawyer's office on the following Thursday, September 11, 1952. Perhaps it is the first time in history that two people have been excited about buying a house they shuddered at the only time they saw it before the papers were signed.

When they were signed, we hurried to 115 Germania Place and as we stood alone with Him in the narrow, dark living room the old, ugly mauve walls glowed with a heavenly glow when we said:

"Here it is. We give it back to You now on the first day after we signed the papers, Lord. Thank You for giving it to us. Thank You for taking it back now. To use exactly the way You want to use it. We know You'll handle the remodeling. And the money to pay for it. We know You'll send the right people to do it and oh, God, most of all we ask You to shine so brightly in this little house that no one can ever walk into it again without feeling the presence of the Living God! Bless dear Brother John, and we thank You, Father, in Jesus' Name. Amen."

"When two are gathered together in my name, there I am in the midst . . . lo, I am with you alway."

We realized His Resurrection in a new way that day because He stood there with us in Little Toot's living room.

And we knew, too, that if He hadn't died, none of this could have happened at all.

"Seek ye first the Kingdom of God . . . and all these things shall be added unto you."

31

According to His Riches

Brother John, through whom God had made our Little Toot possible, took one horrified look at the house and saw that we would need careful and *Christian* remodeling. And so he sent us posthaste to Mr. Henry Staalsen, one of Chicago's best building contractors and one of God's great saints.

We had no doubt but that Jane was correct when she kept repeating that first day that the "little building" was "fundamentally sound." But because we knew Mr. Staalsen to be not only a man of sound judgment, but one also very well acquainted with "fundamentals," we relaxed a little more when he stood with his head bowed beneath the low basement ceiling and laughed his big Norwegian laugh and assured us that Little Toot was definitely *not* "modern" but *was* "fundamentally sound!" To this great-hearted man we owe much more than a few hundred remaining dollars as I write this. He has been, along with Brother John, like a father to us in our "major" undertaking.

But with all of Mr. Staalsen's "pencil sharpening," Little Toot's "resurrection" was going to cost money. And with Philippians 4:19 tucked in our hearts, we began to seek loans for repairs. We knew the Lord had a way all planned, and we would just have to try doors until one opened. Several closed. Radio writers, particularly when sponsored by religious institutions, are not considered good risks at all. And I well remember the Saturday night of September thirteenth, when my "Unshackled" organist, Lucille Becker, dropped by Little Toot with us, heard our financial problems, took one dim view of the patched-up, shadowy little building and sighed:

"My, but you girls are brave!"

We weren't a bit brave. We were just excited and not very patient as we waited to find out how He was going to handle the repairs. If we had not been so sure we were in His will, naturally it would have taken great bravery. If we had not been so sure of His character, the whole thing would have been sheer madness.

But we were sure and we went right on making plans. Two dear and favorite people of ours are a couple named Ebba and Roy Baumann. Roy is a member of the Board of Trustees of the Pacific Garden Mission and owner of a large appliance store. They picked us up one night during the middle of that week and with Brother John, we inspected Toot's decadent kitchen with the idea of Roy's masterminding it into something attractive and usable. He and Brother John measured and talked over our heads for quite a while and then Roy said he would draw plans for a kitchen that would be what his trade called "ideal." We believed him literally. And if you could see our kitchen now, you would say we should have done just that.

We were willing to do just what had to be done in order to move in and had already begun to laugh about the idea of bare, ugly floors and no light fixtures and no draperies and even considered that it might be good for a laugh if we soaked the soot out of the sagging lace curtain which hung at Toot's big front window, restarched it and hung it back up to prove that a Christian can travel first class or third class and still be happy.

"We're not even planning to remodel completely now. Or until we have the house paid for and that will be nine years!" Ellen explained, "He'll provide a way for us to be warm and it will be ours and He'll be there and that's all that matters."

Brother John smiled and said nothing.

But out in the alley while we were all standing beside his car saying good-night, he asked me to step aside for a moment. And in the light from his car, it seemed as though God smiled at me, when Brother John smiled and said:

"Now, you girls go on and have Henry Staalsen fix this little dump up! Do whatever it needs and do it now. The Lord's going to need *you* too much to have you all torn up remodeling a bit here and a bit there over the next nine years. Tell Henry to fix it up now. I'm loaning you girls the money *without* interest. Then if you get sick and can't make a payment for a few months, you won't have to worry. Just glorify the Lord in it, Genie. Just glorify the Lord."

We dropped by to see one of my old friends that night for a few minutes and she understood, for the first time, what I had meant when two years before she called me a fool for closing my own production office.

"Did you ever know me to *save* enough money for a down payment on a house plus repairs during any year I made good money in show business?"

She had to say no.

If I had dared I would have quoted a Scripture. "My God shall supply all your need according to his riches in glory by Christ Jesus!" I didn't quote it. I remembered how I used to feel about text fingers.

But maybe I should have because I certainly had proof that night.

32

All Colors!

Ellen made a few flying trips to the Loop with scraps of paper torn from decorating magazines and another phase of the "Miracle of Little Toot" began to appear. We are both women of definite opinions and tastes. But He was controlling the entire process to such an extent that not once did she bring home a "first choice" that turned out to be my "second choice." We agreed right down the line.

But we agreed so quickly that we were suspicious and so we packed off to Des Plaines for a rendezvous with the autumn leaves at a friend's cottage, with an extra valise filled with more decorators magazines, stacks of wallpaper samples, enthusiastic letters from various houses all of whom said they were thrilled that we had chosen to let *them* "help us plan our new home!" The big valise full of samples rattled because in it, too, were squares of asphalt tile and multicolored plastic wall tiles and Formica samples on bright little beaded chains.

Everywhere we looked we saw *color.* And day-by-day the leaves over our heads as we walked along the quiet autumn riverbank seemed determined to rival the colors we had spread out and propped up all over the big living room of the cottage.

We were children again. We had been converted and had become as little children and were playing happily in the Kingdom with the King. Every night when we went upstairs to the big front bedroom, we gathered up all our playthings and took them to bed with us and spread them all out again up there. Then in the morning, while Ellen made our coffee, I gathered them up once more and propped them up again downstairs in the living room.

We played and prayed and sat with Him in the quiet and saw Him in the colors spread out before us and heard Him above us living in the dying leaves and whispering His love as they brushed our hair and cheeks on their way to the ground. I wrote well and easily and did in one week what it normally takes three to do in the city. We prayed more and often for our "people" who couldn't "get at" us out there, and in two instances He "got at" them in a way we might have blocked.

Life was so good we felt almost afraid and ashamed to take it. We knew so well about all the suffering. And we knew we didn't have our joy because we *deserved* it. And out of this we realized also that when our cup is sweet we can do nothing but drink it deeply and thank Him for giving it to us.

We promised Him one afternoon that when and if our cup was bitter, we would do the very same thing.

And He pressed nearer as we walked together through the leaves with all the color everywhere. He was very interested in the colors for our little house. Our life was all of one piece. And all His. We felt as near Him when we propped up our colors and laughed as when we knelt before Him in the silence and prayed that our families and friends and everyone in all the wide, wide world would somehow find out as we had found that His burden *is* light.

33

In Him Is Motion

The beginning of my fall speaking date schedule brought us back to Chicago on October first and our Cornell Avenue apartment was merely a place to stay, filled with memories and dust. Our hearts had leaped Near North and dwelt in a little narrow building whose dimensions sounded more like a bowling alley than a house.

Mr. Staalsen's men had knocked out the flimsy wall between the front and back parlors and wrecked and removed the old pantry and a strange and ghostly shed someone had built on what had once been the kitchen window wall; although this was all shoveled out, Little Toot showed no signs of her new look yet. She just seemed more forlorn than ever to the people who came to "admire" her with us. But they were polite and now and then someone with an eye for Near North Side property and an imagination on wings saw in it what we saw. This was most particularly true of a woman who has since become a dear friend. Her name is May Von Hagen and she owns Halco Sanitarium on North LaSalle Street, where "up-and-outer" alcoholics dry out and get physically set to try it again.

May Von Hagen loved our little house and not only gave us three lovely pieces of antique furniture for what would have been a bare living room, but offered to let us live on the third floor at

Halco while the house was being finished. Moving day from Cornell Avenue had been pushed up to December first, but there was no hope of getting ourselves into Little Toot before December fifteenth at the very earliest. And so we were going to save hotel rent for two whole weeks because of May's kind invitation. Eating at Halco is an experience in itself and we were really looking forward to our stay there. The manuscript for my first book *Discoveries* had to be finished by January first, and we figured Ellen could run back and forth around the corner from Halco to Little Toot while I hibernated in the third floor in the big room where AA meets to peck away at my publisher's deadline.

Two extremely important and joyful incidents need to be told here. One concerns a gift the Lord made to us of a new brother. A friend from Wheaton named Ward Oury called to ask if I would talk to a lifelong friend of his who was just about willing to admit to the end of his rope. This man was a well-known actor and announcer and had agreed somewhat reluctantly to see me.

In Chapter V of *Discoveries* is the story of how we met and talked one Saturday night after "Unshackled." Ward and his unhappy friend and I sat in London House over supper and mostly I talked. The actor with the unhappy face and the seemingly hopeless eyes listened politely. I spoke of being a slave of Jesus Christ and therefore completely free.

Sometimes he didn't even seem to be there. And then he would surprise me with a penetrating question. As we parted that night I could not have told you what he really thought or how he really reacted to what I had said about my new life.

But the next Monday, Ward Oury called to report that his friend had stopped his car by the side of the road, quite alone, and had surrendered his mixed-up life into the hands of the living Christ that same night.

This man is now one of the most radiant Christians I know. He is our Christian brother on whom we can call and depend in any Kingdom emergency! He gives himself constantly and is free because he no longer has to be concerned about his own rights. In a bit over one year's time as I write these lines, he is writing, directing and producing the "Christian Brotherhood Hour," he shares a microphone with me on the nationally syndicated radio series entitled "The Way Out," and he is my announcer and right-hand man on "Unshackled."

His name is Jack Odell and I am forever grateful that he did what he did that night of November 15, 1952, the night we dramatized Leonard Pollari's story on "Unshackled." We believe God's perfect timing was in this, too, because it brought Leonard into our lives and he took complete charge of keeping Little Toot tidy as each crew of workmen finished one chapter after another of her "resurrection" story.

The second important event which seemed to dispel the last wisp of doubt in anyone's mind that Ellen and I were simply standing by watching God work took place in a railroad station in Chicago just before I took a train for somewhere to speak.

We sat enjoying good conversation and fair coffee with Dr. Frank Mead, editor of Fleming H. Revell Company, in response to a letter he had written after having read an article about me in a magazine. We were overflowing with the miracle of Little Toot. Dr. Mead caught it at once and Ellen remembers his exact words:

"If you can write it the way you tell it, we'll publish it just as soon as you get it down on paper."

I called to Ellen over packing barrels and boxes of books a few days later.

"I think the Lord just this minute dropped the title to our story Revell wants. 'The Burden Is Light'!"

"The Burden Is Light!"

I tossed in another armload of books. "If we like it in the midst of this mess it must be right!"

And if you will notice the cover of this book you will see that it was.

From the beginning of "Unshackled" in 1950, until he went to a rival station early in 1953, Bill Oliver had been my announcer, and by moving day December 1, 1952, Bill had not only become our Christian brother, but offered to pick us up in his station wagon and follow the moving van as we made our pilgrimage back to our beloved Near North Side. Bill picked us up and, replete with my typewriter, a couple of suitcases, a ream of typing paper, some scripts, and the Thanksgiving turkey in a plastic bag, we set out for Germania Place. Ellen and the turkey got out there and Bill took the rest of the luggage, my Smith-Corona and me to Halco Sanitarium. Many loyal listeners would no doubt have raised puzzled eyebrows had they seen Bill Oliver, "Unshackled"'s warm, convincing announcer, helping Eugenia Price, "Unshackled"'s writer-producer, bag and baggage into an alcoholic sanitarium!

But the days sped by and upstairs in the AA room, the pages left the typewriter one after another and the work progressed on Little Toot. We owned our studio beds, my big desk, a gray driftwood kitchen table and two benches, a big rug we couldn't use, three bookcases, the Chippendale mirror, the two walnut chests Mother had sent, and four lamps. We owned a few sheets and pillowcases, a strange variety of towels that didn't match any of the five washcloths and box after box after box of books. Our tea towels had holes in them and our lamps were period pieces. And into the back "studio room" of Little Toot the husky, noisy movers piled our earthly possessions while John Karum, the head carpenter, aged seventy-two, hid *his* annoyance with us for moving in on top of them by daring the other workmen to complain. John was Mr. Staalsen's "man" on our job, and although he thought we were mostly "off the beam" on about every idea we had, he doggedly stood up for our rights with the other workmen. John holds a special place in our hearts and we take this opportunity to ask his forgiveness for all those extra moldings we "forced" him to put up.

The day we chose to move was really a day of movement. Because working in our narrow little abode on December first were John and his son, two tile men, three plumbers, two electricians, and a furnace man! I was trapped once behind my big desk and the bookcases piled on top of each other, and although I am not the athletic type, I remembered the Red Sea and made it to freedom and the "other side," three more packing crates away by the time one of the marble-based floor lamps Mother had given us toppled into the spot where I had been standing.

This same swift tempo had put the two people, out of all the city of Chicago whom God wanted to live with us, into our upstairs apartment. We had hoped to find a couple of business girls like ourselves who loved Him and who would make not only good tenants but good prayer partners. One after another turned it down, although it was reasonably priced and close in. And now we know why. When Ellen called Harvey Jordan to ask him to make an estimate on our painting, Harvey asked to rent the apartment. The story of Harvey and Birdie Jordan is one of the most loved of all the "Unshackled" stories, and Harvey and Birdie are truly redeemed people. For years, in spite of the way they love each other, they drank and drank and drank. Until at the Pacific Garden Mission, one day very near the time He reached down for me in New York City, Christ touched Harvey and Birdie, and now we only have to open the door and call upstairs to have immediate proof positive that the new life in Jesus Christ is the only permanent release to the alcoholic.

We were advised to ask a much higher rental for our apartment. We had been given one thirteen-hundred-dollar estimate for the top to bottom painting of Little Toot. Both Ellen and I felt that even though "the market would take it" Christians should ask "Christian rentals." We believe Jesus intended the Sermon on the Mount for landladies, too, and so we held our rental down and it proved, of course, to be right. Since Harvey insisted upon doing his own decorating upstairs, we saved three hundred dollars more than we would have made had we raised the rent above their means.

"Seek ye first the Kingdom of God and his *righteousness* and all these things will be added unto you."

The Lord sent His tenants and He painted His house through Harvey, and we never wonder that everyone remarks about the magnificent decorating job in Little Toot. God makes a different sunset each evening, why wouldn't He blend exactly the right mellow stain for His pretty birch kitchen cabinets and the pine paneled walls in which He writes his books and "Unshackled?"

He took equal care of the less aesthetic aspects of His little building, too. The furnace men and the electricians were working in the house late one afternoon, neither group aware of what the other was doing. But with cosmic precision the furnace men ripped off the baseboard in the living room to replace it with baseboard radiators, at exactly the moment the electricians ripped out an old refrigerator motor from the back closet. And when the baseboard came loose in the living room, out marched an army of bedbugs! But, when the electrician broke the connection of the antiquated motor in the rear closet, the entire house was carefully filled with sulphur dioxide gas as the Lord did His own exterminating at no extra expense whatever!

We have never seen a crawling creature and it happened at four o'clock in the afternoon when it was time for the men to close up the house and go home anyway. Not even a working hour was lost in the process.

We told this incident one happy night after a repeat broadcast of the Billy Sunday story, when our dear friend, Ma Sunday, and the missionary Carlsons came to inspect the Miracle on Germania Place with us. Mrs. Sunday tossed her handsome head and laughed with delight at the workings of the Lord she had loved so long. Neither the Carlsons nor Ma Sunday were at all surprised at Him. And as though He hadn't kept us spinning with new things for weeks, Marguerite Carlson told us that night we could have whatever we needed to complete the furnishing of our little home from their home in Wheaton.

"He's sending us back to Hong Kong. We're leaving for sure right after Christmas. We want to be able to think of you girls using our furniture for the five years we'll be gone."

In Him *is* motion.

The next Monday's mail brought a warm, cheery note and a check for two hundred and fifty dollars from two more friends whom we had loved for a long time, and whose prayers and love and understanding are still warm and necessary around us both. The note was signed Mr. and Mrs. Stuart S. Crippen, and we only had to add a few dollars in order to carpet Little Toot's battered living room floor from wall to wall.

The carpet is soft and deep and on Saturday nights when Ellen and I can sneak home alone after "Unshackled," we love to lie on it and read the Sunday papers. Our dear Crippens' love is there especially then and He loves us through the pretty rose carpet they bought for us.

The Lord painted His house, He was repairing it, He carpeted its floor and placed furniture in its rooms and as one piece after another came from sources far apart, each one blended with the other because they had been Divinely selected.

Alice Crossland, the commercial artist who had become a Christian with us two years before on Cornell Avenue, descended upon our cypress wood kitchen table and benches with hammer and muscles flying and in no time the once sturdy-looking set was protruding from any direction around her Plymouth backed up at Little Toot's kitchen door. And very high among the gifts of love, we hold the results of her hours of back-breaking scrubbing and sanding, as she completely removed the driftwood finish and replaced it with a rich brown stain, rubbed and polished to the same brown in the tree trunks of the kitchen wallpaper we love so much!

She took upon herself also the painting of the basement front room, where we plan a prayer room after we get the furnace pipes wrapped so that the temperature does not suggest the Enemy's abode. And through her "fun with a paintbrush" the night before, as she painted and praised the Lord alone in Little Toot's basement, He also spoke to us when we needed it most. Ellen was weary with the rigors of remodeling, and I was pushing hard at the publisher's deadline on *Discoveries*. We were near tears of exhaustion as we were unpacking books one night a week before my Mother and Dad were due to arrive for a Christmas visit. It looked as though we wouldn't even be living on Germania Place. Everything was at that pre-final stage of holding up everything else. But there on the unfinished end of Al's paint job on the basement wall in big, definite letters we saw emblazoned:

"The Lord Is Risen!"

At cost, our dear friends the Baumanns had found the right electric refrigerators and stoves for both the Jordans' kitchen upstairs and ours. And just before Christmas, when we had managed to pay Roy for the Jordans' but not for ours, we received a check drawn on their tithe account to cover the balance in full.

The Father's care of Ellen was my joy in those hectic days just before we moved in and the last lingering workmen moved out. He knew I simply had to finish the manuscript. And every few days I went to a railroad station and took a short trip to speak and then back again at the book. "Unshackled" continued to demand its scripts and Saturday night came often. I was no help to her whatever. But Lucy was. Lucy, a great-hearted gal who had just a few months before been given a new life, and who showed her gratitude by becoming Ellen's right hand. By becoming Ellen's two arms, in fact, because Lucy, like me, is able, and Ellen had probably ducked under one hundred pounds during those days of perpetual motion.

Together, evening after evening, they scrubbed and waxed the asphalt tile floors, unpacked kitchenware and books and all the while Lucy was learning more about Jesus from the one who had taught me so much.

The Lord not only remodeled and painted and furnished His little house, He sent Lucy to help Ellen, and He sent me the willingness to stay away from the happy activity until *Discoveries* was in the mail.

Our dear Al Crossland surprised us with a pen and ink drawing of Little Toot which we had printed into our Christmas card for that year. On it were the words: Merry Christmas from our house to you because of Him! Even the "one way sign" on the lamp post in her drawing pointed *up*. And those who know Him recognized the symbol of the Holy Spirit on the roof of the little building. They're just pigeons and not really doves and they're everywhere, but He is in all and over all. And the day the specially made venetian blind for our kitchen arrived as another gift from our friend, May Von Hagen, we were not one bit surprised to find it matched Harvey's cabinets exactly.

By then we were catching on to the art of "expecting" and then praising. He gives when we plead, but I believe His heart longs for our expectancy.

We *expected* a deep and joyful Christmas, our first in our blessed little house. And deeper because Mother and Dad were coming to share it with us.

Muriel and Jim Bremner came bringing a suitable little tree as a gift from Brooke and Belinda, their two charming daughters, and were very "Muriel and Jim" as they tied bows and tiny candy canes all over it. Jim had gilded a pineapple in a tuna fish can and it reigned with dignity throughout the holiday on top of Marguerite Carlson's lovely china closet. And around the little tree, Mother and Dad and Ellen and I were more certain than ever that the Word had become flesh and that He still dwelt among us.

This same Christ had so changed Eugenia Price *and* her mother and father by then, that they knew a oneness together unlike any they had ever boasted about before.

There is a oneness around Him and *in* Him for everyone who wants to know it. Ellen and I had been in it for over a year by then.

We were glad to share it with Mother and Dad on our first Christmas in the "little building" which was no longer shadowy and could never, never again be lonely or piled up with worry too heavy to carry away. It was just beginning to be the place where people came and left convinced that He meant what He said about His "burden" being light.

34

"Continue Ye in My Love"

No "gift shower" deliberately manipulated to "receive" can compare with the steady shower from Heaven which is still being poured into our lives. And the material "gifts" continued to blend with each other because One Person selected them!

Mother and Dad came at Christmas bearing a lovely copper and brass chafing dish without knowing we had copper hardware in our kitchen or that I had given Ellen a "moving in" present of a $5.95 copper skillet clock for the wall. I spoke in Rockford, Illinois, and Marian Carlson who entertained me in her lovely home took me to the train the next morning joyfully bearing a large and beautiful antique Swedish tray with a complete copper and brass coffee service! My organist on "Unshackled," Lucille Becker, slipped a package into Ellen's hand one night as she dropped us at home after the broadcast, and in the package was a pair of candlesticks.

Copper and brass.

People gave us copper and brass for the kitchen, wooden pieces that are right with the birch cabinets, and every piece of furniture, from May Von Hagen's antiques to the lovely whatnot from Alice Crossland's mother, could have been purposely selected to blend with the desk, bureau, chairs, and china closet loaned to us for the five years in which our dear Carlsons will be teaching their beloved Chinese in Hong Kong about Jesus. Mrs. Crossland donated six lovely pairs of nylon curtains which finished off our living room windows and completely curtained Birdie Jordan's front casements upstairs. And for the four new windows along one wall of my pinepaneled studio, Muriel Bremner remembered an elegant pair of custommade draw draperies which rested on a closet shelf because they didn't fit the windows in her present apartment. The hand-blocked design not only blended perfectly with the color scheme of the studio, but when a skillful lady named Mrs. Niehoff cut them in half, no one was surprised at that point in the miracle doings to find they were exactly the right length and width for my row of windows.

The members of my cast furnished our little sand tile bath from brown rug to shower curtain to thick beige towels, matching carefully related beige washcloths.

Sand, beige and brown.

And after having cooked for three years in one small double-boiler, one small Pyrex stew pan, one skillet, and a pressure cooker carried over from B.C. days, Ellen had just about agreed to let me buy a set of pans on the installment plan. Then Marie Crossland and daughter arrived and left one quick evening, and I walked in sometime later to find Ellen leaping for joy that the Lord had forestalled my first possible charge account in my new life.

Stacked all over our new, sawdust-covered Formica cabinet tops was the most amazing display of very slightly used aluminum pans either of us had ever seen outside a kitchen utility department! A Crossland cousin had bought copper and we have now shared with Ellen's brother and his wife and still have more pans whose technical names we may never know.

Our electrical wiring had been done by a saintly Christian man named Ewald. And we were fresh out of words to thank the Lord when Mr. Ewald's bill came, showing all fixtures at exactly half-price. Mr. Perry Larson, who had done our beautiful plumbing, waited good-naturedly for the completion of my first series of "The Way Out" and still cares about little washers and drains in a most reassuring way.

The morning Marian Carlson put me on that train in Rockford, bearing the lovely copper and brass coffee service, it was "padded" with a banquet-size Irish linen tablecloth. We admired it and wondered what use we'd ever have for such a banquet cloth. The Lord knew Ellen's brother Bill and his Lorraine would be getting married in our living room on January 22, 1954 and the yards of lovely white linen gave the festive touch to our kitchen table and the big, white wedding cake was so beautiful and we were all so happy, no one noticed the extra yards of linen nestling on the floor.

In my purse after I was settled on the train bound for Chicago from Rockford that morning, with the Swedish copper and the Irish linen, I found a white envelope. In it was a check large enough to make Mr. Staalsen's payment that short month after the move, but most important to me then and for all the time between was the message Marian Carlson gave me from Christ:

> Ye have not chose me, but I have chosen you, and ordained you, that ye should go and bring forth fruit, and that your fruit should remain; that whatsoever ye shall ask of the Father in my name, he may give it you.

Living in the Kingdom of God is living in the presence of the King, and we feel it is the least we can do to keep things as nice for Him as possible. The seventy-two feet of our little house run along an alley, and within two or three days we realized that the two shiny garbage cans we ordered from the hardware store for ourselves and the Jordans upstairs would not begin to accommodate the bundles and boxes and empty bottles of even one family in the buildings nearby.

And so, having "teethed" on the Sermon on the Mount, I suggested that we buy several big oil drums so that our neighbors would take the hint and deposit their bundles inside and not beside "our" garbage cans which they had already filled. May Von Hagen gave us the name of her scavenger company for an oil drum delivery. Ellen called and the owner, Mr. Albert Clausen, said we could mail a check for the amount of the drums and he would have them delivered within a few days.

On Mondays I am usually "coming home" from some railroad station; the following Monday morning I got out of a cab on LaSalle Street and walked the half block to our house in the pale winter sun. And as I crossed the alley, I beheld two lovely, freshly painted black drums with large white letters reading:

E. PRICE
115 Germania Place

For a brief moment to smile at His humor and little reminders of love, I remembered the mornings with God at the garbage cans during my "janitor era" in the first year. *Now*, He had given me oil drums with my own name on them.

Mr. Clausen had delivered the drums himself in my absence, and as he handed Ellen back my check, he said:

"We didn't know this was the Miss Price who wrote 'Unshackled,' and my wife is such a loyal listener, we want to make you a present of the oil drums. We're Christians, too!"

People in trouble came and kept coming to our little house. People in varying stages of the "new life" called and kept calling on our telephone which now had two lines.

The people who saw that I was happy when I spoke in churches and schools and hospitals began to come and call, too. And bitter, cynical, disillusioned men and women who held an arm high against any kind of organized Christianity wanted to come and talk to the woman who dared write the things that were broadcast over WGN on Saturday night on a program called "Unshackled." And particularly people began to come and to call when I went on the air myself with Jack Odell on a quarter-hour program called "The Way Out" in which Jack and I both declare we have found the "way out" of our own once messed-up, trouble-twisted, selfish lives.

People began doing this soon after we moved and are still doing it in ever-increasing numbers.

We are *watching* all this happen.

We don't feel pressed or imposed upon or harried as long as we allow Him to do it through us. When we take one of "those days" upon ourselves, we sink. Neither of us could stand up through one day of answering difficult letters and writing scripts and listening to neurotic stories with no ending and checking train schedules and taking trains and packing and unpacking and speaking and interviewing and being interviewed and writing more scripts, casting shows and making billings and writing books and shopping for groceries and making guest appearances and pressing clothes and studying and interceding and writing more scripts and calming nervous Christians and telling actors there is no work for a month and counseling and reading galley proofs and holding auditions and writing more scripts and listening to more thirty-minute telephone tirades in the middle of dinner and explaining to well-meaning Christians who crave fellowship and big dinners that we don't seem to have enough hours in the day as things are.

"I have chosen you that you should go and bring forth fruit. . . ." And when God is good enough to give fruit in one's own country, it is a transforming thing. God is that good. In March of 1954, I, who had hated every brick in the building in my teens, was invited to hold a week of meetings in Central Church in my hometown of Charleston, West Virginia. Memories flooded in and the Glory poured down and one night, down the long aisle of the crowded church where everyone knew him, my Daddy walked

and knelt at the altar. And I was there, too, when he made it forever with this Jesus Christ who had made us both whole again.

On another night of that week, my brother Joe knelt at the same altar with his wife, Millie, and left a load of crackling resentment and worry—an act which left him with a smile that is no longer merely a sign of a personality which he could always turn on and off at will.

Some who know Ellen and me think us too simple. We have found that the Holy Spirit *simplifies*. Some consider us subjective. But we are excited about our Object. And we are playing and working in the complete freedom of the Kingdom of God which makes it all right to be considered subjective or objective. We don't have to be either one at any given time anymore.

But we do have to be His.

This is not a book to prove God's supply. Certainly it is no guarantee that your experience can duplicate ours, or ours, yours. It is a book to remind you that even though you are not aware of Jesus Christ now, He is aware of you, and is seeking you as He sought me for all those other years.

This is not a book about "one way" to get a house. Little Toot may burn to the ground.

It is a book about the life by miracle. The miracle of *redemption*. The life He meant us all to live when He finished His work on the Cross and went to sit down at the right hand of the Father. Ellen and I have no corner on the market of "abundant life." We have merely been willing to let Him prove His redemption in us.

At first I did not understand anything about what was meant by the finished work of Jesus Christ. I understand very little of it now, but I have taken it for my own. I have found living here in Little Toot—just east of the West Side Skid Row and just west of the Gold Coast—that in Him we become as one.

And complete.

Mink coats and sale tweeds and grease-soaked lumber jackets pass our little house. All these stood at the foot of the Cross and

jeered as He was making possible their freedom from the ghastly contradiction of sin.

All these stood at the foot of His Cross and we stood there with them.

You were there.

Ellen was there and so was I.

Mink coats and bargain tweeds and grease-soaked jackets are all welcome in our little house because the ground at the foot of the Cross is level, and the alcoholic and the overworked office girl are as dear to God as the widow in her furs. All are stooped beneath their loads of self-pity. All have been set free on the Cross of Christ. All can take this free gift at any moment they choose to take it.

We can assure them of this because we took ours.

And we are free. Free and resting in the *absolute* of the Cross. Not as a symbol, as a literal resting place.

"There is a rest unto the people of God" because when Jesus had, by Himself, purged our sins, He sat down on the right hand of God—and when we believe this, we can begin at once to rest with Him.

And to live lightly in the depths of God.

On this earth, in the century which is called The Age of Anxiety, those who have been converted and have become as little children can rest as the wild stream rushes by, because they sit with Him in heavenly places and no longer need to fight that which rushes by. They can move with it and not mind the corners wearing away. He has done a completed work and there is a rest.

"Except ye be converted . . ."——from the jerky struggle to the rhythm of God—from the stiff arm and the clenched fist to the opened arms and the emptied hands—from the love of self to the love of Christ—from the haughty look to the hungry heart: "Except ye be converted and become as little children . . ."

It is your loss.

And His wounds cry out to yours.

". . . they could not enter in because of unbelief."

Ellen and I have "entered in" simply because we have believed as best we can, and have in some measure taken Jesus Christ at His word. And He said:

Come unto me, all ye that labour and are heavy laden, and I will give you rest. Take my yoke upon you, and learn of me; for I am meek and lowly in heart: and ye shall find rest unto your souls. For my yoke is easy . . . and my burden is light.

Jesus Christ meant every word He said. And because He said it, we tried it and found to our great, glad delight that He had said it because it is true.

"Come unto me. . . ."

We did.

And found the burden to be light.

35

From the Perspective of Twenty-Seven Years

In the year 1954 when I finished writing *The Burden Is Light* I had reached my thirty-seventh birthday. As I add this chapter, I am sixty-five and closer to sixty-six. In that interim, *Burden* has not only continued to be read, but for twenty-seven years, I have seldom opened my mail without at least one letter from a reader who had just found the book. Many of these letters contain a full page of questions—questions which range from a sincere desire to know about my family, about Ellen, the little house on Germania Place— the state of my faith today.

And so, I am grateful to The Dial Press for the unusual opportunity of writing these additional pages from the perspective of twenty-seven years. Few authors are so fortunate.

First, if it's important—and to many it seems to be—*The Burden Is Light* was not my first published book. It was my second. Some time ago I was asked also to revise the first one, *Discoveries,* of which I wrote in these pages. *Burden* is number two of a now rather long list of twenty-nine published titles, each molded by my continuing confidence in Jesus Christ.

Now to the house on Germania Place. Little Toot is no more. Because not many in the neighborhood bothered to care for or to restore the once-gracious houses—large or small—the developers, as developers are wont to do, took us over. In 1959 and 1960, as

I recall, I began writing my long book, *Beloved World,* with buildings crumbling all around me—the wrecker's ball crashing again and again into houses which had once been the proud addresses of people who had wept and loved and laughed inside their thick, sheltering walls. I well remember wanting to weep each time I walked to my office window on the second floor of the Germania Place house (I had by then taken over the entire two floors) because each time I looked out, a new scar had appeared— another once comfortable room—blue or green or yellow—stood naked and exposed. I'm rather proud of having finished *Beloved World* at all. The din was deafening, the dust-thick air hard to breathe, still I hadn't agreed to give up Little Toot. Of course, I knew I had no choice ultimately but to sell it, not at a "fair market price," but at whatever my attorney could squeeze out of the powers that be. And so, one day I moved away from Germania Place and set about restoring another old house on Wrightwood Avenue. I never drove back to see the gaping hole where the little house with the white eyebrows had stood so bravely for so many years. Carl Sandburg Village stands there now, sprawled over the entire block. So, don't drive around looking, as hundreds of readers have evidently done. You won't find Toot, or the lilac tree in its postage-stamp front yard, except in the pages of this book.

Before the little house fell, in fact, soon after Ellen's marriage (to one of my longtime B.C. friends, Charles Urquhart), Rosalind Rinker came to share my ever-burgeoning speaking schedule for about three or four good years. Until her schedule outgrew mine. I had already begun to curtail my own appearances since I'd never had a single aspiration to become a speaker. None whatever. And more and more strongly, I was drawn only to writing books. The speaking engagements, due to the radio programs "Unshackled" and "The Way Out," along with the lengthening list of published books, mushroomed. In those new, eager, first years of my Christian life, I interpreted every request from an organization hard up for a speaker as a direct request from God Himself. Many were, I'm sure. But my books began to be tossed off too rapidly. They sold more every year, but even though I believed all they contained, some were carelessly done. Gradually, God got through to me that I was merely (very) human, that I was not an absolute necessity to the advancement of His Kingdom and that He had every right to expect me to do *well* that which I agreed to do. The only solution appeared to be to begin to agree to do less and less and improve the quality of what I did. Any book is more readable if written in thoughtful silence at a desk than if tossed off between planes or (as in those now-almost-vanished days) on a train heading somewhere.

Little by little, I began to be selective. I resigned first of all from the writing and direction of "Unshackled" and "The Way Out." Rather enjoying my stiffening spine, I also began to refuse to commit myself to a speaking schedule more than a year in advance, then six months, then three. Then, it began to dawn on me that God would still love me if I spoke only a few times a year. And so, about the time I began to live more deeply and sanely and to reach more realistically for balance, God made it possible for me to write all day almost every day *and* for my longtime friend, Joyce Blackburn, to share the Wrightwood Avenue house with me.

His timing is always right, because Joyce had also begun to write the first of her now-long list of excellent books for children. Life was even more centered down in Jesus Christ, but it was also a new beginning for us both. Joyce Blackburn, among the first to have learned of my conversion all those years ago, had gone on being in my mind at least, my most perceptive friend. The one person whom I felt knew exactly *where I was* with God. The one person who neither expected too much nor too little of me—not at the outset, not today. She is still my best friend and we have shared our writing and learning experience for twenty-one years. We lived on what was an "innocent little coastal island" until the developers caught up with us again, and although we have both come by very different routes, God has brought us rather amazingly to the same place in Him.

I'm sure I will always write books about what God is teaching me. Books called in the publishing business "nonfiction religious." I much prefer them to be called books about living, because after a quarter of a century as His follower, I am even more convinced that no one can *adequately* cope with life alone, separated from God.

I am in my sixties as I write this, an age I've always believed should be the very best of all. I believe I have learned much about understanding in the past years, but I haven't yet (and probably never will) understand why a woman lies about her age. Because she's unprepared, I suppose. Well, I doubt that I'm actually prepared to grow old, but in Christ I have come to long, not only for righteousness, but for wisdom. And for more balance. The decade of my fifties was—without doubt—the most meaningful, the most creative, the most alive ten years of my life. I have become wiser than to take for granted that this good period will last until Joyce and I are (according to present plans) buried under a leaning live oak in Christ Churchyard on St. Simons Island, Georgia. No one is immune to tragedy or failure or change. Neither God nor the Constitution guarantees what man calls happiness. Little Toot became a pile of rubble in the hole that was once our nice, clean basement; the developers could so change the quality of life on St. Simons Island that we might have to leave here, too. Yet God remains God when our cups are running over, as now, or when they are only half full.

Like most sixty-year-olds, I'm stiff when I first get up in the morning, I wear glasses, and I tire more quickly than when the first chapters of this book were written—of course. But I want it known that—oddball or not—this woman is looking forward to her seventies. Most of our mistakes should have been made by then—made and learned from, if we are alert at all—and at least a measure of wisdom should have come. Before my conversion to

Jesus Christ, I held only one strong philosophical concept—that nothing is permanent but change. I still hold that concept, but lightly and with hope now, because I've added to it. I now know that nothing is permanent but change *and* Jesus Christ.

Only yesterday, twenty-seven years after *The Burden Is Light* was published, a dear lady wrote to commiserate with me that the Germania Place house fell to the wrecker's ball and that Ellen had married and left me alone. I thank her for her offer of sympathy, but once and for all, let me make it clear that God was in both events. He understands the permanency and value of change, too. I was too pleased with all the circumstances of Ellen's marriage to my beloved friend, Charles Urquhart, to be anything but glad. Through having read *The Burden Is Light* and from having sat in on Ellen's Bible classes in our living room at Little Toot, Charlie met Christ and the good years they shared were my joy, too. Now that Charlie is dead, Ellen, as a widow, is, as always, giving Christ a chance to be His best self in her and through her. She is brave and strong and full of hope. Her husband was a hard man to lose—one of the most talented and lovable and amusing men on earth—but because he had for years been captivated by the prospect of our "being caught up in the air" one day, we know Charlie will be on hand when we *arrive*.

My beloved father and brother are gone, too, and Mother no longer lives in her stone house on the hilltop. I have written at length about that heartbreak in other books. But because of Mother's cheerful and loving neighbors, Mary Jane and Nancy Goshom, the still-courageous woman who is my mother lives more "on a hilltop" than ever before. She is still wise and gay and her beautiful speaking voice sounds as young and encouraging as ever when I pick up the telephone to dial her long distance.

Many other persons mentioned in the original edition of *Burden* are gone from this earth too, now, but they are not dead, because "Whosoever liveth and believeth in [Christ] shall never die." I find I believe that more firmly than ever.

If you have read the first version of *The Burden Is Light* you may miss small sections toward the end of the book in this revised edition. I asked to write this added chapter and so some of the old version had to be cut to make room for it. A few names are missing, but my memories of them are not.

Now to my main reason for wanting to add this chapter from the perspective of twenty-seven years. Over and over, in spite of the twenty-eight other books of mine still in print, I am asked: "Do you still feel the same about Jesus Christ?" Yes. Only more quietly and far more deeply. Before I began this chapter, I reread *Burden* for the first time in more than eighteen years. I cried a little. I laughed. I lived through incidents, both sad and funny, which had entirely gone from my mind in the interim. I read what the young Christian, Genie Price, had written both about herself and about Jesus Christ and along with some quite understandable horror at the youthful glibness and bald, sweeping statements, I found myself helped by what she had written. In one way— because His goal for all of us is maturity—my reactions edged in places toward outright embarrassment at what I had written, but I changed none of those places. The first thirty-four chapters of this book are not my story now in the year 1982. They are my story twenty-seven years ago, just five years after He apprehended me in my darkness.

One such seemingly sweeping phrase was: "For the first time in my life I knew I was free!" That I now know that He goes on year after year *freeing* us still more in no way alters the truth of what I knew then. I am *being* freed daily and the years have shown me the eternal value of the continuing process. In other instances where I appeared to be always "dying to myself" or constantly "surrendering the right to myself," I realize twenty-seven years later that, somewhere along the line, I've found a wider truth. I don't recall exactly *when* the shift took place (thank heaven, I haven't dwelt much on my own spirituality or lack of it) but a shift did occur. *Today, I see the almost unbelievable freedom of looking past my own feeble surrendering to His surrender to us all on the Cross!* Rather than flailing myself into a state of what I once labeled a total commitment to Jesus Christ, I have somehow learned the larger glory, the wider freedom, the deeper peace of concentrating upon *Christ's total commitment to each one of us.*

Yet, I disagree basically with nothing of what I wrote in these pages so long ago. You see, Ellen introduced me to Jesus Christ Himself, not to some marginal issue *about* Him. For more than a decade, my luggage and I banged around from one church to another, from one organization to another—many of them incompatible on numerous marginal issues. I mainly escaped religious controversy in my little talks and with my books since, because I've stayed on Center by Grace, straying to no issue other than the altogether discoverable nature of Jesus Christ Himself. My belief in the absolute necessity of knowing something of what God is really like, of His intentions toward us—toward the whole human race—is down in the pages of what I consider my most important nonfiction work: *What Is God Like?* The thread of that book winds through everything I write because it is my only dogma. Once we know His nature (what knowledge of it we can contain), we will have faith—not by self effort, but because we have learned that God did reveal Himself in Jesus of Nazareth, and because He generates faith. There are still many biblical passages which I simply do not understand, but I have gained definite insight on the one which declares that Jesus Christ *is* the Author of our faith. I have faith in Jesus Christ, not because of my *fidelity—Because of His.*

I was especially warmed by an interesting letter which came a few years ago from a straightforward, fun-sounding young woman who, with a friend, had been discussing me and their reactions to me ten years after they had each read *The Burden Is Light* for the first time as college students. "We were being very honest about our opinions of you after we had spent ten years growing in the Lord and after we'd read most of your other books. Do you know what we decided? Very simple. That Genie Price still loves Jesus."

Absolutely nothing anyone could say about me could please me more.

On the island where I live, I've learned an invaluable lesson which I could never have learned had I continued the hectic travel schedule of the first few years. I've learned how to live in *community*. I'm not only involved day in and day out with the sorrows and joys of the island's people, I'm also involved in preserving its history and its natural resources and beauty. As a packing, unpacking, panting, self-styled "ambassador," I had no time to keep my mind alert to the changing history of the years through which I was living. There was simply no time to read enough, to listen to opinions other than my own. There was little time to *think*. To *learn*. Certainly no time to learn to love in diversity. It's far easier, you know, to hear someone out in a short few minutes, toss off a few quick phrases by way of "answer," repack the suitcase and escape before the unintentional glibness backfired. Some of my old friends prophesied that once I moved to a tiny coastal island, I'd climb into an Ivory Tower and become a "literary recluse." One woman wrote: "How do you dare put a padlock on your high gate and still call yourself a Christian? I read your book, *The Burden Is Light*. You didn't feel you had a right to yourself in those days. I'm utterly disillusioned that I couldn't get through that locked gate to spend even five minutes with you!"

Well, this seems a good time to tell you about another important thing God has managed to teach me in these twenty-seven years: the somewhat difficult art of being willing to be misunderstood. I write rather widely read and extremely hard-to-research novels about the people and the history of the region where I now live. The latest one used up three years of working time. I live in a resort area where three of the novels were laid. My past-middle-aged brain simply could not keep all the complex historical research straight if I stopped to spend "five minutes" with the dozen or more carefree, vacationing tourists who drive past my PRIVATE ROAD sign every day. I wish I could. I'm anything but a recluse. But I am only one person. And so, I'm more than grateful that He has let me in on the secret of being willing to be misunderstood.

I am also asked, "Do you pray as much as you did then?" Yes. More. I've caught on, I think, to something of what St. Paul meant when he wrote that we were to "pray without ceasing." My devotional times are not as "scheduled" as they once were, but then I was knocking myself out trying to be a "good and faithful servant." You see, I've learned that He meant it when He said that He would no longer call His disciples servants, but *friends*. I have a very simple goal now: To be God's friend.

I no longer panic at dry or so-called dark periods. Through my dear Anna B. Mow, I learned long ago that if those times didn't come, we wouldn't be normal. How we feel—how I *feel* "spiritually"—seems less and less relevant. What matters is that God is *constant*. He is the *only* constant anywhere in the world.

At lunch today, before I began this added chapter, Joyce Blackburn asked one of her typically provocative questions: "Does it seem, after all this time, as though you've always belonged to God? Can you remember what it was like not to belong to Him? Is the dividing line between your two lives still so distinct?"

The dividing line is still there. I have not forgotten what it was like to live a roofed-in life. Horizons, thank God, are still falling down for me. I strongly glimpse now and then, not only the limitlessness of God—but also the limitlessness of His life lived in us while we are still on this earth. People who do not know God live under a very low roof of self-effort and fear.

Joyce pursued her questioning: "*How* does it still seem different? What, looking back, was/is the big difference in the daily routine between life with and life without Him?"
Having become a Christian when she was quite young, her question was valid.

I answered something like this: "Life isn't all up to me anymore. Someone is always there, listening, answering, being with me in the silence." And then I laughed. "You live in the same house with me. You, of all people, know that the fact that He is always there accounts for what balance I have! I never thought I'd turn out to be a remotely balanced person. But then, before I knew Him I didn't think God could really be the way He is, either."

The irrevocable fact that God *was* in Jesus Christ is still and will always be a great stretching amazement to me. And that fact *is* my balance and my peace.

EUGENIA PRICE

St. Simons Island, Georgia

January 1982

Christian Herald Association
and Its Ministires

CHRISTIAN HERALD ASSOCIATION, founded in 1878, publishes *The Christian Herald Magazine*, one of the leading inter-denominational religious monthlies in America. Through its wide circulation, it brings inspiring articles and the latest news of religious developments to many families. From the magazine's pages came the initiative for CHRISTIAN HERALD CHILDREN'S HOME and THE BOWERY MISSION, two individually supported not-for-profit corporations.

CHRISTIAN HERALD CHILDREN'S HOME, established in 1894, is the name for a unique and dynamic ministry to disadvantaged children, offering hope and opportunities which would not otherwise be available for reasons of poverty and neglect. The goal is to develop each child's potential and to demonstrate Christian compassion and understanding to children in need.

Mont Lawn is a permanent camp located in Bushkill, Pennsylvania. It is the focal point of a ministry which provides a healthful "vacation with a purpose" to children who without it would be confined to the streets of the city. Up to 1,000 children between the ages of 7 and 11 come to Mont Lawn each year.

Christian Herald Children's Home maintains year-round contact with children by means of an *In-City Youth Ministry*. Central to its philosophy is the belief that only through sustained relationships and demonstrated concern can individual lives be truly enriched. Special emphasis is on individual guidance, spiritual and family counseling and tutoring. This follow-up ministry to inner-city children culminates for many in financial assistance toward higher education and career counseling.

THE BOWERY MISSION, located at 227 Bowery, New York City, has since 1879 been reaching out to the lost men on the Bowery, offering them what could be their last chance to rebuild their lives. Every man is fed, clothed and ministered to. Countless numbers have entered the 90-day residential rehabilitation program at the Bowery Mission. A concentrated ministry of counseling, medical care, nutrition therapy, Bible study and Gospel services awakens a man to spiritual renewal within himself.

These ministries are supported solely by the voluntary contributions of individuals and by legacies and bequests. Contributions are tax deductible. Checks should be made out either to CHRISTIAN HERALD CHILDREN'S HOME or to THE BOWERY MISSION.

Administrative Office: 132 Madison Avenue,
New York, New York 10016
Telephone: 212-684-2800
www.chaonline.org

To My Mother

Early Will I Seek Thee

Contents

Preface

Longing, natural to us all, leads to—*seeking*. God did not create us as a divine pastime. He created us to *find* that for which we seek. Jesus said: "Seek and ye shall find."

It is my belief that every man or woman or young person in the world is longing for something more of life. Some do not realize this, but I believe it is true, just the same.

And longing leads naturally to seeking.

Jesus could say, "Seek and ye shall find," because He knew we were being *sought*! He, Himself, was seeking us for Himself. He, Himself, is still seeking us for Himself.

When we receive Him, we find.

We find because we are *found*.

And once we have been found by the One who Himself is our destiny, a new and deeper kind of longing is set up which does not leave us dissatisfied, but which leaves us forever *unsatisfied*.

The more we see of His face, the more we want of Him.

The more we know Him, the more we long to know Him.

I believe the longing heart is shared by those who are and those who are not followers of Jesus Christ. This book is a journal of sharing my own longing and finding. And of being found. It is written because I believe He Himself is the end of *everyman's* search.

For the time required to read *Early Will I Seek Thee*, will you lay aside whatever might throw a shadow between you as you are and Jesus Christ as He is?

Even if you have tried "religion" and feel a failure . . . even if you are "sure of your doctrine" and are dry in that certainty . . . even if you still do not believe God revealed Himself *only* in the Lord Jesus Christ, expose yourself as you *are* to Him as He *is* for these few pages, and leave the results with Him.

Even if you are already *one* with Him, there is more for you.

There is more for me.

This is a book for all longing hearts everywhere.

EUGENIA PRICE
Chicago, Illinois
January, 1956

Introduction

If you are self-satisfied, you will not be interested in this book. But read it anyway, and you will see what you are missing.

If we are self-satisfied, we can never know the supreme joy of being Christ-satisfied, of having our every need and desire fulfilled in Him. We read in the Scriptures, "Our sufficiency is of God," not realizing what immensely practical results it could and should have in our everyday lives.

This book is primarily for the wistful, eager heart—weary, as it were, of the copies, longing for the Original.

Once more Genie Price brings us to our Saviour, removing the confusion of thought that so often enshrouds Him, so that we see Him as He is—right beside us, invisible to our mortal eyes but infinitely more real than we are, the source of our longing and its satisfaction.

I consider it a privilege to recommend to your thoughtful and prayerful reading a book which has already meant so much to me.

RUTH BELL GRAHAM

1

God Created Longing!

If you long for nothing as you begin this book, you are either dead or deceived!

This is not an attack on your ability to have built a successful and satisfactory life for yourself. It is no attack on the merits of your family, or your state of mind. If you are a believer in Jesus Christ, neither is this an attack on your spiritual status.

I merely believe longing is natural with us all.

I believe our longing is simply the *result* of God's original intention toward us. He made us in His own image. He made us with a capacity for the highest enjoyment. He made us with a capacity to enjoy Himself! There can be no joy higher. Because there is no one higher than God.

". . . for I am God, and there is none else."

God's original intention toward us has not changed at all. He still wants the *very best* for each one of us. If your heart longs for higher ground in any area of your life, from your work to your personal relationships with your family and those you love, this is all God's idea!

He planted longing in us when He created us.

Our capacity to desire comes from the very *desire* in God's own heart.

Then what went wrong?

Why has the word *longing* come to mean misery?

Why has the word *longing* come to mean frustration and loneliness?

Why, instead of associating a longing heart with the potential of the promised joy up ahead, do we invariably *sigh* when we remember our longing heart?

Is God's original intention really still the same?

Does He still want to fulfill us?

Yes, He does.

". . . I am come that they might have life, and that they might have it more abundantly."

"These things have I spoken unto you, that my joy might remain in you, and that your joy might be full."

". . . seek and ye shall find. . . ."

Then what happened?

Why do we seem to search and still not find?

Do we long for too much?

Should we be satisfied with less?

No.

We belittle God when we beg for crumbs, while He stands before us in the Person of Jesus Christ and declares Himself to be the entire bread of life!

Far from expecting too much, we expect too little.

". . . I am the first, I also am the last."

". . . by him all things consist."

"For it pleased the Father that in him [Jesus] should all fulness dwell."

By Him all things consist!

In Him all fullness dwells!

But what does this have to do with our longing?

The answer to that question is the theme of this book.

It cannot be answered in mere words and yet it is all contained in the startling words of Jesus Christ Himself as He confronts us at this moment, still declaring: ". . . *I* am the way, the truth, and the life. . . ."

In Him is everything.

In Him is everything for which I long.

I may not know it, but it is there.

This is true for Christian and non-Christian alike. We were all made in His image and His highest will for every human being alive today is that He be allowed to fill every longing in every life!

"Behold, I stand at the door, and knock: if any man . . . open the door, I will come in. . . ."

"For it pleased the Father that in him should all fullness dwell."

Therefore, when He comes in, *everything* for which I long is there for me to enjoy!

Is this true?

The Bible says it is.

Then why are we restless and worried and anxious and filled with longings that are *not* fulfilled?

Does God taunt us because we are mere humans?

Has He somehow lost His power to keep His promises?

Why is the world filled with people whose lives are empty except for the eternal desire and longing for what they never hope to get?

Are we always to be hungry for our soul's sincere desire?

The Bible says God will fill the hungry with good things.

Is this true?

Yes. God wants to fill us. Jesus Christ still stands declaring: ". . . I am the way, the truth, and the life. . . ." *But* He also still adds that ". . . no man cometh unto the Father, but by *me*."

In *Him* . . . in Jesus Christ Himself do all things consist.

It pleased the Father that in *Him* should all fullness dwell. And that "fullness" *includes* the fulfillment of your own truest longing as you read these lines right now!

"Then," you say, "if I am *not* a Christian I cannot possibly hope to have my longings fulfilled. But if I receive Jesus Christ into my life, then automatically all of my desires are met."

I would have to answer, "No."

Because most of our particular desires and longings have become twisted by the sin that entered man *after* God had made man in His Own image. Your desires may be out of God's will for your life. We were made in God's image when He created us, but the selfishness in our own natures twisted our God-given longings into desires He could never grant. And so I could never tell you that you will have everything you *now think* you want if you will become a follower of Jesus Christ.

Sin has so twisted you, if you have never asked Christ to blot out that sin, that the self *you* know you to be has become in one sense a *false* self. Not the one God intended at all. God made us in His image, but we can become so hemmed in by our selfish selves and peers for so many years from our own viewpoint, that we create an altogether different "image" of our selves and begin to live from that false position, thus living against the grain of the universe and against the God who created it!

In other words, we play God.

Re-creating, as it were, an opinionated, pampered, narrow, self-concerned image of ourselves—and psychology calls us neurotic.

God will not satisfy your neurotic longings.

He would be a fiend if He did.

But, He did create your *capacity* to long, and I know from my own experience that before I became a Christian I absolutely did not know what my real self was like! So, of course, I didn't know what I really wanted. As a result, eighteen years of my so-called adult life were spent in trying to satisfy longings which were impossible to fulfill! They were sinful, false, self-deceived longings conjured up from my sinful, false, self-centered viewpoint.

God could not grant them.

Jesus Christ is a Saviour, not a destroyer!

If you are not a Christian, you may not believe this, but on the Cross of Calvary, God, who hung there *in* Christ, made all the necessary arrangements, released all the necessary power to re-create that twisted self of yours *back* into His Own image so that your real needs and longings and desires *can* be satisfied by Christ Himself.

I do not force my *opinion* upon you in this matter.

I merely share my *experience*.

In the year 1949, at the age of thirty-three, I "opened the door" when the Holy Spirit of this same Jesus Christ began to move upon and move within my empty, twisted, frustrated life. I did not know it was the Holy Spirit then. I would have laughed at the idea, had anyone suggested it. But He was working, just the same. He not only began to attract my attention. He gave me the power to forsake my old life and dare to step out into one so new that I trembled at the very thought of beginning to live in a world popu-lated by people who went to church and understood the Bible and let God guide their lives!

I had never really believed in God at all.

Of course, I trembled. I was well rutted in my false life.

I was familiar there. But, this same Holy Spirit began to put strange, uneasy feelings of a new kind of "homesickness" in my heart and the name of Jesus Christ made my heart beat until I could hear it in my ears at night.

I didn't belong to Him yet, but I wanted to.

I was afraid to let go at first, but I *longed* for Christ Himself.

The very realization of the longing frightened me, but it was there. And it was about to begin to be fulfilled.

When I opened the door, He came in.

And with Him the *beginning* of my first *real* fulfillment. But with Him also came the beginning of my first *real* longing. Longing that came from the heart of God to my heart.

The kind of longing God *can* answer.

Did all my desires change immediately? No, not all of them, by any means. God not only created my mind. He knew, as no one knew, how twisted it had become through the years. He "under-stood my thought afar off." His eyes saw "my substance" . . . even the substance of my new intentions, "being yet unperfect." In His Book, all my members and intentions and neuroses and notions and self-deceptions were written . . . He knew me.

He knew the real person I *could* be in Christ Jesus.

He knew the false, sinful self which had strangled His purpose in my life for so many years.

Gradually, my desires began to change. I began to long for different things and to experience those new longings fulfilled almost as quickly as they came! He knows exactly how fast to work in new Christians. He knew exactly how rapidly to work with me. And how slowly.

He knows exactly how rapidly to work in you.

And how slowly.

"Such knowledge is too wonderful for me; it is high, I cannot attain unto it."

He knows.

He knows about you as you read.

"But," *you* say, "I *am* a Christian! I *have* received Jesus Christ as my Saviour. I did this many years ago and, oh, how I strive to be a good Christian and obey God! But, in spite of this I'm not fulfilled! This is wrong and that is wrong and sometimes my defeats come so close together I almost doubt that Christ came in at all! What's wrong with me? Why am I so lonely? Why isn't my longing for a companion satisfied? Why do I long to look young and fear getting old?"

Or perhaps yours is *another* longing. Maybe you've had an alcohol problem. Maybe you've sincerely received Jesus Christ as your Saviour and you still have that problem! Do you feel like beating your head against a wall and shouting "Why?" at God?

Perhaps *you* have been trying for thirty-two years to hold your tongue and in spite of all your sincerity toward God and your work in the church and your correct doctrines, you're still "blowing your top" when a certain type of person crosses your path *and you*!

You received Christ. Isn't He in you?

Yes, He is.

He said He would come in. And He is a God of His Word.

Then, what's wrong?

Think.

Could it be that you have been living your life in compartments? Trusting Christ for your material supply and not trusting Him for the power to lose your temper forever? Trusting Him with your new job, but not really believing He can take the place of that bottle?

Compartments.

Here.

But not *there*.

Could it be that even though you assent intellectually to the *fact* that He did really come in to live in you when you received Him as your Saviour, you have not begun to *act* on that belief?

Intellectually, I believe in the laws of aviation and in the adaptability of the modern airplane to those laws.

But I *prove* that belief when I walk calmly aboard and allow a plane to carry me from coast to coast.

Could it be that in *almost* every area of your life you have begun to act on your belief that Christ did come to live His life in you when you received Him? Could you have begun to do this to such a fine extent that most people consider you a spiritual stalwart? And yet, *you* know and God knows about that one area. That one place where you are still not victorious.

To long for victory in *all facets* of our lives is from God.

Constantly He is urging us to come up a little higher.

Longing is from God. But He also wants to fill that longing. And then He will send another . . . each one to move us on up a little higher! But He cannot send a new one until the old ones are filled. Why do we keep the same old longings year in and year out?

I believe it is because we have not begun *fully to participate* in the very life of Christ which is in us!

327

The remainder of this book I share with you from my own life and from the lives of persons whom I know intimately. I am merely witnessing.

No one could have been *less* indwelt by the life of Christ, nor less interested in being indwelt by the life of Christ than I was just a few years ago.

Then I received Him and He came in.

And as I have decreased, He has increased.

And as I have allowed Him to increase by taking myself out of His way (however slowly and stubbornly) I have found to my great joy and constant wonder that as I remember to participate in His life within me, *I am fulfilled.*

When He comes in, everything we long for comes in with Him.

Our part is to *take it.*

Even when it means inconvenience for us!

When it would be easier to say, "I'm afraid I'm not courageous enough to do this thing" . . . *we can take of* His courage and do it.

His courage is in us when He is in us.

". . . Paul . . . thanked God, and *took courage.*"

Paul *participated* in—shared the life of Christ within him. ". . . yet not I, but Christ liveth in me. . . ." The great Apostle had access to the very courage of Christ Himself. And he took it. In almost every instance, it did inconvenience Paul, humanly speaking. But it fulfilled his deepest longing at the same time because to Paul to live *was* this Jesus Christ Himself!

"O God, thou art my God; early will I seek thee: my soul thirsteth for thee, my flesh longeth for thee in a dry and thirsty land, where no water is."

"O God, thou art my God; early will I seek *thee* . . ."!

Longing is a gift of God for God Himself to fulfill.

With Himself.

2

I Did Not Long For Salvation!

I, personally, did not long for salvation.

I laughed at the word.

Many persons *do* long for it. Many others do not. I have heard Christians say: "I'm not wasting any more time with *Him*. He's not interested in salvation!"

My heart has longed to run to the fellow, who is probably not one bit interested in the Christian's "salvation," and tell him about my Saviour!

Most unconverted adults in our portion of the twentieth century are a product of the humanistic materialism which flooded our schools and colleges during the twenties and thirties. They do not, as I did not, even know what salvation is!

And so don't care. Or pretend not to.

But something within us all is strangely *attracted* to the Person of Jesus Christ. For years I contended that Jesus and Socrates were my two favorite characters in history.

Still I don't once remember having called someone of high character a *Socrates*-like person.

The loftiest compliment I could pay a man or a woman was to say, "There is a *Christ*-like person!"

Many do not believe He is the Son of God, the only Saviour of the human race, but something in His personality *attracts everyone!*

Even though Jesus declared that He and the Father were One, and even though a man may say this is *not* what he believes, still I have yet to find one who will commit himself by accusing Christ of lying or misrepresenting things.

The usual answer is . . . "Well, you have your interpretation and I have mine . . . et cetera, et cetera."

Something in us all *responds* to Him, because whether we believe it or not, He *is* God's revelation of Himself and we were created in the first place to belong to God.

To be one with Him.

The life union was broken. But once we experience the healing touch of Christ in our lives, we begin to feel more and more "at home" again.

The air of heaven was meant to be our native air.

If you call salvation a "way out" of your troubles, or think of it as a process whereby God becomes a heavenly "Yes-Man" to you, then you may long for salvation. Most persons don't think of it one way or another. This may shock the average Christian, but it is true.

Those of us who believe that God sets forth His plan for salvation in the writings of the New Testament know that man simply needs to "believe on the Lord Jesus Christ" in order to be saved. Those of us who have tried it have seen that "belief" shifted *for* us by the Holy Spirit to something we *know*.

Something knowable only to the heart.

Those of us who have moved our central confidence from ourselves to the Person of Jesus Christ have begun to believe on Him and we know we are experiencing personal salvation. We can't explain it. Unless we're still counting upon the merits of our *own* wits and wisdom, we don't even try to explain it.

We receive it.

We enjoy it.

We experience it.

We use it.

Paul said to his Philippian jailer: ". . . Believe on the Lord Jesus Christ, and thou shalt be saved. . . ."

The jailer "believed" and he was saved. Changed. Transformed from a man who inflicted stripes to a man who washed them. From a man who locked other men in prison to a man who set them free and gave them of his own meat and bread.

The jailer *believed* on the Lord Jesus Christ and he was saved.

Jesus taught that those who do *not* believe are cut off from Him. ". . . ye believe not, because ye are not of my sheep. . . . My sheep hear my voice, and I know them, and they follow me: And I give unto them eternal life; and they shall never perish, neither shall any man pluck them out of my hand."

If you do not believe on the Lord Jesus Christ as you read these lines, then you simply do not have eternal life. This is not my idea. It is God's plan. And God is not on trial. We are. We will either believe or we will not.

He won't force us.

Sometimes I wish He would. But He cannot because free will is also His idea. Not ours. Most of us would prefer *not* to choose. We do a lot of rebellious talking about our need of freedom. We bruise our hearts and our minds and our egos, battering at the wall of what *seems* to pen us in. But actually, most of us would prefer to have someone else make our choices for us.

Particularly in the choice of believing on the Lord Jesus Christ. And few are willing to face the indisputable fact that even when we do not choose *for* Him, we are still choosing—*against* Him.

"He that is not with me is against me. . . ."

Jesus Christ declares Himself to *be* life itself.

". . . I am the way, the truth, and the life. . . ."

". . . I am the resurrection, and the life: he that believeth in me, though he were dead, yet shall he live: And whosoever liveth and believeth in me shall never die . . ."!

". . . Believe on the Lord Jesus Christ, and thou shalt be saved. . . ."

To be saved is to have eternal life.

And if Jesus Christ *is* eternal life, then being saved is *having* Jesus Christ.

Salvation is what He does for us because He is the Saviour. And being human and most interested in ourselves, we tend to talk more about our salvation than we do about our Saviour!

But we can stop this.

We control our conscious minds and we can bring this off-center emphasis to a sudden stop right now. We can bow our heads before this Saviour and ask His forgiveness for making the theme of our Christian song the worth of the gift instead of the still greater worth of the giver. I pray every day for a more grateful heart . . . a heart that somehow learns to respond with thanksgiving for the unspeakable gift of my salvation. But mine is the kind of heart that wants to respond to a giver even above His gift.

Do I dare point you to my salvation?

Can you receive eternal life because I have received it?

No.

You can be convinced that eternal life is available to you by looking at my eternal life and believing that if this wonder is for such as I, it can be for such as you, too.

But my salvation cannot save you.

Only my Saviour can do that.

Not my salvation . . . my Saviour.

Not my salvation . . . my Saviour.

Look at my Saviour.

Look at *the* Saviour!

And find your own eternal life, "Looking unto Jesus the author and finisher . . ." of it all.

My paternal grandmother, whom I called Gram, had a native knack for using a tone of voice, just a touch above a whisper, to call me, as a child, into happily isolated, completely cozy moments alone with her as the two of us inspected a bird's nest or a new and nestling violet patch. Sometimes she would call me in this particular "Genie voice" to come and stand beside her at our kitchen door and "smell that good sweet air!" Still more delightful to me were the times she called me over her shoulder as she stooped beside a prize rose bush (which she more often than not called her "Genie rose"). And when I came tripping up beside her, all set for sharing two or three of those cozy moments, when no one else stood on the earth but my Gram and me, she would cup a long lovely rosebud in her hand reverently and say:

"Would ja' jist look at that? Would ja' jist *look!*"

My grandmother was not an educated woman. And she was not even proud of the fact that she could practically stick a pencil into the ground and make the pencil grow! She expected things to grow. She was simple enough and wise enough to revere the very *life* of that rose.

She was in awe of it.

In a deep and profound and marvelous way this simple woman and this simple child bowed before the *life* in that rose.

Gram wouldn't have thought of trying to describe the rose.

She knew perfectly well that it could speak for itself.

It was right there and she simply called me to look at it, and without a thought of analyzing her knowledge, she knew I would know what she meant when she said: "Would ja' jist look?"

Has anyone ever spoiled a sunset for you by attempting to describe it while standing right beside you as you look at the same sunset? Some things won't yield to description. Good writers don't even try. People with no reverence for the sunset or with an exaggerated notion of their own descriptive powers will always stand right there beside you and "describe" the view at which your very heart is *looking!*

My very heart and my brain—even my hands on the keys of this typewriter long to describe the Saviour to you.

But I know I cannot.

There is something I *can* do, however. I can call you into a close, complete moment with me as I share with you the ways in which He has become my everything. For the next few pages will you come and look with me at Jesus Himself?

He is the One who is living in you, too, if you have received Him.

Will you just *look*—at *Him*?

3

I Longed to Look at God!

A few minutes before I received Jesus Christ as my Saviour, I asked my friend who was helping me find my way . . . "What does God look like to you?"

Without taking time for one small thought, she replied: "He looks like Jesus Christ."

Jesus Christ.

". . . I, if I be lifted up . . . will draw. . . ."

He does.

He drew me. Perhaps He has drawn you. If not yet, He is seeking your attention. Seeking *you*.

I was not attracted to my friend's "salvation." I was attracted to her *Saviour*. Just minutes before I became His, I was longing to *look* at Him!

Then, the Holy Spirit lighted up His face and in the next moment, I was His and He was mine forever.

One of the great creative works of the Holy Spirit is to make us *sure*. Sure that we are sinners and sure that we need a Saviour!

Every native in every dark jungle knows the burden of a guilty conscience. It is inevitable that any one of them could miss it. ". . . all have sinned, and come short of the glory of God." Everyone in the world. Everyone who has ever been in the world.

And for that reason *everyone* needs a Saviour.

The jungle-man doesn't know why, perhaps, but something within him goads and drives him to try this and that sacrifice to this and that god in order to relieve himself of the heavy weight of guilt for his sins.

In this respect the native is more advanced than many members of so-called civilized society. In this respect the native is less neurotic. Neurotics don't see themselves as they are. Neurotics see themselves in the *images* which they themselves have conjured up. The jungle-man is clearer here.

He sees himself as needing to be relieved of sin.

He tries ineffectual methods, but he tries.

The so-called "Christian movements" which teach that we already contain within us all the "good" we need—that God approves of us as we are—that we only need somehow to "latch on" to this nebulous divine approval, contribute a great deal to the making of neurotics. God's estimate of us is in the Holy Bible and there He says, "There is *none* righteous, no, not one."

To say God approves of us is to hide behind our own neurotic image of ourselves and thereby refuse to be *changed* back into the image of God.

But, in spite of the swamp of teaching abroad today that we need only to develop the "good" that is already in us, one after another continues to "come out" of these cults and fall relieved at the feet of Jesus Christ to receive forgiveness!

The Holy Spirit *convicts* of sin.

The "groups" may teach "goodness." But the Holy Spirit will bring to our remembrance that which we *must* know in order to find victorious life under *all* circumstances, and this is that "all have sinned" and all need a Saviour.

A Saviour is One who touches us at the place we cannot reach.

Those of us who have been struck to our knees and caused by the Holy Spirit to cry out for forgiveness at the foot of the cross of Jesus Christ . . . those of us who have *seen* ourselves through His eyes, as God sees us . . . those of us who have been stopped short in our mad hurtling to eternal destruction by the merciful hand of the One who reaches toward all men . . . those of us who have stared in blank horror at the *fact* that we are living corpses until the life of God has been *put within* us, *know* beyond any doubt that because *that* life is holy it cannot—it simply *could not* be put within us as we are because we are sinful! *Until* our sin is forgiven by Jesus Christ.

He touches us and cleanses us in the depths we cannot reach.

Then, and only then, can He come into us to dwell in the Person of the Holy Spirit. Then and only then is there true *goodness* within us.

Jesus Christ had to *become* sin *for* us on the cross of Calvary and we have to receive Him *before* His righteousness *can* be put within us!

"For he hath made him to be sin for us, who knew no sin; that we might be made the righteousness of God in him."

He is our righteousness.

His righteousness comes right along with Him when He comes.

Any virtue or goodness we might have inherited or developed naturally *is* as "filthy rags" compared to the righteousness of God. Those of us who have experienced His righteousness being *put within* us at the time of our turning to Christ and those of us who have given this righteousness, this life, room to grow, *know* that the "filthy rags" simile is altogether true.

The contrast is breath-taking.

And so . . . when we face reality in both ourselves and in Christ we can do nothing but trust Him COMPLETELY for our salvation. We see that we cannot earn it. We cannot deserve it. We cannot achieve it. We cannot capture it. We cannot learn it. We cannot absorb it.

We can only *receive* the *gift* of God.

And the gift of God is Jesus Christ Himself.

He is our salvation. His very life which He puts within us at our "new birth" is the dynamic of our salvation. ". . . I will *put* a new spirit *within* you. . . . And I will put *my* spirit within you. . . ."

We trust Him for a special process called salvation . . . but *then* . . . (and this is why I have asked you to look with me at the Saviour Himself) . . . but *then*, once He has saved us, we begin to take things into our own hands!

We begin to *try* to grow.

We begin to *try* to increase our faith.

We begin to *try* to abide.

We begin to *try* to be peaceful.

And hour after hour, day after day, week after week, month after month, this Jesus Christ stands reminding us with the simplicity and majesty of God Himself that ". . . without me ye can do nothing"!

". . . without me ye can do nothing."

Why do we continue to try?

Is it because we think Christ Himself was confused about the reality of things when He said what He said to His disciples as it is recorded in the fifteenth chapter of the Gospel of John? Or is it because we feel we need to help Him accomplish that good work which He has begun in us? Do we think He is inadequate to one or two things which we feel we had better work out ourselves?

What is it?

Stop and think.

"Search me, O God, and . . . see if there be any wicked way in me . . ."!

Surely it is wicked to try to take God's place.

Surely it is wicked to doubt His power.

Surely it is wicked not to believe Jesus Christ meant what He said.

And He said quite clearly and with the simplest simplicity that *without Him* we can do absolutely nothing!

In utter, frantic helplessness at the sight of the sin in us when the Holy Spirit points it out, we turn to Christ for forgiveness. For salvation. And then . . . and then we take things into our own hands. Why?

Could it be ignorance on our part?

Could it be that we haven't been still before Him long enough to find out what He's really like?

Could it be that we haven't spent enough conscious time in His presence?

Could it be that we haven't fed our starving spirits on the Word of God?

Could it be that we haven't depended upon the Holy Spirit to open our understandings as we read what He inspired?

Could it be that we have missed the central point entirely?

Salvation *includes* growth, life, faith, abiding, prayerlife, peace, simplicity, as well as forgiveness of sin. And if the Saviour Himself is our salvation, wouldn't it be plausible to realize that in HIM *all things do* consist?

If salvation implies being saved, then looking unto the Lord Himself is the answer.

"Look unto *me*, and be ye saved. . . ."

"Come unto *me*, . . . and I will give you rest."

". . . *I* am the way, the truth, and the life. . . ."

My heart sings with joy because of that personal pronoun when it is used by Christ Himself. I'm so glad He's a person and not just a principle! I did not long for salvation. I longed for a Saviour.

"O God, thou art my God; early will I seek *thee* . . ."!

And now that our eyes are *upon* Jesus Christ the Person, we'll move on to see how it is that He *can* become all things to us. Even more to the point, we'll see how it is that He has already *become* all things to us and our part is to find out how we can begin to *experience* it. First we'll have a look at *growth*.

We all long to grow. Unless we are blind to our need.

Be prepared to feel pretty silly at your past efforts to add that "cubit" to your spiritual height.

I do.

4

I Longed to Grow!

Up to this point I have written to those who do and those who do not believe in Jesus Christ. In this chapter I will write primarily to those of you who not only believe in Him, but whose hearts long to follow Him as Lord of your lives.

This does not rule out non-believers or nominal Christians.

I believe that if you will read on (you who do not follow Christ with all your hearts) you will become jealous of what is in store for anyone who dares to follow Him the second half!

Again, I witness.

That happened to me. I became jealous of the freedom, the life, the perpetual upward motion in the lives of those whose gift of hinds' feet enabled them to leap and skip around the mountainside always in sight of Him, who was just up ahead. I grew jealous of their abandon, their gaiety, their joy, their ease in the rough places. Their growth.

Their fulfilled desires.

If you are yet undecided, please read on.

If you are stumbling on the way, please read on.

If you are singing on the way, please read on.

Longing springs from the heart of God.

He would give you a new and deeper longing for more of Himself.

I will write on.

Knowing, as I now do, that each new longing comes from the God who fulfills it.

The sincere Christian longs to grow.

It is as natural for the Christian to grow while he is looking at the *Son* as it is for the daisy to grow while it looks at the *sun*! Growth is natural when the conditions of growth are met. Growth does not exist of itself. It is the result of life.

Growth is not the result of itself.

It is the result of the presence of *life*.

And life does not come from the roots of a plant; it comes from beyond. From below the roots.

From God.

Life *is* within us, but it does not *come* from within us.

Life comes from God.

The life of the daisy and our life too.

There is a kind of life which the daisy cannot get, however, even from God. That is eternal life. Eternal life is for us only. Because only we are made in the image of God. And eternal life *is* God's life.

But following the already laid down natural laws of life, even eternal life does not come from within. *Especially* eternal life does not come from within.

It comes from *beyond*.

It comes from Christ. It *is* His very life.

It comes to invade us when we receive Him in His resurrection fullness. Then it is surely *within* us.

But not until we receive Him.

". . . if any man will open the door, I will come in . . ." And *then* there will be *growth*. Because *He* is life.

". . . I am the resurrection, and the life. . . ."

Letters I receive leave me with varied feelings. One kind inevitably leaves me feeling—helpless. It is from the earnest soul who writes, "I don't seem to be growing in my Christian life. Tell me, please, what is the secret of your growth?"

I feel limp when I receive a letter like that.

And somewhat dismayed that someone should ask me when Jesus Christ Himself anticipated that question and answered it in the plainest of language!

"Which of you by taking thought can add one cubit to your stature?"

Do not jump to quick conclusions here. "Thought" is required to know what Jesus meant. Thought or plans or mental-gyrations will not make you grow one cubit, but thought is always required to know what Jesus means. Even after the Holy Spirit reveals it to us, we must weigh it with our enlightened intelligences. And what the Lord Jesus said in effect is that *effort on our part does not promote growth.*

He Himself is our growth!

Because He Himself is our life.

Where there is life, there will be growth, and there will continue to be growth as long as the conditions of life are met.

Growth is an all-inclusive, wonder-filled sense of love living!

Growth is love—*living*!

The Beloved Disciple John late in his life lifted his voice and declared that ". . . God is love."

Where God is, love is.

Where God is, life is.

Where life is, growth is.

And so growth is love living!

There are many signs of growth in the Christian. We will look at only two. First . . . am I honest with myself and with God?

Am I honest with myself and with God?

It is impossible to be one without the other. If I am not facing facts as they are (especially facts about myself) with myself, then I cannot be honest with God when I discuss myself and my problems with Him!

Of course, God knows this. But my will is the spring which releases His power to untangle me in the depths which I cannot reach and if I am misrepresenting the facts, even to myself, how can my will be an act of clear-cut decision on the *right* issues?

I listened, not long ago, for over an hour to a disturbed woman who poured out her longing to see her husband become a Christian. Her desire seemed right. On the surface, it was even scriptural. But after that hour, I managed to get in a word or two, and I asked a question which I knew could and probably would end the interview abruptly one way or another: "*Why* do you want your husband to become a Christian? Do you want him to do this because you see how much Jesus Christ needs a man with his capabilities and personality? Or do you want him to become a Christian so that *you* can be proven right?"

Her quick flush and sharp answer showed me that her motives were definitely *mixed*. She was not being honest with herself and, of course, God could not answer her prayers.

In my own experience I have found over and over that I have prayed vainly for a Christian brother or sister who seemed to need an enormous amount of changing. At first, my prayers consisted of a long complaint to God (sometimes in the King James Version, sometimes not), *about* this brother or sister. Usually the complaint reminded God with regular frequency how Christ-like I was acting in the situation and that if God didn't change this one who offended *soon*, I'd surely have to take some steps to help Him in the correction!

After months of this, God finally got through to me with: "If you see sin in that life, it's only because I have given you the perception. Your part is to double your own efforts to protect My reputation with those involved who do not know Me."

In one case in particular, I obeyed on this point.

That was one sign of growth.

But still God could not answer the prayer completely. This brother was still hard at it and everywhere I turned I seemed to run into more of the results of his flaming ego at work among a certain group of non-believers with whom I had been quite proud of my own Christian witness.

This brother was *not* behaving like Jesus Christ.

Not at all.

But I could almost *feel* myself grow when once more God got me quiet long enough to realize that my motives were not altogether unmixed! I was not being completely honest with myself.

Praying for this brother to change was right.

But *using* his un-Christian behavior to point up my own Christian behavior was not right.

I had been doing this and was not willing to admit it to myself.

And certainly I wasn't admitting it to God!

But, of course, God knew it anyway.

Are we really honest with ourselves?

Are our motives mixed or unmixed?

If we are honest with ourselves, we are honest with God.

And if we are honest with both ourselves and God, we can relax and *know* we are growing up in Jesus Christ.

Jesus Christ always faces facts as they are. He did not always answer the surface questions which were put to Him when He was on earth, but He *did* always answer the *real* questions which lay squirming beneath the ones formed into words.

He is my honesty if I permit Him full sway in my life.

Christ in me is my *only* hope of—honesty!

With God and with myself.

And if I am honest with myself about myself, I am growing.

He is always honest.

He is my growth.

Anyone can grow. No one has a corner on the market of spiritual growth. Once the life of God has been put within us at the moment we receive Jesus Christ as our Saviour, growth *can* begin.

He wants to be your Saviour and He also wants to be your growth.

He can be because He *is* your life if you have received Him.

One more among many signs of spiritual growth (almost too obvious to mention!) is *maturity*. When we grow, we grow—*up*. We grow to maturity, don't we? Or at least we are supposed to be growing *toward* it. But how many of us confuse Christian busyness with maturity? How many of us confuse noisy meetings and numbers of forced testimonies with true spiritual maturity? Noisy meetings *can* be meetings of mature Christians. And certainly many busy Christians are mature, or at least maturing. The point I want to make is simply that the common signs we use are not always accurate.

Mature Christians are Christians who *act* more and more every day like Jesus Christ.

Some of the most immature Christians I know read their Bibles every day and many of them can recite pages of Scripture from memory. But in the tight places they ridicule and criticize and blaze away in judgment and condemnation of other Christians who might not interpret those well-memorized Scripture verses just as *they* do and nowhere in their behavior or personalities can we find any family resemblance to the Saviour.

Or any evident signs of true maturity.

To me, the most evident sign of true maturity is the ability to adjust.

How quickly do you adjust?

How quickly do I adjust?

When you've planned for a quiet afternoon alone and an alcoholic for whom you've been praying rings your doorbell—how quickly do you adjust?

When I've set aside a long-cherished evening to digest a new book on "the deeper life," what do I do when a dear soul who has been praying for me for years "just thought she'd drop by for an hour or so between trains to bring me a tin of cookies and chat awhile"?

How quickly do I adjust?

Especially when I'm dieting and can't eat the cookies!

If the contractor promises moving day in plenty of time to get settled before Thanksgiving and you find yourself not only trying to prepare Thanksgiving dinner amidst packing crates, but see no hope of putting up the Christmas tree in your new home—how quickly do you adjust?

In my B.C. days, and during a good part of my early Christian life, I excelled at maladjustment. If something didn't go to please me, I felt I had a right to let off some steam about it!

At least I had a right to make the other person uncomfortable too.

But that was before I woke up to the blessed, glad truth that *only* as I give up the *rights* to myself along with my SELF, am I free!

I had read about rejoicing in *all* things.

But somehow it had to do with St. Paul, not with me. And then slowly I began to see that I would be mature only when Jesus Christ was living His life *fully* in me. I would be mature *only* when once and for all, I took Galatians 2:20 as the standard for my personal, everyday life.

"I am crucified with Christ: nevertheless I live; yet not I, but Christ liveth in me. . . ."

I, as I, am not mature!

But "I am crucified with Christ." Still I am living and moving about this earth in a mortal body, ". . . yet not I, but *Christ liveth in me* . . ."!

I, as I, could not adjust quickly.

I, as I, did not even want to.

"Nevertheless not I—but Christ" who *does* want to!

And since the moment I took Galatians 2:20 as the standard for my hourly living, He has given me chance after chance to try it.

One fine opportunity came several months ago when I finished a week's speaking engagement on a Sunday morning in Portland, Oregon, and was scheduled to fly to Seattle, Washington, in time to speak at the evening service in a Seattle church.

The week in Portland had been one of those weeks which look comfortably full on Monday and end up "pressed down and running over" as I staggered "pressed down" physically toward its close. I was exhausted and I had a virus. How I longed to take a plane back to Chicago and my own bed!

Instead, I began my next engagement with a two-hour wait in the Portland airport and when my plane could not take off due to engine trouble, I was put on another plane whose pressurization apparatus was not working quite right.

I am a good flyer, as long as the pressurization apparatus is working. But that day, I sat huddled in a cramped, overheated coach plane, swallowing madly in a futile effort to unstop my ears . . . unable to convince the woman next to me that I had all but lost my voice from too much speaking the week before . . . coughing, massaging my aching head and neck, trying to comfort myself with the reassuring thought that I'd soon be on the ground in Seattle and bathed and resting in my friend Sylvia Hatfield's comfortable apartment.

"Things could be a lot worse," I told myself. "You could be hungry and you could be landing just in time for the evening service so you'd have to speak in this horribly wrinkled suit. You could even have a radio or a TV interview this very afternoon. But you don't. So things could be a lot worse."

Determinedly I put my *will* into thanking the Lord for the whole thing. I didn't *feel* thankful, but I thanked Him anyway. Although I allowed myself the luxury of thinking how sorry Mother would be for me if she could see her darling daughter sitting there courageously thanking God while the growing pressure pain in her head and ears forced tears to trickle down her cheeks!

By the time the plane landed, I was almost deaf and the pain had moved down to include both shoulders and my arms. "It could be worse though. After all, your ears will open up and you are going straight to Sylvia's apartment and then you can bathe and rest and change into fresh clothes. Plenty of time before your next appearance for at least an hour's sleep."

As I trudged down the steps from the plane to the ground I saw Sylvia waving frantically from the airport gate. I wondered why she was so eager to see me and as I came nearer, my ears popped enough so I heard her shout: "Hurry, Genie, hurry! We have just twenty minutes to make a radio interview and it takes almost that long to drive to the station from here!"

Now, I had rather looked forward to losing my luggage as a Christian. You see, I'd lost it a couple of times in my old life and each time I blistered the ears of any hapless rail or airline employee in sight. Both times I was completely convinced the railroad or airline had held a special board meeting at which detailed plans were laid to lose *my* luggage! The entire railroad and airline operations had been "out to get" Eugenia Price.

And so I wondered how I would react and what I would do as a Christian under the same circumstances.

That day I found out.

As Sylvia propelled me along toward the luggage counter, I "surrendered" having to make an appearance at a radio station in my wrinkled suit, but thanked God I could have a freshly pressed one from my luggage for the evening service.

And then the big chance came.

"Miss Price, I'm so sorry to have to tell you this, but your luggage was left in Portland by mistake."

With my head still spinning with pain, I wondered vaguely why the poor airline chap felt he needed to add "by mistake," but beyond that I just stood there surprised at the sudden wave of compassion for the young man which swept over me!

And yet, there it was. Unmistakably I felt sorry for him as he stood there adjusting his tie and straightening his trim cap preparatory to giving me "apology number 1-A for ruffled passengers whose luggage has just been left behind in Portland"—by mistake.

He opened his mouth to begin, but I said: "Better save your speech for someone else who needs it. I'm a Christian and I've *never* been more delighted to be one than I am right this minute. And you may not know it, but you should be glad I'm a Christian too!"

The fellow couldn't answer me, so I went on as Sylvia and I both began to laugh. "I'm dog-tired from the week I just finished and more thankful than I could ever tell you that I don't have to waste any more energy being sorry for myself or cutting you down to size. It's all right. The Lord knows where my luggage is and when you find it, please send it in a taxi to this address."

Did *I* make that adjustment?

No.

Jesus Christ made it in me.

". . . yet not I, but Christ liveth in me. . . ."

The interview at the radio station had a fresh ring to it too, not because I was especially original (I was especially unoriginal!) but it was not I, but Christ who gave me the fresh proof that I *was* growing up.

I can be mature because Christ Himself is mature.

Jesus Christ *in* me, my *only* hope of maturity!

I became a Christian when I was physically thirty-three years old. At thirty-three years of physical age, I was an immature "sixteen" emotionally . . . still frantically trying to prove *my* point in everything.

Now? . . . Jesus Christ *in* me, my only hope of maturity.

Christ *in* me, my only hope of—growth!

5

I Longed to Believe

The most difficult thing about becoming a Christian as an adult is to begin to believe. And yet the only qualification for becoming a Christian is to begin "to believe on the Lord Jesus Christ."

When we do that, He comes in.

But at first I couldn't believe.

All the arguments about *why* I should believe, only seemed to make it more impossible. I was trying to do it with my mind. I listened to the reasons why I should believe and I listened and digested them with my mind and then went right on trying to take the step also with my mind.

We take the step with our *will*.

Our will empowered by the Holy Spirit. Unless He gives us the power to place our wills in the hands of Jesus Christ, we can't do it. I believe we definitely have the choice to make. Some will disagree with me. But while I do believe God continues to respect our free will, we are powerless to turn that will toward God without the work of the Holy Spirit! We can choose to turn toward our selfish selves alone. But not toward God. I believe it is a two-way transaction, with our part entirely dependent upon His grace poured out in His mercy and His love and His caring about us. He showed the extent of all of that caring on the cross, so we can depend upon it that He will stand ready to give that power wherever we will make our choice to *take* the power.

I am inclined to think that down deep enough or up high enough there is a point of agreement here among all Christians who differ so widely and sometimes violently on the terminology used.

Personally, I know I was *given* the very ability to turn to Christ in that hotel room in New York City in the month of October, 1949. A decision like that was totally unlike me, as I was that day *before* Christ came to live within me.

And so, one of the first longings set astir within me when He began to press in upon my heart was the longing to *believe*.

I longed to believe.

First I simply longed to believe something.

Anything.

I was lost.

I couldn't admit it, but I had never really had a "way" that was clear cut. One I could see and follow. I needed a way to live and I knew it and I longed to believe in something beyond myself.

But it was not until it was *revealed* to me, from *outside* myself, by way of my longing *heart*, that Jesus Christ and God *are* one and the same, that I began to be able to believe that He could give me a new life.

When at last my eyes were opened to see that God's every intention toward me was *in* this Jesus Christ, I believed.

". . . I, if I be lifted up . . . will draw. . . ."

He did. He drew me, gave me the very ability to open my heart to Him, and then He came in.

As every other Christian, I trusted the Person of Jesus Christ to make this eternal transaction in me.

And then, as with almost every other Christian, I began to long again. As they, I also longed for faith and more faith. And although I trusted Him for my salvation, I began to try to whip up *faith* myself!

It is said that the devil flees from the sight of a Christian on his knees. I am inclined to doubt this. Certainly the devil has gotten in some of his best licks with me while I have been on my knees! On my knees working feverishly to conjure up a *mental attitude* which I could recognize as *faith*. On my knees in an attitude of tense striving to whip up in my imagination a picture of the thing for which I prayed—as I thought it *should* be. On my knees with set jaw and clenched fists explaining anxiously and in detail to God just how He can go about helping me out of the difficulty . . . or how He can use this device and that method to change the person or persons whose disposition clashes are making trouble for me.

On my knees "manufacturing" faith.

And the devil is having the time of his evil life!

Making full use of my futile self-effort.

But I hang my head in shame that during so much of the time I have spent in such a manner on my knees, only God and the devil seemed to know about the futility angle!

I was slow to learn.

Then some months ago a certain tragic situation arose which involved persons who are very, very dear to me. My heart ached constantly. I set a regular prayer time each day about which I told no one. I kept it religiously. Every day at the appointed hour I was on my knees—fists clenched, eyes wet with tears, jaw set, mind working, *working* to "whip up" the attitude of faith. Long and detailed instructions poured forth to the Father in heaven in the name of the Son. I imagined the persons involved smiling at each other again . . . arms around the neck . . . heart to heart as Christians are supposed to be, according to the Scriptures.

Regularly I prayed and wept and pleaded and conjured up "faith" and outlined procedures to God and—nothing whatever happened.

Then one day I was exhausted. I just knelt there drooping and said, "Lord, I can't think of anything else to say!"

And He said: "Good."

Then He took over. With simple, swift strokes the Holy Spirit seemed to be drawing a picture which even I could interpret. No words came, but suddenly I knew that I had no faith outside of Christ Himself. Suddenly I realized that He Himself is my faith too!

Within a few months there was the miracle of another answered prayer.

". . . the life which I now live in the flesh I live *by the faith of the Son of God. . . .*"

Would Jesus Christ come to indwell me in the Person of the Holy Spirit and leave His faith in heaven?

No!

The thought stabbed me into awareness that here was a deeper rest about which I had not yet heard. He is my *faith* too. I could from that time on pray in the name of Jesus Christ and *in His faith.* The very same faith that gave Him the courage to commend His Spirit into His Father's hands as He hung as a man on the cross of Calvary.

The same faith that overcame that same Satan when he tried to put suggestions of self-effort into the Lord's mind in the wilderness, just as he had tried to put them into my mind as I too knelt in prayer. The same Lord who turned Satan down flatly in the wilderness was right there to turn him down for me too.

And He did.

In no uncertain terms.

I didn't even try to pray any more about the tragic situation. I did try to thank Him and then got up and went about my work as though for the first time, the fact of His presence and His intense interest in the same situation had just penetrated my dense mind! Of course He was with the persons involved in my "tragic situation." Of course He loved them more than I did. Of course He wanted the whole thing straightened out too. Even more than I did. His stakes in it were much higher than mine.

Of course He didn't need me to tell Him how to handle it.

Of course He had faith in Himself. *Of* Himself.

Of course He brought that faith along when He came to live in me.

Of course He Himself *is* my faith!

What a relief. What a rest. What a leap forward.

And then it began to clear up still more for me. The two blind men who heard that Jesus was passing by outside of Jericho, did not cry out—"Thou son of David, we have conjured up great faith and are declaring that we can see again!"

No.

They cried—". . . Have mercy on us, O Lord, thou son of David"!

And Jesus stopped and looked at them.

But He did not say, "Because I see that you have done a splendid piece of work whipping up your faith, I will help you."

He just looked at them and said, ". . . What will ye that I shall do unto you?"

"What will ye that *I* shall do unto you?"

What do you want *Me* to do for you?

He Himself was their faith.

And that faith made them whole.

Faith is having confidence in God. Naturally, we cannot have faith in someone whom we do not know. So, the more we know God, the more confidence we have in Him. But who knows God better than God Himself? And why would not God's faith be the ultimate?

It would be.

It is!

Jesus Christ Himself is our faith. "In whom we have boldness and access with *confidence by the faith of him*."

Growth is love—living.

Faith is love—*confiding*.

God is love.

God has supreme confidence in Himself.

He declared Himself in Jesus Christ . . . "In whom we have boldness and access with confidence by the faith *of him.*"

Therefore true faith is love confiding.

We can relax and draw on the riches in glory by the faith of Christ Jesus Himself. *If* . . . *if* we *know* that "the life which (we) now live in the flesh (we) live by the faith of the Son of God, who loved (us) and gave himself for (us)."

I longed to believe . . . I longed to have faith.

From now on I can pray with His faith.

What a relief to know that He *Himself* is my faith!

6

I Longed to Be Constant

Christ *in* me . . . my only hope of *growth*.
Christ *in* me . . . my only hope of *faith*.
He is my growth. He is my faith.
And He Himself is my very *abiding*! My constancy.

How is this so? Perhaps you think, "I can comprehend what is meant by saying He is my growth. I can see this because Jesus Christ Himself tells me that He is 'the resurrection and the *life*.' That He Himself is 'the way, the truth, and the *life*.' And so, since I know *growth* is a natural result of *life*, and since I have His Own Word for it that He Himself comes in to be my very *life* when I receive Him, then I can comprehend that He is my growth. Since the Word of God also tells me that 'the life which I now live in the flesh I live by the faith *of* the Son of God . . . ,' I can understand that he is also my *faith*."

"I have God's Own Word for *growth* and *faith*."

"But how is it that Jesus Christ Himself can be my constancy, my *abiding*?"

"Does He not tell me that I am to abide in *Him*?"

Yes, He does tell you that. He tells me that too. And every Christian believer who hungers for the deeper things of God *longs* to know a constant abiding in Jesus Christ. This is natural *after* we have been invaded by the *super*natural. The Holy Spirit coming in

356

to dwell in us creates this longing for constancy to Jesus Christ. This is His Work . . . to make us long for unbroken communion with the Lord Jesus.

What sincere Christian, longing for more and more of Christ, does not promise God every morning that in this day he *will* abide?

"Oh, God, today I will . . . I *will* abide! I will remember that You live within me. I will remember that everywhere I go I have the reputation of the Son of God in my hands! I *will* remember to let You do the reacting through me every minute of this day!"

"*Abide in me*. . . ."

"Yes, Lord . . . I will abide in You."

This tender exchange takes place in our morning quiet time and by ten A.M. *that* person calls on the telephone or the washing machine breaks down and . . .?

What happened to all that "abiding"?

Didn't we mean it when we promised the Lord just two short hours ago? It seemed such a logical, practical, simple thing to do. Sitting in our "chair of heavenly bliss" as we meditated upon God's Words to us, we thought ourselves rather silly not to have seen before now that *striving* is the hard way! Today we would truly *abide*!

And then the washing machine broke down.

And so did the abiding!

The automobile stopped in heavy traffic.

And so did the abiding!

Why?

Didn't we promise? Yes. We promised.

Didn't we realize the seriousness of a promise to the Creator God? Yes. We realized the seriousness of such a promise.

Then why did we stop abiding?

Why?

I read everything I could find on the subject of abiding for over two years. I read and reread the fifteenth chapter of the Gospel of John. "I am the vine, ye are the branches. . . ."

Through and through my heart and mind came His voice asking me . . . commanding me . . . "Abide in me . . . without me ye can do nothing."

"The voice of my beloved."

I agreed with Him.

What a relief it was the day I discovered that without Him I *could* do absolutely nothing.

I agreed with Him that I should, that I must abide in Him.

I truly wanted to.

And yet . . . those times kept coming. Although He always forgave me and restored me to the closeness with Himself we knew before I broke my promise to abide, I grew sick of the failures and I cried out to Him one day to teach me the secret of abiding in a way even I could understand!

He did.

And this is the story of that lesson.

At thirty-seven years of age I remained a spoiled brat in one big respect at least. Even though I had been a Christian for four years, my parents were still buying most of my clothes. This had been a way in which we had "spoiled" each other in the years past. Naturally I cut down on the quantity after my conversion, but the time came when I faced the fact that I must not only begin to buy my own clothes, what was worse (to me), I must begin to shop for them myself!

This was the part I resisted most.

For years I had made fun of people who attended sales. My things were selected for me by Mother and the faithful saleswomen in an exclusive store in my home town where they loved me (or tried to) in spite of my unpleasant arrogance every time I had to "bother" to try on something.

They were accustomed to me.

I suspect they realized some of my fussiness was due to my self-consciousness at wearing such large sizes and went on placating me through the years because Mother was such a dear friend and good customer.

This haughty attitude on my part was not like Jesus Christ.

I had known it for sometime. Finally I informed Ellen (the friend who led me to Christ and who is now my associate) that I was ready to launch out on a shopping trip—*and* at the after-Christmas sale season!

She gasped quietly and said: "All right. I'll go with you. But let's have a prayer first—and *you* pray."

I prayed.

A very spiritual prayer, I thought. I told God I knew He knew my needs and that I was sure He had just the two suits I needed at just the prices I could pay and I promised Him frequently throughout the prayer that I *would* abide in Him every minute of the entire shopping expedition!

The first sales lady we approached had obviously lost all her Christmas spirit. I smiled at her (proud that for the first time in years I had lost enough weight to wear an eighteen right off the rack!) and said: "Could I see some eighteens, please?"

Her *look*, which swept right down over the end of her patrician nose, said: "Sorry, Madam, we don't carry circus tents in this department!"

What she actually said was: "Sorry, we don't have anything that *large*!"

She intended to wither me. What she did was bring a mighty resurgence of the old Gene Price with all her soap opera dialogue banners flying! My great "spirituality" following my prayer was fractured as a razor-reply tore through my "abiding" mind and hung there teeming to be put into words.

In my old life I would have relished every moment of my "reply." I would have re-told the incident over and over, improving my "reply" with each telling. *Naturally*, I responded with every atom of Eve in me to such an exchange. It was my forte. I thoroughly enjoyed cutting people down to *my* estimate of their true size.

Naturally, this was true of the old Gene Price.

*Super*naturally, something new had happened!

I said nothing to her for a moment. And by pure self effort I held the "reply" I longed to make. *But* I could *not* hold back my "look." I returned hers intensified. I even cocked my eyebrow as I hadn't done in almost four years (a bit of business which I always felt increased the venom in any "look"), and said, with ice breaking from every word: "I'm terribly sorry to have disturbed you."

And walked away.

Ellen followed me in silence.

Outside on the street I could stand it no longer. My heart was broken at what I had done!

That woman had every right to wither me if she wanted to. I, as a disciple of Jesus Christ had *no* right whatever to return even her *look*! As I stood there on the sidewalk with Chicago's Loop pushing past me I wanted to cry. The only reason I hadn't exchanged more words with her was because I was afraid she might recognize me as the author of a Christian radio program I was writing at that time, which originated in Chicago.

The only reason I said as little as I said was pure spiritual *pride*!

What had happened to my *abiding*?

Hadn't I promised the Lord just one minute before I stepped out of the door of our house that I would abide in Him?

My shame was intense.

My heartache more intense.

I was irritated with Ellen when she suggested maybe we should go home and try it another day.

Then notions of doing this crossed frantic desires to run back and find the saleswoman and apologize! All I could do was stand there in the noise and the crowd and try not to cry.

And then . . . the lesson came. Quietly, over the noise of Chicago's Loop. And at the first convenient stopping place I grabbed my New Testament from my purse and began to read the first sentence of John 15:4 over and over and over!

"Abide in me, and I in you."

"Abide in me, *and I in you*."

"Abide in me, *AND I IN YOU*."

Sitting on a stool at a glove counter in a big Loop department store, He taught me the lesson I had prayed to learn.

I had been trying *of my own self to abide in Him*!

Jesus Christ would not have *dared* command me to abide in Him if He had not fully intended to be abiding in me even during the time in which I did *not* abide in Him!

We stop with the first half of that sentence: "Abide in me.

His whole sentence reads: "Abide in me, and *I in you*."

You abide in me, and I'll be abiding in you.

If He had *not* been abiding in me, I would not have experienced my heartbreaking need outside that store. Without Him I would have enjoyed the incident as in my old life. Where Jesus Christ *is*, sin is abashed! Sin is abashed and dumbfounded in His presence! In Saint John's first letter he tells us that "No one who is born of God makes a practice of sinning, because the . . . life-principle continues to live in him . . ." (Williams Translation). We cannot *practice* sinning because He is always, every minute *abiding in us*! He can trust Himself. He knows what He will do.

Abide in me, and *I will be abiding in you*!

This is the way I learned the lesson that "abiding" does not come in a separate package of my own making.

He Himself *is* my abiding!

7

To Be Peaceful

Men gather around big polished tables and argue about how to make and keep peace in the world.

Magazines and books are filled with theories about peace.

Christianity is called "the gospel of peace." But Christianity has been in the world for almost two thousand years. And the world is still sitting on an atomic "powder keg"!

America is called a Christian country and one group of citizens of one color still throws rocks through the windows of the homes of another group of citizens because their skin is yet another color.

Every year billions of dazzling greeting cards go out across the world which read: "Peace on earth."

Every year murders increase and divorce rates increase and a new war, either hot or cold, springs up from somewhere.

Peace?

It gives one a vaguely uneasy feeling to think of the horror smeared across the bloody face of the world because of the shortage of peace. It gives one a far less vague case of jitters to think those atomic mushrooms *could* "grow" in our own front yard because there is no real peace in the world. One can almost hear the silent breaking of hearts across our world on the days when we "honor our war dead." Cemeteries are quiet places and the hearts of those who kneel beside the little cross-marked tombs break again each year silently because cemeteries are silent places and there is no answer anywhere to the world's heart-cry for peace.

No answer to the individual heart-cries for peace.

No answer anywhere in the world in anything.

Not for you and not for me.

Why?

Because we are seeking peace in the wrong places. By wrong methods. We have misunderstood, or purposely twisted what the angels said when the Prince of Peace was born that first Christmas. We are expecting peace to come from some nebulous turn of events. We act as though the angels *prophesied* peace that other silent night.

As though they prophesied something yet to come at one crashing, silver moment.

The angels did not prophesy peace at all.

They *proclaimed* it!

They proclaimed that peace itself lay in that manger and would hang on a cross and then walk bodily out of a tomb, and save the people from their sins. Peace only comes to the world when the people in that world are peaceful people. And peace only comes to a people when they are rightly related to the Father by faith in His Son, Jesus Christ.

Peace comes in when Christ comes in.

Most books that offer a way of peace are popular.

Most peace conferences make the headlines.

Vacation spots where "peace grows in you as the green grass grows upon our greening hillsides" pour out their "peacefully" written literature.

Weary, harried men and women are urged to "come out to the old ball park and enjoy a peaceful afternoon away from your troubles."

Lots sell well in the suburbs because it's "peaceful in the country."

Books about the "religion of peace" contained in right thinking pile up and vanish from the bookstalls and men and women leave the "peace" of their new lots in the country for work each day in the hectic unpeace of the city. The books on peace pile up and vanish and the "peaceful" fans leave the "old ball park" and go home to the battle of the bulge in friend wife's ego because supper got cold when the game ran into extra innings. The books on peace pile up and vanish and the hot wars and the cold wars continue to break out and the quiet hearts break again beside the quiet graves in the cross-marked cemeteries.

"Where is God in all this?" cries the grief-torn woman whose husband died of shock because their two boys were murdered in cold blood by other human beings gone diabolically mad in this same civilized world whose bookstalls are piled high with books on peace!

"Where is God in all my suffering? And why should *I* be the one who has the kind of cancer no one can cure or even cut out?" A once pretty woman of thirty-eight buries her head in her pillow and tries to choke off the sobs of rebellion against the tragedy that turned her "peaceful" life into one of fear and dread and pain and certain death!

Someone brought this woman a book about how to be peaceful by teaching herself to think right thoughts and she threw it across the room and swore for the first time in her entire life! She had thought she was peaceful once. But her peace didn't hold.

True story after true story of speeded-up desperation under the heavens and the earth gone mad in its search for peace. Books about peace pile up and vanish from the bookstalls, and God calls down from His heaven saying: ". . . they have healed the hurt of . . . my people slightly, saying, Peace, peace; when there *is* no peace!"

There *is* no man-made peace that holds when the ghastly circumstances of life pass our understanding! Man-made peace . . . peace in the peaceful bookstalls among the books about.

peace only heals the hurt slightly and men and women go on saying "Peace, peace . . . when there *is* no peace!"

"Peace on earth?" Is it possible?

Yes.

". . . peace through the blood of his cross. . . ." Peace *only* by the One who Himself said just before they killed Him: "Peace I leave with you, my peace I give unto you . . ." ". . . if it were not so, I would have told you. . . ."

Jesus Christ was not prophesying peace at random.

He spoke those tender, strong words to *His Own* disciples. He was on His way to the cross to die for every man and woman and child in the world. To open the way for everyone, with no exceptions, to know personally the "peace . . . which passeth all understanding. . . ."

He gives His peace now to *all* who are His Own. And He *wants* us all to be His Own. But because peace only comes through union with God, peace cannot exist where sin is. He is a Holy God.

Sin must be wiped out before the Holy One comes in.

Perhaps that is one reason He said what He said about leaving His peace, just before He went willingly to the cross to shed His Own blood that our sins might be washed away. He made the promise of peace and then went about making the way for us to receive it.

Peace is not a separate thing.

We make the mistake of searching for it as though it is.

It is not.

Peace is a result of an unbroken communion with God, which includes unbroken communion with our fellow man as well. This is only possible when we are out of the way and Christ is living His Own peace-filled life in us.

We are not peaceful by nature.

Sin has invaded our nature as God made it in the beginning and sin is not a peaceful thing.

Peace is not something the Lord left for us in a package.

Peace cannot be put into a package or a book.

Paul sang it out as he saw it in the heart that broke on Calvary for *him*, when he wrote: ". . . now in Christ Jesus ye who sometimes were far off are made nigh by the blood of Christ. For *he is our peace. . . .*"

He is our peace!

Jesus Christ Himself is our peace!

Where He is, sin is abashed. Worry, anxiety, fear, self-pity, murder, rebellion at life . . . rebellion at God Himself which shows itself in alcoholism, neuroticism, skepticism, atheism, communism, or criticism, curls up and vanishes in the presence of the One who went to the cross and let His Own sinless heart break wide open under the horror-filled burden of our sin!

We cannot *think* our way to peace.

We can only know peace when we allow Him to do away with all the enemies of peace. And when we begin fully to ". . . walk in the light as he is in the light . . . ," his blood will *keep us cleansed*, minute by minute of the sin of even understandable self-pity!

The woman dying of cancer at thirty-eight and the woman whose husband died from the shock of his sons' murders have a perfectly understandable *human* right to pity themselves.

To cry out, "Why?"

But that very rebellion and self-pity robs them of the peace He left for them. If it were not so, He would have told us.

His peace does not come in packages. Nor does it come only to those who have walked with Him over a long period of years. Peace comes at once to the newly converted sinner who has felt the weight roll away. He doesn't know where it went. He may not know the front from the back of the Bible. I didn't. But I knew a peace I didn't even think existed when Jesus Christ forgave me of my sins.

Before my conversion, I had sung lustily at so-called sophisticated parties of this very thing. An amazing number of "pagans" know the lyrics to the old gospel songs. Over and over I led out with:

> *At the Cross, at the Cross, where I first saw the light,*
> *And the burden of my heart rolled away,*
> *It was there by faith, I received my sight,*
> *And now I am happy all the day.*

I sang it and laughed with everyone else and hours later, as I lay wide-eyed on my pillow trying to get the somewhat stilted melody out of my reeling mind, the tears on that pillow seemed more ridiculous than the song as the lyrics of the last line kept circling around in my brain . . .

> *And now I am happy all the day.*

I tried many "peaceful" pastimes. Sometimes I felt peaceful. I had a splendid classical record collection at a certain period. Bach and Handel and Haydn and some of Beethoven made me feel peaceful.

I owned some "peaceful" books with fine old leather bindings.

But mostly my peaceful pursuits only made me long for peace.

The peace I now *know* in Jesus Christ.

The peace He said He'd leave with me.

The peace that came when He came. His peace. What kind of God would He be to come to live within me, according to His promise, and leave His peace in heaven?

Peace does not come in packages or by methods or in books. It is in Christ Jesus. And it is not reserved for those who have known Him a long time at all. A few months after my life story, *The Burden Is Light*, was reviewed in the *Chicago Tribune* book section, a letter came from Claude M., a prisoner at Joliet Penitentiary, saying that Mr. Lawrence Heron's arrestingly written review had attracted his attention.

"Where may I purchase this book? If it is 'for the scoffer,' as Mr. Heron claims, then I want to read it."

Sometime later we tied up this man's story with the front pages of every Chicago newspaper! Claude M. was a famous member of the underworld who had turned state's evidence at the time he wrote his letter of inquiry about my book. Through letters, prayers, a radio program I was writing, and a visit with him at Joliet Prison, this "big-time policy racket" boy became a son of God.

As we sat facing him across the visitors' barrier desk at the prison, we discovered that he had truly surrendered *his* life into the hands of Jesus Christ as he read through the pages of *my* life in *The Burden Is Light*.

There was no mistaking it.

He was a very newborn babe in Christ, but the life of Christ was *in* him and we relaxed in the presence of our new brother. He and I had both longed for the wrong things. I remember his smile when I said: "You didn't need a Saviour any more than I did. And I didn't need one any more than you did. The ground *is* level at the foot of the cross of Jesus Christ."

His smile was good and direct and redeemed.

His face was peaceful.

Because *Claude* was peaceful.

A man who is imprisoned for protection from the quick guns of the underworld is—peaceful? A man who, according to the federal office conducting the investigation, is in grave physical danger every minute he is outside the walls of the prison? This man is peaceful?

Yes.

In a letter received from my new brother in Christ only today he writes: "No one here can understand my seeming indifference to the drastic situation ahead of me. But how can they possibly know about my peace when they do not understand about our Saviour? I have belonged to Him such a short time, but I have found out in a way better than a hundred sermons, that He *is* my peace!"

Peace is *holding* this man.

When he leaves prison, nothing of this world is sure.

Claude M. may or may not read this book. But ". . . underneath are the everlasting arms. . . ."

The Saviour who is this prisoner's peace is also his eternal life.

The gang guns may blaze, but no one can kill my brother in Christ. The One who is *in* him, *is* life.

". . . I am the resurrection, and the life: he that believeth in me, though he were dead, yet shall he live: And whosoever liveth and believeth in me shall never die. . . ."

It pleased the Father that in Jesus Christ should all fullness dwell.

"All fullness" includes Claude's peace and yours and mine.

Nothing can shake that peace because nothing changes Jesus Christ.

And He is our peace.

8

To Be Sensitive

Jesus Christ is our "look" at God Himself.

He is our salvation.

He is our life, therefore, our growth.

He Himself is our ability to believe. He is our faith.

He Himself is our constancy. Our abiding.

And He is our peace.

He is all these for which we long and more. Because we all long for more than these. Each one, however important, is merely a part of the fullness God holds out to us in His Own life which He longs to live *in* us as we go about in the daily patterns that make our lives *our* lives. He longs to show Himself within the confines of *our* personalities which form our friendships and set the direction of our beliefs and influence our work on earth.

God is willing to walk the earth again incarnate in us.

This thought is too high for me.

I cannot attain to it.

But I can participate in it. Because of what the Lord Jesus has done on Calvary.

And as I dare to take part more and more in the very life of Christ which has been put within me, my heart leaps up in wonder each time I discover that contained in His life is so much more than the average Christian dreams of!

I confess to that stunted dream.

But I mean to break out of it more and more each day.

Books are written and sermons spoken on the pursuit of peace and constancy and faith and growth. Books should be written and sermons should be spoken on the tremendous fact that in Him all these things for which we all long *do* exist.

And yet, we should not stop with these.

The gift of the life of Jesus Christ within the believer is never quite discoverable in a long lifetime lived in looking *at* it from *outside*. Least of all by those of us who waited so long to receive it. My heart prompts me to waste no more time failing to look *inside* into unusual corners and under different lights in my search for more of the secret riches God offers us in the indwelling Christ!

". . . it pleased the Father that in him should all fulness dwell."

What more is there in this unspeakable fullness which is ours?

What treasures have we missed in the darkness of our own refusal to explore?

". . . I will give thee the treasures of darkness, and hidden riches of secret places. . . ."

How glad I am for His patience because darkness will come again and again into my life as it comes into every life, and even though I sulked at the darkness and forgot to look for the treasures during all those other times, He will be waiting to point them out when I look again at some other dark time still to come.

". . . I will give thee the treasures of darkness, and hidden riches of secret places. . . ."

Peace, faith, growth, constancy.

What of the other longings of my old life before Christ came in? What of the longings which had right origins, longings which even then came from God, but which He could not fulfill because I was cut off from Him by sin?

Your special longings may not be the same as mine. But I am inclined to think that mine will find a response in your heart and yours in mine. If they are longings that come from the heart of the God who created us both, this is bound to be true.

I would share with you four *particular* longings from my life before I turned to Christ *and* after. They did not change. They came from God.

And for brief, tempting periods in my life without Him, I touched these four things for which I longed. I cannot say I possessed them. I only touched them and found them good and then lost them again.

Each one.

Particularly did I long for these things as a writer. Writers have great need of all four of them. So do painters and composers and artists of any kind.

So do mothers and doctors.

And salesmen and teachers and missionaries.

Everyone may not be aware of the need, but everyone does have need of all four.

It so happened that I recognized my need of them. I also knew I lacked them most of the time, in spite of the fact that my longing kept right on.

I needed these things and longed for them before Christ came in.

I needed these things and longed for them after He came.

To my great surprise and delight and relief, I have now discovered that I have them!

They are mine every minute of every day and night and all I have to do to enjoy them is to partake as freely as I like!

They are all in Him.

They all came in abundance and to stay when He came in His fullness to stay forever.

And the first of these things for which I longed was *sensitivity*.

As a writer, I particularly needed to be sensitive to the reactions and viewpoints and personalities of other people. Actually, as a writer of daytime serials, I obtained most of my contracts because I wrote what was called "sensitively realistic" dialogue. I have never said that I wrote dialogue as people really speak. I wrote as people *think* they speak! Or as they *think* others speak.

My child "characters" were supposed to be realistic.

They weren't. I knew practically nothing about children. I simply wrote what mothers *think* their children are like! Which, I suppose, is a kind of sensitivity to mothers. But, I will admit to a *limited amount* of true sensitivity in my *writing* during my old life, and there it stopped.

My "sensitivity" in the main, beyond radio dialogue, was in reality only *touchiness*!

Many confuse the two words.

Purposely.

Someone said to me not long ago: "Oh, I know God won't let me have to live with *her* again! He knows I'm far too sensitive to be around someone as crude as that."

Sensitive?

No.

Touchy.

When I first became a Christian, I simply could not attend a church where the soprano was likely to sing off key. I suffered too much at the hand of my "sensitive" nature if I did.

Sensitive?

No.

Touchy.

Do not misunderstand. The true sensitivity which came when Christ came in His fullness, the sensitivity which increases in me as I decrease, has made me a better radio director, a better writer, a better conversationalist. It has not made me deaf to the lady hiding behind the trembling anthem because her high c slipped. I can still hear her. I still know she didn't make it. But instead of squirming and feeling sorry for my own "sensitive" self, Someone *else* in me wants to *pray* for her and His influence makes *me* want to pray for her too!

Jesus Christ is all sensitivity.

No touchiness.

All sensitivity.

They are not the same.

If my feelings are easily hurt, that is no sign that I am sensitive in the true sense of the word.

But it is a sign that I'm touchy!

True sensitivity meets other people where they are. Jesus always met each person where the other person stood. He did not shade the truth in order to do it. He was the truth. He remained Himself, but He anticipated the other person's reactions to Him. He was sensitive to their heartaches, their twists, their sins. He put Himself in the position of having to say "thank you" to an immoral person when He asked the Samaritan woman at the well to give Him a drink of water. He asked her for a drink *first*. It did not excuse her sin. But it softened her heart toward Him a little and in return she gave Him her attention and He could give her living water.

He met her where she was, needing to think that someone needed her, even for a drink of water.

He was *sensitive* to her.

Because He is the origin of all sensitivity.

The Creator of every leaf sensitive to every wind.

". . . without him was not any thing made that was made."

The bird's quick eye and every gentle hand.

". . . by him all things consist."

Including the sensitivity for which I longed. And which I now have *only* because Christ lives in me. I knew it for brief, tempting times before He came. Enough to make me long for more. And more consistently.

Christians desperately need the very sensitivity of God. We need to see that although *we* have light, others may not. If we realize that we are all apt to stumble through a darkened room, even though it is a familiar room, we must be sensitive enough to see that those we may be trying to reach for Christ are still in darkness and the normal thing to do when it is dark is to stumble.

And to look at things from a wrong perspective. People are off balance in a dark room. If we are sensitive with the sensitivity of Christ, we will not condemn or click our tongues at the man who drinks heavily. If he has not received Jesus Christ as His Saviour from sin, I wonder that he doesn't drink more! If we are sensitive with His sensitivity, we will not condemn the person whose starved emotions seek to be fed in an illicit relationship. We will remember that it is dark where that person is. Jesus Christ is the only light of the world.

Christians who expect those in whom Christ does *not* yet dwell to act as though He *does*, make His cross "much ado about nothing"! If we possess His sensitivity, we will not do this.

". . . where are those thine accusers? . . . Neither do I condemn thee: go, and sin no more."

My sensitivity need not come and go now that He has come to live in me.

It can remain constant.

Jesus Christ is the same today as He was yesterday and He will be just the same tomorrow.

And *He* is my sensitivity.

9

To Be Objective

When Christ came to live His life in me, He came a light into my self-dark world and in that light I have begun to see "hidden riches in the secret places" of our life together.

Riches for which I had longed. Sensitivity and now— *objectivity*.

Writers especially need to be objective.

As do mothers and doctors and teachers and missionaries.

As do people. If they are to live balanced, sane lives. Objectivity is very lacking in our world. Most of us are looking out *from* ourselves as we look out *for* ourselves. We are boxed off one by one by one in our extreme *subjectivity*.

"I'm this way because my grandfather was before me."

And his grandfather before him.

"I don't know . . . I haven't always been this way. It just seems like my life's so *hard!*"

And my mother before me.

"I'm *like* this . . . when the going gets too rough, I just have to get off by myself. I can't take confusion and other people's troubles! That's just the way I am."

And my father before me.

And the human race before *him*.

Looking out for *us* from the viewpoint of *ourselves*.

How I longed for *objectivity* in my life before Christ. How I longed in the very depths of my being to be objective about life. I remember very little else in James Joyce's book *The Portrait of the Artist As a Young Man*, but I do remember the gist of one very joycian declaration: *The true artist is one who sits in the corner and pares his fingernails as he works.*

I remember that declaration because it made me jealous for two reasons. First, I had no fingernails to pare! I had bitten my nails since childhood and no amount of parental cajoling and bribing had caused me to stop. (Fingernails came too when Christ came. And not until.) The second reason that declaration stirred me to jealousy was the thrilling picture of pure objectivity as the artist sat paring his fingernails in calm, unemotional appraisal of the very work he was creating!

An artist like that would be out of his own way.

What he had to say could come through. Of course, I had very little or nothing to say in those days, even if I could have captured and held that longed-for objectivity. I could be objective about words themselves, but when I began to put them together, my own garbled emotions got in the way. I was so subjective in my own personal life, I was all over the place when I wrote!

The only persons I knew who were *not* subjective and emotionally slopping over the sides of their efforts were those who had dropped love out of their vocabulary of living. Who had hardened into what they called "objectivity."

I wasn't quite that old yet.

I still wanted to be warm and loved and to love in return.

And so I circled around in my subjective circle, ringed around by myself. And longed for the freedom of being off my own hands and *objective*.

I knew my writing would be improved if I could stop taking personal pokes at the people I knew and begin setting down characterizations objectively from the corner as I "pared."

But I saw my "characters" from *my* viewpoint and I had so many grudges and criticisms and, of course, no nails to pare.

So, I kept on longing for the objectivity which I had now and then touched and then lost.

Objectivity and sensitivity, like peace, do not come in packages. They come from within.

They are all contained *in* the One without whom nothing was made that was made.

Human beings can only be naturally objective toward things about which they do not care. I was nicely objective about Arabian oil, for example. And double-barreled shotguns.

My father and brother could get into heated, emotional upsets over shotguns, but guns left me cold. Therefore objective.

True objectivity is demonstrated only when we are able to remain undisturbed at the center of our beings in the midst of the crashing of our own defenses or the sound of our own breaking hearts. True art and true living come from such as this.

I was incapable of it.

Until He came. And with Him came my longed-for objectivity.

I no longer need to be ruled by my circumstances. I need no longer to be a victim of my emotions. Or the emotions of someone I love. Or dislike.

I am free at last to sit in the corner and pare the fingernails He gave me when He came, bringing my eternal life and my blessed objectivity for which I had longed.

Christ lives in me and I *can* be off my own hands and into His hands, looking and living and writing and loving from His point of view and no longer my own.

This is a great, great relief.

Jesus Christ . . . the only Person outside of ourselves who is attractive enough to pull us out of our subjective boxes and set us free to live—objectively!

". . . I will give thee the treasures . . . and hidden riches of secret places . . ." "I will not leave you comfortless: *I* will come to you."

And bring with Me *everything* you need.

"O God, thou art my God; early will I seek thee . . ."!

10

To Be Simplified

For as long as I can remember caring at all, I have been attracted by *simplicity*.

It has been well said that John, the Beloved Disciple, saw into the very heart of the gospel of Jesus Christ, when late in his earthly life, writing what we now know as his first letter, he framed the essence of the gospel in pure simplicity: ". . . *God is love*."

I believe John had grown into that insight as the life of God increased in him and what he saw was *simplicity* itself!

How I longed for simplicity before I became a Christian. Little did I know I was longing for the very essence of the gospel of Christ! I would have laughed had anyone told me I longed for Christ Himself. I merely longed for simplicity knowing that all great art—painting, music, writing, sprang from simplicity itself. And so I longed for this simplicity in my own life so I could transfer it to my writing. Picasso's paintings, Matisse's line drawings, Marin's water colors, Gertrude Stein's daring singleness of pen in which she allowed the *thing* to describe *itself*, made me strain with desire to capture the same brave simplicity for my own. You may laugh at Miss Stein's oft-quoted and oft-ridiculed line "a rose is a rose is a rose is a rose." But *is* a rose anything else but a rose? Doesn't a rose best describe itself?

I have known since I was old enough to care that the truly well-dressed woman is the *simply* dressed woman. A frantic scramble of flowers and veils and plastic bobs turns the eyes away for "rest" on something simpler! Our eyes are drawn *to* simplicity. This is natural because God made us to be at home in a world with large expanses of sky and ocean and mountains.

We *rest* in the wide-open spaces because they are *simpler* than the clutter and jerk of shapes and rattles in a city block.

The truly well-turned-out home is the simply decorated home. Too many ruffles in the kitchen curtains will claw at the splatter of wallpaper most likely designed by a neurotic craftsman who needs the *simplicity* of the gospel.

Of God Himself.

Do not misunderstand. Your taste in houses and dress have nothing to do with your growth in the Spirit of God! I use these merely to illustrate my own longing for simplicity.

Being aware that you may share it.

Of course, I could affect simplicity in my dress and houses before Christ came to live within me. But I threw away reams of paper seeking it in my writing.

Write, whittle, pare. Then throw it away.

Not simple enough.

Too many adjectives describing description itself!

And failing often.

Now and then the thing I sought to say said itself as simply as I longed for it to do. But only now and then.

And almost never in my personal life was there simplicity at all.

Even then I knew I could never write simply and greatly until I had somehow become simplified. But I could only long for it. I was webbed around by the perpetual complication of a critical nature. By over-emotionalism. By unevenness of disposition. By a bumpy set of values based on too many things for simplicity. I struggled to master a simple writing style and then I had nothing simple and clear to say!

Everything seemed off-center and uneven and muddy.

And it seemed that way because it was.

As I was.

Now Christ lives in me. And with Him came the blessed simplicity for which I longed and struggled. I find I seldom think on simplicity now. I simply use it as I use my brain. It is a part of me. It came when He came. It is the needed single-eye *given* to those who would see Jesus Christ as He is. The Holy Spirit knows about this needed single-eye and, of course, He gives it to us when He knows we are willing to accept it!

To use it.

To dare to see what is possible even for *us* on this earth with Christ living in us. To dare to look at who it is living there!

A great, restful, simplification sweeps into the life that is truly given over in every area to Jesus Christ. We stop going seven directions at once. We are pulled together into one whole.

Excesses are lopped off.

The way *is* blessedly narrow, we discover with a shout of joy!

No need to lose our way now because there is only one road like this one and it is single and simple and straight and leads to eternal fulfillment for the most limited among us.

Eternal fulfillment of everything for which you long.

Of everything for which I long.

Simplicity.

"Come unto *me*. . . ."

". . . *I* am the way. . . ."

". . . Follow *me*. . . ."

". . . *I* will come to you."

". . . *I* will dwell in them, and walk in them. . . ."

". . . *I* will come in. . . ."

Simplicity.

No confusion. Only one way to go. Where He goes.

Jesus Christ Himself is my simplicity.

11

To Be Original

To me, this is the perfect sentence in all recorded literature: *"In the beginning was the Word, and the Word was with God, and the Word was God."*

Its content is the greatest.

Its style is the greatest.

Its impact upon history and upon me greater than any other because it seems to contain all that God is.

All of God that *can* be contained in words.

These words go beyond themselves. They are simpler than simplicity. Deeper than deep. Higher than height itself.

They are *purely original*.

They contain God and they come from God.

God Himself, through the Holy Spirit, directed John, the Beloved Disciple, to write them. As he wrote them.

Only God could have directed a sentence like that.

Only God knew how things were "in the beginning."

"In the beginning God created the heaven and the earth . . . ," *but* only God could have known that *with* Him, as He Created, was the Word, Jesus Christ. That ". . . the Word *was* God."

"And the Word was made flesh, and dwelt among us. . . ."

Only God knew the content of John's second sentence in his Gospel: "The same was in the beginning *with* God." Only God could have written the third sentence: "All things were made by him; and without him was not any thing made that was made."

The writing itself in those three verses would make a human writer give up if that writer did not believe God wrote them! They contain perfect writing. Impossible to man. And perfect truth.

And they contain the sublime proof that still another of my old longings has been met in the Person of Jesus Christ dwelling within me. *Originality*.

Even before I could recognize it as such, when I was a very small child, I must have been longing to be original. As I grew older, this turned to disaster. My "originality" became troublesome "individuality" with its elbows out in every direction!

At nineteen I was too old in boredom for my years. And eccentric.

At twenty I had almost run out of ways to be "different."

And yet, I truly believe that longing came *originally* from God. Everyone longs to be original. If we make a little hopeful joke, we enjoy the warm wave that rises when someone is kind enough to laugh. If we write a little poem—even one we know should not be graced with the name of poetry—we want it to be admired and thought fresh and different. Women like to be thought original in planning parties and wardrobes and dinners and husbands. Men like to be thought original when they tell you "by the yard" after dinner just what happened on that trip last summer, often explaining longer than the color movies of it which they also hope are original. Children love to plan surprises. Any kind. From Easter baskets to lovely dead frogs under your covers at night.

The longing for originality is good.

It comes from God.

What we do with it can come straight from His enemy!

I longed for originality as a writer. This was good. It made me diligent when I might have been just vain and careless. And some of the time there *was* originality in what I wrote. And in the way it was written. But only some of the time.

As with sensitivity and objectivity and simplicity I was only able to catch at it and watch it go. I longed to be original. Consistently original.

New.

Spring was a fact. It always came. And it was always new. But I wasn't. I was getting old. In everything.

And then Christ came to live within me.

The same Jesus Christ who *was* in the beginning . . . who was with God and who *was* God! In me, in me, in me, *this* Christ?

Yes.

". . . I will come in. . . ."

The One without whom nothing was made that was made!

The great Creator God had come to live in me.

Had become my Saviour and my Holy Guest forever.

Jesus Christ was not another *creation of God*. He was there when all creation was created! He is the One who made all the heavens and all the worlds and all the universes and all that each contains.

He, who created *me lives* in me.

This is too high for me. I cannot attain unto it. But I can accept it and begin to partake of the originality that springs from Origin itself!

I need never run short of ideas.

I need never *force* another idea as long as I live.

I need only to take of the very life of the Creator God.

And that life is in me.

Christ Himself in me . . . my *only* hope of originality.

Never a copy.

Never a duplication.

One constant new beginning with the One who was there "before the world was." Who said: ". . . before the day was I am He. . . ."

I no longer need to struggle to be original.

". . . without him was not any thing made that was made. . . ."

And He lives in me.

Forever.

12

I Longed to Know Him As He Is!

I shall know Him, I shall know Him,
As redeemed by His side I shall stand . . .
I shall know Him, I shall know Him,
By the print of the nails in His Hand!

If you have ever sung this old gospel song, you know what I mean when I say that when I reach the line: "As redeemed by His side I shall stand" . . . I am not at all surprised at the next line which repeats the irrevocable fact that we *will* know Him when we stand one day by His side—redeemed! But those of us who have been redeemed by the love and the blood that flowed from the cross of Calvary know that if we had not been *redeemed* we most certainly would *not* know Jesus Christ!

We simply do not *recognize* something with which we have no ties and no affinity.

No resemblance.

Those of us who have come to know Jesus Christ as our own *personal* redeemer, know that we, in our unredeemed selves can have *no* family likeness to our Saviour! But we also know that when He comes to dwell within us . . . when we receive Him as our Saviour and then permit Him to take us over and master us, there begins to be an actual family resemblance. That this could be in *us* as we are and Jesus Christ as He *is*, is the wonder of redemption. And yet, does He not come actually to live His life in our bodies when we receive Him?

Either He does or Jesus Himself was not sure of His ground when He said that *if* we would open the door He would come in. That He would send the comforter. That He Himself would come.

Those of us who are "learning of" Jesus Christ know that He was and is very sure of His ground. If we have received Him with sincere hearts, He *has come in!*

We can begin to resemble Him.

Not because we are learning how to be Christ-like, but because we are gradually permitting Him to rule our lives! He never lives contradictory to Himself. The Spirit of Jesus Christ is always unmistakably the Spirit of Jesus Christ.

The Spirit of Jesus Christ is always unmistakably the Spirit of Jesus Christ!

Christian work does not make us resemble Christ.

Christian church attendance does not make us resemble Christ.

Christian thoughts do not make us resemble Christ.

Christian witnessing does not make us resemble Christ.

The actual indwelling presence of Jesus Christ makes us resemble Him and nothing else can counterfeit this likeness!

"Take my yoke upon you and learn of me. . . ."

I say I long to know Him as He is.

You may say, "What if I don't *want* to learn of Jesus Christ? What if there is no desire within me to 'learn of Him.' What then?"

If He is within you, ask Him to *create* the desire *for* you. After all, if He created you, can He not create a *desire* within you? If Jesus Christ tells us (and He does) to "learn of Him," would He be the kind of God we know Him to be when we look at Him on the cross, if He did not intend to change us until our very desires were His desires for us?

He can convert our desires too.

He can actually *become* our desire!

Do you think for one minute that Paul had a corner on the market of the burning heart? To Paul as Saul of Tarsus, "to live" was *not* Jesus Christ until this same Jesus Christ made it so! He creates in us the desire to know Him and then fulfills that desire for us. Saul of Tarsus might have shouted "To me to live is to persecute this Jesus Christ!"

When Saul, the destroyer, was transformed into Paul, the disciple, he cried out of a heart that had been healed and filled with a hunger for still further healing: "That *I may know him* . . ."!

"That I may know him, and the power of his resurrection, and the fellowship of his sufferings, being made comformable unto his death"!

We know, even as we sing through the wobbly verse of the dear old song about knowing Him "as redeemed by His Side we shall stand," that *then* in that day when we do see Him face to face, *we shall know Him* . . . but what of now?

Can we know Jesus Christ now?

Really know Him?

Yes.

We *can* know Him now.

The spirit within us witnesses to His Spirit within us that we are children of God.

Citizens of heaven.

Still living on this old earth at our address!

You, living where you live, and being named your name, *can* know Jesus Christ. Otherwise He would not have said, ". . . learn of me. . . ." He does not urge us to the impossible with Himself. He urges us to follow Him and then proves to us that nothing is impossible with God.

I long to know Him as He is.

To know Him is to live.

"In him was life. . . ."

". . . I am the bread of life. . . ."

". . . the water that I shall give him shall be in him a well of water springing up into everlasting life . . ." "If any man thirst, let him come unto me, and drink."

To know Him is to know life. "And this is life eternal, that they might know . . . Jesus Christ whom thou hast sent."

To know Him!

As He is.

"As the hart panteth after the water brooks, so panteth my soul after thee, O God."

Living with Him and knowing that He lives in me have made me long to know Him better. As He is!

With Augustine I cry . . . "My heart is restless until it rests in thee!"

Seeking to know Him as He is.

Not as He has been described, but as He is.

Longing to know Him beyond the printed page. Beyond the spoken word.

Beyond.

He Himself planted that longing within me. In His kindness which is always all around me, He shows me *how* I may know Him . . . as He is.

He shows me carefully and clearly, as He had showed Paul when he wrote: "That I may know him, and the power of his resurrection, and the fellowship of his sufferings, being made conformable unto his death."

In this cry from the heart of Paul, the bondslave of Jesus Christ, we find clearly set forth the *only* way to *know* Him. As He is.

For the next three chapters we will attempt to show that knowing Jesus Christ as He is, personally, is only *three steps away* from us all.

It is my prayer that you will be given the power to take these three steps into the life He wants you to live!

13

Enough to Be Made New?

"That I may know him . . ."!

The cry from the heart of St. Paul is still rising from the hearts of those of us who long to know Jesus Christ as He is. In Philippians 3:10, Paul exclaims: "That I may know him, and the power of his resurrection, and the fellowship of his sufferings, being made conformable unto his death."

If we do *not* long to know Him, this verse is an anathema. It sticks in our spiritual throats and we cough and sputter and try to forget at least the last two steps set forth so clearly in the verse that vibrates with Paul's own personal longing after the One who had transformed his life. But the cry within this one verse contains the three steps into *Oneness* with Jesus Christ.

The three steps into peace.

Into victorious living.

Into the joy He promised the night they were planning to kill Him.

Into some knowledge of what He is really like.

Three distinct steps away and yet no one step can be taken without the other two! One step must follow and one step must precede and there is no real beginning and no real ending. In this sense they are not steps at all, they are parts of a circle which completes itself as Christ completes the human heart.

If within our hearts He has been allowed to plant the longing for Himself, we leap to embrace this verse, rejoicing even in the thorns in it which pierce and tear as the hard, young buds break open in our souls and the perfume of maturing flowers causes us to forget the blood upon the thorns was ever ours.

> *The blood was never ours,*
> *'Twas ever His!*

And because He walked *out* of that blood-soaked, borrowed tomb that first Easter morning, He is alive today to walk *into* the tomb of our lives. And as He comes *within* such light breaks *upon* us and *within* us that we drop "darkness" from the words we know and vow never to use it again!

When *He* comes within! When we begin really to *believe* in the resurrection, because we have come to *know* Him who arose bodily and who now lives at the right hand of the Father *and* in us . . . praying, praying, pressing, pressing, pressing ever nearer, His Spirit working within the once-dark depths of our beings to make clean and bright the place where He will dwell.

The resurrection?

Yes. But still more—the One who arose!

"That I may know him, and the power of his resurrection. . . ."

This is the *first step* into Oneness with Jesus Christ.

That I may *know* Him in the power of His resurrection!

I do not shudder at this step. It grips me. It thrills me.

No one will shrink from the possession of power. We live in a power-crazed world. In fact, the phrase "powercrazed" is so trite we pass it over with no reaction at all. Political power. Economic power. Military power. Automotive power. Atomic power. Hydrogen power. The "power" of thinking in this direction and that. The "power of the press."

Just words. Almost.

But not unattractive words. We'll *take* power, most of us. Especially Americans love power. And most especially they love it if it is under the hood of their automobiles as they madly try to crowd each other into eternity on their super highways designed to help along the process. Oh, we'll take the first step gladly. We'll open wide our arms and our souls and *take* the ". . . power of his resurrection . . ."!

Is this true?

Will we do that?

Do we really long to know Him as He is? Are we truly willing to be *given* a new life in Jesus Christ? Especially when it means we have to give up our old ones in exchange? Are we willing to be made new?

Are we really willing to be made new?

Are we willing to be given a brand-new life and not just use our own will power to "turn over a new leaf"? Resurrection power is the same power that brought the dead body of Jesus up out of that tomb! Do we want that to happen to us?

Right in the midst of things?

The power that invades us from above when we receive the life of God into our lives is the very same power that brought Jesus to life again. When we are born again from above, we are given life from the dead.

When we become Christians by the invasion of the Holy Spirit, we are brought to life! Eternal life.

And it is surely life out of death!

Because it is resurrection life and resurrection means life from death.

But sometimes it is comfortable to be dead.

To be alive means we have to move.

To know Him is to know life. We have said this. We say it again . . . *to know Jesus Christ is to know life itself!*

"And this is life eternal, that they might know thee the only true God, and Jesus Christ whom thou hast sent."

To be raised from the dead means "sleepers awake !"

To be raised from the dead means to be made new.

Why does it?

Because the Lord Jesus said, ". . . I am the resurrection, and the life . . ." and then He added, ". . . Behold, I make *all things new* . . ."!

Are we willing to be brought to life?

The next two steps tell the tale. The seed of His life must be planted in us by the Holy Spirit upon our turning to Christ, and this is the seed of resurrection life because He *is* the resurrection and the life. And so step one . . . "That I may know him, and the power of his resurrection . . ." must go before steps two and three: ". . . and the fellowship of his sufferings, being made conformable unto his death."

But . . . as a circle completes itself, so must steps two and three go before as well as follow step one!

The seed of the resurrection life must be *put within* us at conversion, but in order that we may go on to ". . . know him, and the POWER of his resurrection . . ." (that is, the *full* power . . . enough for victorious living "in the midst of") we must needs take steps two and three!

We need His life within us to be *enabled* to embrace the fellowship of His sufferings. And surely we need His life within us even to be *willing* to be ". . . made conformable unto his death"!

And so, all follow and yet all come before.

All are one and yet there are three.

"That I may know him . . . (1) and the power of his resurrection, (2) and the fellowship of his sufferings (3) being made conformable unto his death."

Do I long to know Him enough to take the first step? To be made new? To be willing to give up those old thought habits and personality tricks which Jesus Christ would not use?

Am I willing to stop using the "methods" I've used so long to "get my own way"?

Am I willing to stop hitting the pagans I know over the head with my doctrine in order to win them to *my point of view*? Will I begin to win them to Christ by letting Him make *me* new in my disposition so that He can love them *through* me?

Am I willing to change jobs if this one is against God? Or am I willing to stay with this one, knowing the ground on which I stand *is* Holy ground? In spite of my boss's disposition and the fact that I end up doing other people's work!

Am I willing to be made new?

To tell my "beloved story" for the very last time?

Never to indulge in that secret sin once more throughout all eternity?

Am I willing to give up the luxury of worry and the self-indulgence of fear?

Am I willing to be made *entirely new*?

Even to writing that letter or preparing dinner for that person who, of all God's creatures, is the most difficult for me to "take"?

". . . *Behold, I make all things new*. . . ."

Do we still long to know Him if He says that to us *once more*?

"Remember ye not the former things, neither consider the things of old. Behold, I will do a new thing. . . ." ". . . Behold I make all things new."

Do we want to know Him enough for that?

14

Enough to Suffer?

We have been facing the three steps set down *too clearly* by St. Paul in the tenth verse of the third chapter of his letter to the Philippians.

I say "too clearly" because there can be no begging the question, nor dodging the central issue in the way Paul set them down. And so, for those of us who want to beg a question or dodge an issue or hold onto a handful of rights to ourselves, it would be a convenience if the great Apostle had not made it so simple.

We could ponder it all.

We could claim confusion.

We could argue another interpretation.

And still another.

We could stall for time by pleading lack of understanding.

The Holy Spirit directed Paul to make it simple, though.

And He did.

God wants to be One with us. He wants us to long to know Him as He is. He knows we cannot know Him until we are near Him. And so He directed Paul to make it very clear to us. Paul did this in Philippians 3:10. Here we do not find three *easy* steps. But we do find three *clear* steps.

Three clear steps into Oneness with Jesus Christ.

Into knowing Him as He is.

Too clear, if we are fighting His claim to supremacy in our lives.

Blessedly clear to those of us who have been brought to the place of seeing once and for all that without Him we *can* do nothing!

Blessedly clear to those of us whose hearts ache to know more of this Jesus Christ who, by His Holy Spirit has *put* not only a "new song" into our hearts, but has made it a love song that sobs at times because we long more deeply for our beloved.

And then the longing deepens as He works within us.

And deepens.

And when it is deep *enough*, from "step one," when our hearts cried, "That I may know him, and the power of his resurrection . . ."! He leads us right up to "step two," "That I may know him, . . . and the fellowship of his sufferings. . . ."

We can't always *see* the path along which we are walking toward this step. More often than not our eyes are too filled with tears and everything all around us is blurred and distorted because no one can focus clearly through tears. But He can see. And He leads us right up to "step two":

Entering into ". . . the fellowship of his sufferings. . . ."

He stands there beside us and our soul seems to hear Him say: "I know this is one of the steps you wish I hadn't made quite so clear through Paul when he wrote that letter to My children in Philippi. I understand why you're weeping. I understand why you're trying to miss this step. Near the top of Calvary there was a sunken place in the ground where another cross had stood. When they filled it in, some of the earth piled up to the right of it. I could have stumbled over that little rise in the ground. My eyes were filled with tears as yours are now. If I had stumbled it might have postponed the cross a minute longer. But I didn't *need* to stumble. I had prayed that *prayer* back there in the garden. It was all in the Father's hands. And He was with me. He was in me. I *could* have stumbled. I could have called for angel help. But I didn't *need* to and so I just went on and *took* that next step. And then I was at the top of the hill where the crucifixion was to take place. Believe me, My child, I do understand the way you feel about this step right here."

". . . the fellowship of his sufferings. . . ."

An attractive woman named Fannie Davis lived and loved through eleven near-perfect years with her husband, Bill, who was a peace officer in Abilene, Kansas. They both belonged to Jesus Christ, who seemed literally to hold them together in their marriage which anyone knew *had* truly been made in heaven. Made by the One who fed their love for Himself and for each other as they walked heart to heart with each other and heart to heart with Him through those wonderful eleven years. And then in 1949 the rest of us read in our newspapers of the peace officer named Bill Davis, who had been shot to death by an insane man barricaded in a burning house, near Abilene.

The police had to sift the ashes after the fire was put out in order to find Bill's badge for identification.

Fannie Davis stood at that "second step" trying to see *something* in it all that made sense!

She understood why tears were called "scalding tears" when people wrote stories about great weeping. She understood about those who spoke of trying to "*see* through tears."

She couldn't "see" at all.

Everywhere she looked there was a black agony that refused even to express *itself* and nothing penetrated it.

But He had led her there. He had not caused her husband's tragic death any more than His Father had caused *His* tragic death on Calvary. But He was *with* Fannie at that "second step" very near the top of the little hill, where her cross stood. And as He promised, He didn't leave her for a minute.

". . . lo, I am with you alway. . . ."

Fannie Davis was faced with the decision to accept Bill's death. To accept it and not *fight* it. And then to *take* that "second step" into the fellowship of the sufferings of her Lord willingly, in *His strength*! She still couldn't see a thing. But He could. And she *knew*

He was there. Even when she didn't feel His presence. He had said He would never leave her nor forsake her. He was God. He didn't misrepresent things. He was there to give her His hand and to pour into her weak, weary, grief-blinded heart and mind and body, His very Own life . . . His power . . . the same power that enabled Him to take that last step at the top of another Calvary so long ago. The same power that ended that prayer in the garden, and made all prayer forever afterward so simple that even a child can pray.

Fannie Davis took the "second step."

By His grace, which overflowed each minute, she *took* the "second step" in blind faith. But she took it. That's the important thing.

She *took* the step into the "fellowship of his sufferings" and once she had taken it, *her* "radiant moment" broke from eternity into her time-shackled life.

"I was able to sit through my beloved Bill's funeral service *knowing* a feeling of genuine exhilaration! I knew Bill was *not* dead. I knew as I had never known before that Jesus Christ was not dead. That He and Bill were together forever. And forever alive!"

Fannie Davis took the "second step" and she *knew Him* in a new way from that moment on!

In the next chapter, we will look at how this same woman took the third step into Oneness with Jesus Christ ". . . being made conformable unto his death."

We shudder at entering into the fellowship of His sufferings.

We *balk* outright at being made conformable to His death.

But the steps are clear. The call is clear. God knows about these things that we face. And once we have taken all three steps . . . *we* no longer demand to know!

Our questions turn to praise because at last we *know* Him!

"That I may know him, and the power of his resurrection, and the fellowship of his sufferings, being made conformable unto his death."

Do I long to know Him enough to suffer and *accept* the suffering?

15

Enough To Die?

"I have tried and tried and tried to make Jesus Christ become real to me! After reading your autobiography *The Burden is Light*, I am filled with a deeper longing to know Him as He really is. But the more I try, the farther away He seems to be! I force myself to pray for longer periods of time. I keep more frequent devotional times. I pray up and down my prayer list. I give more to God's work than a tithe. I attend all church services and activities possible. I have pictures of Christ in every room in my house. I try to keep my promises to Him . . . Oh, Genie Price, I just try and try and try to get Him to be real to me and I fail miserably! Why should life be like this? What am I to do?"

You are to die.

Did I send this terse reply to the sincere letter which I have just quoted? No, not in those brief four words. I have learned that the quick, glib answer only deepens wounds kept open by self-deception or self-pity or lack of light. This kind of wound is one of the most painful of all.

And it is also one of the most common of all.

It is a wound made usually from years of *unconscious* living for oneself and it is usually infected by the germ of *unconscious* self-pity. But its most striking characteristic is that it *cannot* heal.

This kind of wound in the human personality cannot heal over because it is not *exposed* to the light.

This person writes in darkness.

Not from conscious sins. More from ignorance.

All this wild, flailing, frantic effort to try to make Christ real only increases the irritation.

But by some means coerce or drag or draw this sincerely seeking, but completely self-deceived person out into the light that streams from the cross of Calvary and if he or she will expose the wound long enough—it will begin to heal!

The suffering, seeking saint will see that *death* is the answer.

Death and *healing* together?

Can these two meet on any ground?

They *have* met on the blood-soaked ground beneath the cross on which Jesus Christ died. And they met again in the flower-filled garden in which the birds sand around an empty tomb no one expected even to be opened again.

The rough, splintery cross on which they nailed Him was real.

The blood He shed as He poured out His very life for our sakes was real.

The nails were real.

The thorns were real.

The spear was real. And the vinegar.

The bawdy jokes were real and the suffocation in His heart as He smothered our sin. *The sin was real!*

But the One who *took* the sin into His Own heart was real also.

And He still is.

Because the tomb is open?

No. The tomb is open and empty because He was and is real!

The tomb is open because He is the one *true* God.

True and real.

And alive. Could God stay dead?

Jesus Christ is alive and sitting at the right hand of the Father, praying for you and for me and for the pathetic person who so completely had missed the point as he wrote that letter in the dark!

Jesus Christ is alive and very, very real to those who know Him. *He is real even if no one knew Him.* But to those of us who are beginning to know Him as He is, He becomes more real as we embrace the truth that the life He offers *is* life out of death.

Eternal life is *life* from *death.*

Resurrection life is *life* from *death.*

We must be made conformable to his death!

What does that mean?

It means many things, but for our practical discussion now, it means that you and I must be willing to die out to every personality trait or trick . . . to every mode of thought . . . to every way of life . . . to every relationship . . . to every ambition . . . to *everything* that is not found in the personality and character of Jesus Christ!

We can try until we are spiritually "blue in the face," as the writer of the letter has done, to *make* Jesus Christ real. We can try and try and try to know Him in the power of His resurrection . . . we can suffer agonies as we picture Him suffering on the cross of Calvary . . . we can go with Him bravely through personal tragedy, enduring with clenched teeth so no one will find out that *our* Christianity is not working! We can "protect" Jesus Christ's reputation before others by feigning a chin-up deliverance from grief . . . we can do all of these things until we *are* "blue in the face." And we will only end up with "spiritual blues" unless we die to our SELVES!

Unless we do this, we are merely protecting our *selves!*

". . . Except a seed of corn fall into the ground and die, it abideth alone: but if it *die*, it bringeth forth much fruit."

Jesus said that Himself. And as always He said in a few words what we complicate by many words.

No living, growing wheat waves in any Kansas wheat field *until* the corn of wheat has first *died.*

Even Jesus Christ could not be glorified until after He died, so why should we pine away good hours *trying* to "get Him" to be glorified in us, until *we* die too?

Jesus also said, ". . . I, if I be lifted up from the earth (on the cross), will *draw* all men unto me." The unredeemed human "self" swaggering about laughing at the idea of itself on a cross, is a repulsive "self." Even other unredeemed "selves" find it unattractive because they want to do the swaggering! The unsurrendered "Christian self" is oftentimes *more* repulsive! But the sinful, selfish, swaggering human SELF "lifted up on a cross" with Christ—*draws*! This sweetened self is free to walk quietly and surely through tragedy and grief and hardship and heartache. It does not have to waste energy by swaggering. It is crucified with Christ . . . but it *is* strangely *alive*. Marvelously alive because Christ Himself lives in that redeemed, radiant self.

With many of us this death to self can be effected on the surrender of *one central issue*. It may be that in your life there is one person, one ambition, one habit, one desire, one right to yourself to which you cling doggedly. And as long as you cling to that one "thing" or person you cannot live freely as crucified with Christ. You give *most* of your old self to be made conformable to His death, but not quite all. You are *almost* on the cross. But one hand waves free, clutching whatever symbol you hold dearer than knowing Jesus Christ!

In our last chapter, we told the story of Fannie Davis, who entered gloriously and realistically into the fellowship of the suffering of Jesus Christ, when she *accepted* the death of her beloved husband, Bill, in the spirit of Christ. Fannie Davis amazed her friends. They expected her to collapse. But in her acceptance she had come to know her Lord more deeply and *He held her*.

But without meaning to be stubborn, she told me she had insisted that God permit her at least to continue living in the house she and Bill had built and decorated together. She stayed on there for six years. But her life was not unfolding. She longed to know Jesus Christ better. She prayed earnestly that He would lead her into some new work that would help fill her maimed life. No answer seemed to come. There was only silence.

Until Fannie Davis let go of her insistence that God "at least" allow her to live on in the house she loved so much! That house was the symbol of Fannie's right to herself. And when she gave it back to God, she died out completely to her old self! Almost at once a fine position opened in which this authentic Christian life can touch the lives of thousands of teen-agers! When Fannie *died*, she *rose!*

Now, she has to leave her beloved house and move to a strange city where she knows few people. But she is walking with Jesus without strain.

She *knows* Him.

She has died with Him and now, in the fullness of life with Him, she will draw to herself, with simple, unconscious grace, a new circle of friends . . . an entirely new and fruitful life.

". . . Except a seed of corn . . . die, it abideth alone. . . ."

Do you really want to know Jesus Christ as He is?

If you do . . . if I do . . . we will, by His grace, step into the power of His resurrection then enter into the fellowship of His sufferings . . . and not protest when He calls us even to the death of the cross.

He has been there first.

And where He is . . . and *only* where He is, will we find the true desires of our hearts met at last.

"That I may know him, and the power of his resurrection, and the fellowship of his sufferings, being made conformable unto his death."

Do I long to know Him enough to die?

16

Stop Longing And Die!

Do I long to know Him enough to die?

If you honestly believe that you do, and yet you seem unable to die or to stay dead, read on. Right now, you no doubt think my chapter title is glib and unfeeling and smug. Perhaps you are wondering about me. What right have I to tell you to stop longing and die?

Have I done it?

No!

I tried for five years of my Christian life and ended up exactly where you may be right now—living in a state of constantly attempted suicide! I have "reckoned myself to be dead unto sin and alive unto God" until I was nothing but exhausted and that is just what the enemy hoped I would be. You too.

But doesn't the Bible tell us to ". . . reckon (ourselves) to be dead indeed unto sin, but alive unto God . . ."?

Yes.

Then what's wrong?

I am witnessing again. So many deep and wise and light-filled essays and books and commentaries have been written on this very subject that I almost hesitate to touch on it myself. I am not learned and I am not an authority on anything except what I have tried in my own life and found to be true.

And workable.

And free for the asking. For anyone.

My only value to you is this: If a thing works for me, it can also work for you. No one, absolutely no one has a corner on the market of the freedom that always follows ". . . the law of the Spirit of life in Christ Jesus. . . ."

No one with a string of theological degrees after his name has an "exclusive."

And certainly not I.

But let me try to tell you step by step how I came to the beginning of a new freedom. I say to the *beginning* of a new freedom, because it is still opening before me every day.

I see no end to it.

Because there is none. It is eternal and that is forever.

For the first five years of my own Christian life, and particularly for three of them, I "reckoned."

Sometimes I reckoned calmly. Or tried to.

Sometimes I reckoned with great vigor.

Sometimes I reckoned with high feeling.

Sometimes I reckoned with no feeling at all.

At other times I just—reckoned.

But within a day or two, or occasionally within an hour or two after the great "reckoning" had taken place, I would find myself quite alive to—pitying myself for my heavy schedule or forcing my opinion on someone while cutting him down to size spiritually.

In other words, I found myself still quite alive to sin.

What was wrong? I believe I was trying to bring a certain state of my inner-life into being by *means of my reckoning.*

In other words I was still attempting suicide.

And not making it.

Looking back now, I see there were two reasons why I was not making it. First of all, I am always going to have a *self.* The point is not to kill myself, but to die to the down-pull of indulging that self according to her earth-bound instincts! The other reason why I believe I failed was that I was reckoning on my *reckoning*.

I was reckoning on my reckoning.

Now, this is not new at all. You may have read it in a dozen other books. After all, it is in the Bible. We are not to reckon ourselves to be dead . . . but dead to the need to give in to temptation.

In other words, we *can* pass a "point of no return." Trans-oceanic airplanes carry enough fuel to bring them back to their take-off point should they develop engine trouble *up* to a certain distance. Beyond that point, if the trouble develops, they have to hit for their destination. They have passed "the point of no return." I came to see gradually and joyfully and somewhat nervously that this was also true for Christians! We too could pass a "point of no return." I was nervous because I was quite attached to some of the things which I saw I could be finished with forever.

For only one small example, I found quite a bit of delight still in explaining to God in my prayers how far short of the Christian ideal certain of my co-workers fell. This made me feel "spiritual" by comparison. I liked the feeling. As I still liked the relief of alibis and excuses when I failed to do something I should have done.

The idea of never permitting myself the luxury of "humbly worded" destructive criticism again nor the release of "putting someone in her place" made me quite nervous.

I trembled inwardly as I had trembled outwardly the day I faced the fact that I *could*, because of God's provision for me on Calvary, go through all eternity without ever smoking even one more cigarette. Cigarettes meant that much to me.

That moment still shakes me and five years of that eternity without a cigarette have passed.

I want you to see that I understand your trembling at the prospect that it is quite possible for you never to give in to that particular temptation again as long as you live. And that is forever.

My "reckoning," however sincere, had not worked for at least two reasons. I was trying to kill off an eternal self and I was reckoning on my "reckoning." My self is eternal. It is to be "alive unto God" and only "dead unto sin." Reckoning on my own "reckoning" is a squirrel-cage procedure. I walk to the wall and snap on the light in my workroom "reckoning" on the *fact* that the switch is connected and the current is there waiting. I do not reckon on my reckoning about the current. I reckon on the *current*.

The day God showed me that was a big day.

Did I not believe that Jesus Christ had done a finished work on Calvary? That the power to forgive and break the power of sin in my life was let loose that day? Wasn't the current there waiting?

Yes. I wept for joy. And trembled some more.

And then, with this new light streaming, I began to re-read Galatians in my morning quiet time. I read through the first chapter. Then I began the second.

Soon I was reading one of the *first verses* I had memorized when I was trying to bring my lazy memory back to life right after I was converted.

I meant to read the whole verse.

Something stopped me.

Over and over the first two and a half lines my eyes ran.

"I am crucified with Christ: nevertheless I live; yet not I, but Christ liveth in me. . . ."

Over and over and over.

Then I could not get past the first phrase.

"I am crucified with Christ. . . ."

"I am crucified with Christ. . . ."

My heart leapt up!

I am *already* crucified with Christ!

This thing has been *done*. The part of me that *can* respond to sin has already been killed off. They not only killed Jesus on the cross, I was there too. He took me with Him!

I can't crucify myself. I'm too chickenhearted and selfish!

How many times had I said from how many platforms that no one can imitate Jesus Christ? And yet I had been trying in one sense to do what only He could have done.

This began to link up in my mind with other fragments of this great truth which He had been trying to teach me and I saw that if I am *willing* to know Him in the power of His resurrection, I *can*! I *can* be made conformable to His death because He has already taken not only my sin but my sinful, hard-to-handle ego to the cross with Him. Being made conformable merely means I take by faith what has already been done for me!

Suddenly being made conformable to His death lost its sting!

All my question marks about "reckoning" myself to be dead were "straightened out and turned into exclamation points !"

Paul was not trying to make me miserable by holding up a standard for me to *reach*! He was witnessing to his own experience. He was handing me a standard in Galatians 2:20 which I could simply *take* for myself!

Would I dare?

Could it be this simple?

Was there no more need to struggle? I had read that. And at that moment I was able to confess for the first time that every time I read it, I grew rebellious and angry because I was still struggling. People told me their struggles were much more intense than mine. Some of them seemed almost to resent me because my Christian life was working at all. But I knew I had been struggling for a perpetually, minute-by-minute victorious life and at this point when the new light came, I trembled and wondered if I dare begin to act as though Galatians 2:20 were for me too!

I confess now that any time I had noticed another Christian writing Galatians 2:20 after his name in a book or at the close of a letter, I thought—"How does he *dare* do that?"

I was afraid to write it after an autograph in one of my books. For fear someone would say, "Crucified with Christ? She doesn't act like it!" Suddenly I was free to do it. Because I saw at last that it had to do with me too. I was no longer "reckoning" so that something new *would* happen. I was reckoning on something that had already happened!

On the fact of Calvary.

Psychologists and theologians use many and varied terms to express the essential *self*. I am not entering the field of controversy here at all. I do not wish to get into a discussion as to whether we have one, two, or twenty-two natures. I only know that my essential *self* needed to be redeemed. Needed to be made new. Needed desperately to have all the "old things pass away."

And I also know that the part of me which responds to sin was handled once and for all on Calvary—if I take hold of that fact by faith and use it!

I also know that my new self needs to be daily and hourly *aware that it is in the living presence of the Christ who dwells in me.*

More of that in the next two chapters. Here, I would have you see that the first instruction in Romans 6:11 is merely for us to *declare* by our actions that we have already been crucified with Christ. We reckon ourselves to be dead indeed unto sin because we *are*. And to bring this into reality so we can notice it in our daily lives, we need only to take it by faith and begin to *act* on it.

Here is a simple example of how that works.

Not long after I began to see and realize by faith this great freedom from "perpetually attempted suicide," I spoke at length on it at one of my favorite Bible conferences at Cannon Beach, Oregon. I had told my friends there of having read about a missionary who received a card from a friend on which was written this message: "Happy Birthday, I hope you *know* you're dead!"

We were emphasizing the need to know of our cocrucifixion with Christ.

Cannon Beach Conference out on the Pacific Ocean is different from most, because there I have a chance to let the people who come share with me what God is teaching them. We all grow from it. And one morning an extremely attractive lady shared this experience with us.

The night before, she had invited several people from the Conference for a supper after the evening service. The woman confessed to having always been extremely particular. Even when entertaining guests for a bedtime snack, she remained, in her own words "a fussy hostess." She wanted everything to be "just right." She confessed also that although she had been a Christian for a long time, she occasionally gave a waiter a bad time if the service was not as she thought it should be. That night they all ordered beef-burgers and french-fried potatoes.

With my friend wanting everything to be "just right," the french fries arrived *first*!

And they sat and sat and sat.

The people getting fidgety and the french fries getting cold and limp and tired, as is the way with french fries and people.

My friend began to look for the waitress. In her words . . . "I raised up in the booth and began to glare around the restaurant. After all, this was too much! My reflexes were all set to let her have it—in a nice refined way, of course. And then suddenly, I sank back down in my seat. Looking around the table at my guests, who had also been listening to you speak on Galatians 2:20, I fairly choked on my words, but I got it out: ' I can't let that waitress have it—I'm *dead*!'"

The good, easy laughter that is the Holy heritage of God's saints when they see suddenly what God is "up to," rippled around the auditorium where we met that morning with the crackle of a wood-fire and the roar of the Pacific somehow joining in.

From that woman's simple witness, twenty or thirty others who had not yet caught the truth of Galatians 2:20—began to laugh too. The relief *is* tremendous. *We can stop trying.*

We can even cease the struggle to cease struggling.

It has been done for us.

"We are crucified with Christ. . . ." "Knowing this, that our old man is crucified *with him*. . . ."

The part of that lady which could let fly at a waitress had been crucified with Christ. She had never before *dared* to take that fact by faith. And so it had not been hers. We only possess the gifts and promises of God as we take them for ourselves and dare to use them.

"Ye shall be my witnesses. . . ."

The "fried potatoes" witness was used of God to set others free that morning as the wood-fire crackled and the ocean kept on doing what it had been doing since the day He ". . . gave to the sea his decree . . ." and your witness can do the same. From now on.

You can quit longing for a victorious life and *have* it.

We have already been crucified with Christ. More than to "stop longing and die," we can stop longing and *know* that we are already *dead* to the down-pull of sin.

From the moment we *know* that because of what He did, we can stop longing and live!

17

Stop Longing and Live!

All life springs from death.

This is woven right into the fabric of the universe. We can't understand it. But we can recognize it all around us. We can see why Jesus said, ". . . Except a seed of corn fall into the ground and die, it abideth alone. . . ." We have all put seeds into the ground and have seen them appear again as living plants.

We have all seen seeds come from their little brown tombs.

This doesn't surprise anyone.

It follows the pattern we expect from nature as God made it. No one can explain the entrance of sin into the world. No one can fully explain why God permitted it to come. No one can fully understand how it is that by submitting Himself to death as Christ died on Calvary, God could so completely identify us with Himself that we too can know eternal life out of death.

We can't identify ourselves with God.

He must always make the first move toward us.

This is a great relief to me.

It is a still greater relief to know that He has already identified me with Himself both in death and in resurrection! The more I see my own helplessness and inadequacy the more relieved I am that this has already been done.

When Christ died, the uncontrollable part of me died too.

Seeing this is at the very base of freedom.

Power was let loose when Christ died. Dr. F. J. Huegel saw the connection between the graphic gospel account of Christ's death and sin in our lives. He describes the power let loose into the world from the place called Golgotha as a "kind of radium that kills" the tendency to sin in us! I too look in the gospel accounts and I find that when Jesus died, He cried in a *loud voice*, ". . . It is finished . . ."!

His life *built up* to death!

Other mere human lives dwindle toward death.

This power "to kill" is very real power. I find evidence of it wherever I need it and will take it. For a time after this aspect of the truth contained in Galatians 2:20 laid hold of me, I seemed to see reminders in the Bible of this power to kill and bring to life. Reminders in most unexpected places. God seemed almost to be shouting to me ". . . I know the thoughts that I think toward you . . . thoughts of peace, and not of evil, to give you an *expected* end."

He has every right to expect victory from us because He has already made it possible.

"See now that I, even I, am he, and there is no god with me: *I kill, and I make alive; I wound, and I heal. . . .*"

And again, "*The Lord killeth, and maketh alive*: he bringeth down to the grave, and bringeth up." ". . . he bringeth low, and lifteth up."

The way up is down.

Life springs from death.

A fact we are very, very slow to learn as Christians. A fact God will never tire of trying to show us. With all His heart I believe God *longs* for us to learn this elementary fact. Because He wants us to be truly free. Free of our grasping egos. And He knows that "dead men" require no attention!

He knows that dead women require no attention.

He knows we are free only when we are free of the bondage of self-protection and self-defense and self-pity and self-esteem. Only then can we really be trusted with life.

Only then would we know what to do with it.

But then we *can* know! Jesus Christ sets us free to live. Forever. And well.

More about the art of living this new life in the next chapter. But here, having accepted the fact that our troublesome nature or self, if you prefer, *has been* crucified with Christ, let's rejoice together for a few minutes that Paul inserted *this* thought *between* the two great facts in the first portion of this verse.

The first great fact is that we were crucified with Christ.

The second great fact is that Christ lives in us.

But, between these two is the glorious fact that *we are not extinguished!* We are not pushed into the dirt and forced to try to resemble worms when we were created in the image of God! I am forever convinced, that without Him *I can do nothing.* But I am also convinced that Jesus Christ didn't die in order to present the Father with redeemed worms or shattered vessels. He died to redeem men and women for God's use.

"I am crucified with Christ. . . ."

Yes. And I rejoice in the fact that the old girl is dead!

But ". . . *nevertheless, I live . . .*"!

An "I" made whole and clean and acceptable to God *because* of what Jesus Christ did that day when the veil was torn from top to bottom. An "I" whose scars have been made radiant and whose useless years have been restored. Whose "old wastes" have been built.

Whose "former desolations" have been raised.

An "I" which has been given beauty for its own dry ashes. Oil for its abject mourning. A beautiful garment of praise for its death-bound spirit of heaviness. A *redeemed* self *lifted* from the mire of self-destruction, and planted by the Lord Himself in the rich earth at the foot of His Own cross.

A self whose roots were washed by His blood.

Watered by His tears.

Redeemed . . . that I, *even I,* "might be called a tree of righteousness, the planting of the Lord, that *he* might be glorified."

That He might be glorified.

According to *His* purpose, you and I live that *He* might be glorified.

Is that according to our purpose too?

God does not intend to smash us into the ground and exalt Himself by beating us down. This is the very opposite of the good news Jesus came to announce!

God's intentions toward us are that we should have ". . . life and . . . have it more abundantly"! He took us to the cross with Him so He could plant us in the fertile soil of His Own life, spilled out on Calvary. His intentions are to tend us and water us and be our very growth!

"I am crucified with Christ . . ." (so that) I can live!

". . . nevertheless *I live*. . . ."

Christ died so that *you* might live!

In my cabin at a summer conference a shy, introverted little lady in her fifties sat telling me the tragic story of her life. She was the colorless and unnoticed member of a rather brilliant and talented family. For years she carried her pain of feeling unwanted and it twisted her personality out of any resemblance to the one God intended her to have in the first place. Her very pain at being ignored made her more of a burden to her uncaring family. And so her heartache grew.

And when it had reached the breaking point at the tragic circumstances surrounding her father's death, she let it break at the foot of the cross of Jesus Christ. Being Jesus Christ, of course, He healed her heart. And I shall never forget the look on her plain, but radiant face as she said shyly, but with great certainty, "If no one else in all the world had needed a Saviour but me, Jesus would have died—just for me."

She was *experiencing* the wonder of the love of God. *For each one of us.*

She had discovered the secret at the heart of the gospel.

". . . Christ Jesus came into the world to *save* sinners. . . ."

If you are saved from something, you are *rescued*. Would He try to smash you into a nobody after what He did to rescue you? God is not quixotic. He is consistent.

He redeemed us to *use* us. Not to extinguish us.

Please do not misunderstand me. I do not mean to imply for one brief instant that God is to be thought of as a Cosmic Servant to our special personality quirks! He is not "the first and the last" in order to guarantee me success in my new job.

He did not lay down His life that I might live in luxury.

But He has done something better.

He took my sinful self to the cross with Him so that I might live . . . but *not* as the old I. The Berkeley Version of the New Testament reads: "I am crucified jointly with Christ; I no longer live as I, but Christ lives within me."

". . . I no longer live *as I*. . . ."

". . . old things are passed away; behold, all things are become new."

". . . nevertheless I live. . . ." And I am learning more clearly everyday *how* to live. Why?

Because "Christ lives in me."

The One who created me in the beginning has made a way to come and live right *in me!* The One who knows *why* His very presence brings me unspeakable joy. He should know. He created me. The One who knows what my *true self* longs for, *has come in.*

The One who can fulfill every longing of my true self is here.

The One who can fulfill every longing of your true self is there living in you.

Not to squelch you. To *fulfill* you!

If you will relax in His presence, He will begin to give you your heart's desire. Because only He knows what it is!

"I am he that liveth, and was dead; and, behold, I am alive for evermore . . ."!

And He is in you, if you have received Him.

You can . . . you *can* stop longing and live!

18

Stop Longing and Let Love Live!

The best definition of love I know is contained in the mighty three-word sentence John wrote in his first letter:

". . . God is love."

God, in the Person of Jesus Christ, is all we can know of love. It is all we need to know.

Love is the most attractive force in all the world. It is the most sought-after possession in all the world. Men may spend their lives seeking riches and fame, but when it comes time to die, they long for love, with a longing that even death cannot diminish!

We all long for it.

We were created that way.

Then, does that mean we all long for God?

If ". . . God is love." Yes.

And if the Bible is right and if my own experience of the love of God in Jesus Christ is valid, God *is* love. And I long for Him. So do you. You may not know it. I didn't for many, many years. But I now know that whether we recognize it or not, we all long for the love of God with a longing that cannot be measured or weighed. Except perhaps to measure it inversely by the size of the shrunken heart that beats without love and to weigh it against the paradox of the heavy heart where no love is.

As I understand it, the gospel of Jesus Christ tells us of the possibility of the miracle of the life of God *in us*!

By my reasoning, if God is love, and if He actually comes to be in us when we receive Him, then we can love according to the extent of His occupancy in our lives.

Is this reasonable?

If it is unreasonable and impossible, then why did Jesus say we were to love our neighbors as we love ourselves? He recognized our "selves" in this great commandment. Christ Himself tells me He does not intend to extinguish me. He wants to fill me with His very life and thereby change my self so that it begins to resemble His lovely self.

He will be my very capacity and ability and power to love.

Without Him living His Own life in me, there are some people I simply could *never* love! I tried for years with two or three of them and the relief was great when I found it was just impossible for *me*. But it is not impossible for Him. His very nature is love.

Mine isn't.

But His is.

Is it natural for me to love everyone?

No.

Is it natural for me to love everyone as much as I love myself?

No.

But the One whom I seek to follow tells me that I must love my neighbor as much as I love myself.

This is not natural at all.

But it is *super*natural, and possible because He will come and live His Own lovely life right in me.

"I am crucified with Christ: nevertheless I live; yet not I, but *Christ liveth in me. . . .*"

I am still living. I am still to be reckoned with, both by my friends and by God. I still have a self. The part of that self which *prefers* to defy God was crucified. The false, selfish "I" was killed on the cross. When I lay hold of this fact by faith, it becomes mine. I find that the next time I want to assert myself because that old groove is still worn in my brain from such long usage, I don't *have* to do it any more!

Dead people require no attention.

They don't need to have the center of the floor.

They don't need to defend themselves.

But, I rejoice to know God has not snuffed me out. ". . . nevertheless I live. . . ."

". . . yet not I (as the old I), but *Christ liveth in me*. . . ."

There is Someone else living here now too!

We are together in a tender, closeness that is One.

We love each other.

I am His and He is mine.

But more than that we live as One.

Which means we can also *love* as One.

This is not true in its most complete sense with us all. Some of us have only partial union with Christ This is not His idea. It is ours. He wants to be entirely One with us as He and the Father are One. But some of us have not placed our selves under His complete mastery. And, when we have not, there is no reason to expect that we will behave or think or react as though we have! No reason to expect that we will love everyone. We still have the right *not* to love those who do not appeal to us if we are still partially in command of our selves. Even of our redeemed selves.

Galatians 2:20 is the most perfect definition of the Christian life. It is not a goal to be reached. It is a witness to make because of what He has worked out for us.

Paul is simply saying that Christ took Saul to the cross and set Paul free to live. He is simply declaring that he, Paul, has learned the art of real living *because* he has surrendered his entire self to Christ's occupancy and therefore he is living fully because Christ *in* Paul knows *how* to live!

Who else would know as Christ would know?

"In him *is* life. . . ."

"I am the . . . life. . . ."

The Creator of life and life itself.

When He comes in, life comes in and we come under the influence and the control of the One who thought it all up in the beginning!

". . . without him was not any thing made that was made."

He Himself is my very life.

He Himself is your very life.

If He is not, He wants to be.

The world says, "Realize *yourself*." The modern cults of self-development say, "Realize the good in yourself."

Jesus Christ says: ". . . whosoever will *lose* his life for *my* sake, the same shall save it."

The cults say in accord with the voice of the world: "Realize your God-life already present in you."

Jesus says: "Lose your sinful life for my sake."

"I will *then* come and live My Own life right in you."

". . . as many as *received* him, to them gave he power to become the sons of God. . . ."

When we receive Him, He comes in.

Bringing His power, His faith, His abiding, His peace, His very life.

Bringing Himself.

And ". . . it pleased the Father that *in him* should all fulness dwell."

If you have been trying to declare the "Christ in you" and have never received Him, you are trying to beat down the door of heaven with your poor fists!

Receive Him as best you know how right now and He will come in. The capacity for Him is there. The longing is there. The emptiness is there. The big empty space created to fit *only* the Person of the Lord Jesus Christ was created right in you when you were created. But even if you are also sincerely trying to "declare sin away," it remains and keeps His life *out*, until He Himself has forgiven it. Denying does not get rid of sin. That is done only by the blood of Jesus Christ. The cross is not a symbol of our need to do the best we can to live a sacrificial life, thinking of others and doing good deeds. The cross is not a symbol. The cross was very *real*. The blood He shed there was very *real*.

And it is the only *real* way to be rid of the sinful self in us all which keeps His life out because He is a Holy God. Receive Him as your Saviour from sin and He will forgive your sin and come in.

Whether you believe it or not, ". . . all have sinned. . . ."

That isn't my idea. It is God's.

If this is the very first Christian book you have ever read, you can still turn right now and receive His life into yours, when you confess your need of a Saviour.

Very few seem to know this.

Very few seem to know that the Christian life is not merely a way to be good, or to find fellowship with other human beings whose hearts also long. Very few seem to realize that a Christian is not one who can snap his prayer-fingers and God will obey. Few seem to realize that being a Christian is not simply being sure you are going to whatever you conceive as heaven.

Or not going to whatever you conceived as hell.

Very few seem to know that being a Christian is Christ living in us right now!

A Christian is one in whom Jesus Christ lives now.

". . . the life which I now live in the flesh I live by the faith of the Son of God, who loved me, and gave himself for me." Our Galatians 2:20 has a mighty ending!

"I am crucified with Christ: nevertheless I live; yet not I, but Christ liveth in me: *and the life which I now live in the flesh* I live by the faith of the Son of God, who loved me, and gave himself for me."

A Christian is one in whom Christ lives now.

Think who He is!

Shouldn't we be wonderful people?

Look who lives in us.

421

". . . without him was not any thing made that was made." The One who lives in us is the One before whom one day ". . . every knee shall bow. . . ."

He is the first and the last.

". . . the name which is above every name. . . ." ". . . Wonderful, Counsellor, The mighty God, The everlasting Father, The Prince of Peace!"

The Lord, Jesus Christ!

In me?

In you?

Yes.

Then why are we as we are? Why are we such poor examples of what a Christian can be? Why do the pagans down the block have every right to laugh at our Christianity?

Why are we so often unlike the One who is living His very life *in us*?

Just as we have never laid hold of the fact that we were already crucified with Him, so we have never let it break all the way into our consciousness that *He does live in us*!

We operate from another point altogether.

We operate from the point of one, "trying-to-be-humble" earth-bound creature looking longingly to a far-away, benevolent, but distant God.

We are here and He is there.

It is true that Jesus Christ in His glorified body does sit at the right hand of the Father, "ever living to make intercession for us." But by a mystery which we don't even need to try to understand, this same Christ also comes to live His life again *in us*.

God incarnate again, walking the face of this old earth in us!

Incredible?

Yes. But true. And possible.

And it will show too, *when* we have taken this fact and made it ours. When we have begun to *let* Him not only do the acting but the *reacting* for us!

If you've received Him, He's there in you. He wants to bring you into such an indescribably close union with Himself that your very reactions will become His. His will become yours.

Do I understand this?

No.

But I have experienced it. And during the time I experience it, during the time I lose myself in Him willingly, I know I am not only learning the art of true living, I know I am being lived through by the One who created life.

By the One who is life.

Do I experience this consistently?

I experience this victorious life consistently *according* to how much I depend upon His *never failing me!*

". . . I will never leave thee, nor forsake thee."

I have His Word for that.

". . . lo, I am with you alway. . . ."

That is the last thing He said before He ascended bodily to sit at the right hand of the Father until all things will be put under His feet. It is as though, if we forget everything else, He longed to have us remember that He would never leave us.

"I will always be right there with you. In you."

". . . if any man . . . open the door . . . I will come in. . . ."

But, you ask, "How does this work out in my daily life? *How* do I begin to live this victorious life? *How* do I begin to give Christ freedom to live in me?"

Examples from real life are always best.

My friend, Ellen, does our grocery shopping. Our meat is always excellent, and so I asked her if she held a special charm over the boys at the butcher counter.

"No," she replied. "I've just heard the other women fly at the poor butchers day in and day out and I simply take Galatians 2:20 very literally every time I walk in the store. I let Christ talk to the boys behind the counter *for me!*"

The glory here is that, even if the meat should be tough and too fat, *He* would never "fly at" the boys who sell it. Even if they weighed both thumbs with it, He would still be Himself.

Our meat is always good.

The real freedom comes, however, in no longer *needing* to feel "put upon" if it happens to be poor!

Nothing changes Jesus Christ and He will still be *in us*.

My very dear friend, Dr. Norman B. Harrison, whose writings and life have done so much to assure me that I am being shown the *true* light in Galatians 2:20, quite unknowingly gave me another magnificent demonstration of Christ in us when I first came to know him in the summer of 1955. Of course, I had heard of Dr. Harrison, and had met him once briefly. But at the Mound Keswick Conference that summer we were both speakers.

Before I had read a word he had written, before I had heard even one of his power-filled messages, he came up to me, his face radiant beneath his wavy white hair and as he grasped both my hands, he said:

"Now, Genie, we're going to live love here this week, aren't we?"

Conference speakers often have interesting talks together at mealtime, and I had met some of God's great men and women here and there across the country. But this was different.

Christ Himself came up to me in Dr. Harrison and took both my hands and said: "Now, Genie, we're going to live love here this week, aren't we?"

He seemed to gather us all to take part in a new game of joy!

I could see his face, still handsome, shine with the very light of God as he sat that week patiently listening to me share what God had taught me firsthand from Galatians 2:20. He, a greatly venerated, highly educated Bible expositor . . . I, merely a witness. But it was as though God and Brother Norman sat there listening together sharing a big, shining secret!

God was in that dear old man.

And the more I saw of him during that week the more I was convinced that the great discovery of my life had been made! It *was* possible, just as it had come to me from that verse, to live an ordinary life right here on this earth, in *complete union* with and under the *complete control* of Christ! Dr. Harrison's messages thrilled me. Our brief conversations here and there on the grounds were charged with eternity. Each day as I spoke I became more and more convinced. Dr. Harrison seemed to be a man filled with the *delights* and the energy of God. At eighty he was sure and joyful and his face shone. It was as though he had just then discovered God himself!

From the pulpit and at dinner and on the grounds he fairly radiated joy. I wondered about his family. His daughter, Marjorie, was with him and I couldn't help thinking what real fun they must have together! How happy their home life must be.

I wondered if Dr. Harrison had ever known deep sorrow.

Almost everyone else knew already about his life. I, being such a new acquaintance, did not know. I was just taken up with the fact that *in him*, God was showing me the joy of heaven itself.

And then, on the last day I learned, quite by accident, that the dear old fellow was there proclaiming the good news and *living* it before us only a *few weeks* after the tragic death of his beloved daughter, Frances, with whom he had worked for twenty years . . . *and* only a *few days* after the death of his wife!

I was jolted and the jolt sent me still deeper into the truth of Galatians 2:20.

I *knew* Christ lived in Dr. Harrison.

His books and his preaching were filled with the authority of God Himself, but Brother Norman's *life* showed me what I needed to see.

I *saw* Christ controlling his entire being and showing forth His joy which sorrow cannot dim. Even this old man's grieving heart was lit with the joy of heaven.

A few months later in Chicago I watched the same Christ take over in Brother Norman's *reactions* when a friend of mine inadvertently picked up the wrong briefcase as he took Dr. Harrison to a tram. I knew that brief case was the most important piece of luggage he had. The time element made it impossible for him to receive it for at least three days. The same Christ was still living in him and my friend, a comparatively new Christian, was neither hurt nor made to feel humiliated at his careless mistake.

Jesus Christ never hurts anyone.

He goes along right *in us* to the grocery store, to the conference ground, through sorrow, through the minor annoyances, and He will also love that person whom you simply cannot love!

A sincere Christian woman found she had never really let Him *love* through her until her mother-in-law came to live with her. The mother-in-law could easily have been the model for all cartoons and the evil inspiration for all stories about mothers-in-law. We looked at Galatians 2:20 together as we walked across a college campus one day. She *saw it* and this is what she said:

"Well, it's a relief to know I can't love her! To know I don't have to. That He will love her through me."

We just walked along for a moment and then she said, in a voice that was almost childlike in its discovery, "My mother-in-law is very old. She'll be bed-fast one of these days and then I can really let Him take care of her through me!"

When we first began to walk, she wanted me to commiserate with her. The instant she began to *accept* her wretched situation and to dare to think He would do the loving through her, His very presence within her began to influence her entire outlook! He was there all the time. Before she talked to me. Apparently she had forgotten it. Or hadn't known that she could depend upon Him entirely!

Love was living right in her!

Waiting to love even her mother-in-law *through* her.

Another woman, a dear friend, struggling painfully through the heavy humiliation of having her husband divorce her after thirty years of married life, allowed this great truth of His indwelling presence to take hold of *her*, and even though the husband went through with the divorce, even though everyone in the town knew it, even though they also knew about the other woman, my friend won two of her four embittered daughters to Christ by letting them see Christ *hold her* and *react for her* and *love through her* as they went through this ghastly ordeal together.

This woman is alone now. Her big, lovely home is very empty at times. But *she* is not empty. Her humor is strong, she can laugh at herself, she gives of herself and lives a full and creative life.

Her circumstances did not change.

But Christ living in her, changed *her*.

She fell completely under His influence! And they became One forever.

"I am crucified with Christ. . . ."

". . . nevertheless I live. . . ."

". . . Yet not I, but Christ liveth in me. . ."!

Don't be afraid to make it yours. We can, oh, we can stop longing for love, stop longing to be able to love the unlovely. We *can* stop longing and let love Himself live *in us*!

19

David Longed

"David longed. . . ."

David, who had all his life been handsome and courageous and daring in battle and in thought . . .

David, whose talent upon the harp rivaled his talent to create poems of praise to enlarge his melodies . . .

David, praised and adored by the women who ". . . came out of all cities of Israel, singing and dancing . . ." to the lilt and laud of their adulation of David, who had ". . . slain . . . his ten thousands."

David, popular enough to stir the jealousy of a king . . . beloved by one whose human love bore a shadow of the great heart that broke on Calvary. ". . . the soul of Jonathan was knit with the soul of David, and Jonathan *loved him as his own soul*." David, sharing the very soul of a man who had every reason to hate him, but who instead ". . . stripped himself of the robe that was upon him, and gave it to David, and his garments, even to his sword, and to his bow and to his girdle."

David, the skillful shepherd boy who slew a giant, became a prince's friend and then himself king, anointed of God, mighty in battle and gentle in spirit, leader of "mighty men," called by God Himself "a man after God's Own heart" . . . this David, of the house of Jesse, from whose line was to come Christ Himself.

This David—*longed*.

428

Surrounded by his "mighty men," headquartered in the cave of Adullam, King David *longed*.

The Philistines "pitched in the valley" between, held his beloved native city of Bethlehem. King David and his "mighty men" were cut off and waiting in their cave for a chance to attack and regain the city beloved to David.

But David did not speak of his longing for Bethlehem itself.

He did something any one of us might have done.

Sitting there, as he was, surrounded by his strong followers, instead of speaking in mighty phrases of mighty military plans to be carried out by "mighty men," David did what we might have done.

David longed for a drink of water from an old well he loved.

". . . David longed, and said, Oh that one would give me drink of the water of the well of Bethlehem which is by the gate"!

How many times have you, if you have ever drunk water from a well near a place you loved, longed for one drink of that particular well-water? Perhaps you "taste" it from a gourd, as I remember water from the well on my Uncle Steve's farm. Perhaps you "taste" it from a tin cup. But when you long for that water, is it really the water for which you long?

Is it really the *water* for which you long?

Isn't it rather a longing to recapture something you have lost? Isn't it rather a longing to hold again, or perhaps to capture for the first time something you meant to grasp and never let go when you stood by that old well all those long years ago?

Is it really the water you want?

Or is it that "feeling" you had as you drank the water?

Could it be that your heart longs to "go back" and look more closely along the road of the years that lead from that well to now?

Did you lose something along the way?

Would you like to go back and look for it?

Or did you step on a clump of violets as you walked indifferently away from the well the last time? And would you like to go back and straighten them up again and loosen the black earth around their roots and give them a chance to begin to grow once more?

Is it the *water* for which you long?

Or is it the peace you knew back in that uncomplicated time when you stood there drinking and thinking about nothing at all?

Is it the *water* you want, or the chance to "make up" for something you crushed?

Is it the water you want, or the peace you knew as you drank it?

Is it childhood?

Is it your parents you long for?

Is it rest? Art thou "wearied in the greatness of thy way"?

In the length of the journey?

Or is your life going by so fast your heart cries out for time to taste it as you used to taste that clean, cold water at the well?

Are you anxious and frightened by the flying-by of all the things you hold dear? Would you like to hold them all for just a clear, peace-washed moment as you held that water in that green- and yellow-striped gourd by that old well where once you drank?

Are you longing for a higher place, above the dirt and smoke of your own failures and defeats? Or above the dirt and smoke of too much success?

Do you perhaps long for your heart to be mended?

Or for a return to the simplicity of a humble heart?

Is it really the *water* you want?

Or do you long to be free again? As free as you were the days you drank at that well?

Do you long to be wanted once more as you knew you were wanted when you drank the clean, clear water from the well which belonged to someone who belonged to you too? To whom you belonged?

Is there a battle up ahead from where you wait now? And are you sitting there in the temporary protection of your "cave of Adullam" trying to escape what's up ahead by longing for what was so precious to you once?

Is there a parting up ahead?

An ending of all you hold dear?

Are you putting off the future by "putting on" the past?

Even for a moment?

The moment you'd need to drink just one tin cup of water from an old well?

Is it really the water for which you longed?

Was it really the water for which David longed?

Perhaps the answer lies in the finish of that little story about David and his "mighty men" as they waited there in the interim cave of Adullam.

"And David longed, and said, Oh that one would give me drink of the water of the well of Bethlehem, which is by the gate! And the three mighty men brake through the host of the Philistines, and drew water out of the well of Bethlehem, that was by the gate, and took it, and brought it to David: *nevertheless he would not drink thereof, but poured it out unto the Lord.*"

David would not drink the precious water, after his faithful men had risked their lives to bring it to him.

". . . David longed . . . (and then) poured it out unto the Lord"!

Why did David do this?

Was the water *too precious* because it had come to him at the risk of the very lives of the men who loved him and whom he loved?

Yes. Certainly this was one reason.

I know this was one reason because this little story of David and his pitcher of water from the well at Bethlehem has been one of the main melody lines of my entire Christian life!

And for three or four years of that life, it caused me to learn the higher way of giving back to the Lord as a love-offering, memories of my old life which were still precious to me—but less than God's best. I "poured out" my work over and over again. My desire to play god in my own life. Intellectual concepts which had found such wide welcome in my mind through the years in which

I *did* "play god" in my own life. I "poured out" certain music which caused me to reach for the tattered graveclothes I still trailed. Music that made me want to pull those graveclothes close around me again and hide in their dark, still familiar folds. Still familiar and dear because I had hidden there so long before He rolled the stone away and called me to come out and live!

For these dark hiding places I sometimes longed.

They were familiar and I had lived in them a long time.

But I knew the stone was rolled away. He *had* come in. And more often I found gladness in "pouring out" to Him even the memories of things I once held dear before morning came. More often I found gladness and always I found release.

And more Oneness with Him.

If you have been a Christian since you were very young, you may not understand clinging to old things. But here and there in the world are others who like myself, experienced the new birth as adults, and who have been enabled at crisis times to take God's power to resist temptation because they knew David's "water story" had worked for me.

Thoughts can be "poured out."

Habits can be "poured out."

Longings can be "poured out."

A young man now in the service of His Lord confided that although his mind and heart were forever turned toward Christ, he still suffered agonies of longing for alcohol. I reminded him of David and his precious water. When the boy wants a drink now, he "pours out his longing unto the Lord."

And the Lord sets him free of it.

Perhaps you are asking: "Is alcohol precious?"

Yes. It is the most precious thing in the world to the alcoholic! And if God took our sin, surely He will take the outward manifestation of it which has become precious to a man whose values and concepts were twisted by the very sin God died to cleanse away.

This "pouring out unto the Lord" has helped narcotic addicts who have turned to Christ. It has helped those who have been forced to give up work they loved because the work somehow was against God.

The time comes, in most instances, when the freedom is constant.

Only now and then do I have to "pour out unto the Lord" something still dear to me from my old life. The new grooves are formed in our brains. "Old things"—and that means old grooves in our brains too—"are passed away."

Memories remain, however, and memories can make us long.

We need not fear them.

We need not be ashamed or let Satan's superweapon of discouragement defeat us because our desires are not as "spiritual" as we think they should be! I almost "went under" on that one once. Until a saint named Anna Mow said: "So what if you're the one who wrote *Discoveries* and *The Burden Is Light*? You weren't witnessing to yourself, were you? You were witnessing to Jesus Christ!"

I saw her point and Holy laughter came back.

Directed toward *me*.

I had expected too much of my "spiritual self"!

Expect *everything* of Christ *in you*.

But *nothing* of yourself.

And don't fret if you have to continue "pouring out unto the Lord" that one thing which trips you on your way. Or those several things.

Just be glad there is that way to do it!

If you are trying to quit drinking, and you have *already* received Jesus Christ as your Saviour, the next time you think you're going to die if you don't have a drink—the next time you even think of a drink—"pour the longing out unto the Lord!"

This method has worked wonders for me with food too.

And with as many others as are willing to try it!

Not only am I losing the last several pounds which keep me from being a "fit temple" for the Holy Spirit, I am finding still another way of communion with the One I love.

The next time a forbidden dish is passed your way, give it to the Lord as a love-offering! Your craving for chocolate pie or black-eyed peas may not cause as much social disturbance or cost quite as much money as the alcoholic's craving for liquor, but it springs from the same twisted source. You're "taking out" an emotional lack in your life—trying to satisfy a *longing* with pie!

The alcoholic is trying to satisfy an emotional longing with whiskey.

Both escape into the temporary oblivion of self-satisfaction as the liquor and the pie go down!

Perhaps you say you have a sweet tooth and you can't help it.

The alcoholic has a physical as well as emotional longing for liquor too. Of himself he can't help it either.

None of this is the point. *God can help in both cases.*

God can give you complete victory from chocolate pie and bourbon! I have seen the same glint of defiance in the eyes of an overweight housewife *and* a chronic alcoholic when it is mentioned that God can change them *both* so much they will no longer *need* to eat that extra "snack" of solid calories of an afternoon or take even one more drink throughout all eternity!

The glint comes when neither one wants *total* freedom.

But when we do want it—from anything, we can have it by pouring out unto the Lord, the specific thing or relationship or circumstance to which we cling in our frantic efforts to assuage our longings.

If you feel forsaken, unwanted, "pour it out unto the Lord." *Be willing* to thank Him for your very feeling of loneliness because each time you "pour it out" before Him, you experience His love in a deeper way. You belong to each other more completely than you did the moment before. You may not feel this each time. But it will be true. I cannot explain it, but there is a law involved here.

And it always works.

If you are lonely, remember "God setteth the solitary in families . . . but the rebellious dwell in a dry land." Alone. If we rebel at our lot, we dwell alone. If we make a love-offering of our heartache to God, ". . . the Lord will take (us) up." Unto Himself.

Our personality twists will disappear as we praise Him and build our tottering altars before Him, and soon our loneliness will be gone because when He is living fully within us, we *attract* other people. "Christ in me" . . . my only hope of companionship. He draws. He will draw to me, *when* I have cheerfully laid down my loneliness and heartache as a love-offering at His dear feet.

". . . I, if I be lifted up . . . will draw. . . ."

We are beginning to move into a new and deeper meaning of this story of David's water "poured out unto the Lord."

We all long.

David longed.

Only the neurotic or the self-righteous deny it.

We twist our longings until the things for which we long are not what God would choose. But the longing itself is from God. He gives the ability to long. And when we long for something precious to *us*, even if it is sinful in God's sight, He will *take* that thing as a love-offering *from* us, *if* we will "pour it out unto Him."

He will take it and redeem it and give it back *changed* into what He alone knows will satisfy the true longing in us. The longing which always comes from Him.

From His heart to our hearts.

He will always take the "precious thing" we offer, even if it is sinful, because *we* are precious to Him!

Calvary is here.

Here the cross is raised in your particular circumstance.

There He *took* the thing so "precious" to man—self-rule!

Bondage to self.

Sin.

And set man free.

So, He will take *whatever* you are willing to "pour out" unto Him.

But there is more here for us.

If the lonely person pours out his loneliness *with thanksgiving* for the loneliness itself, God not only receives the offering, He gloriously *transforms* the one who has "poured it out," however tremblingly. He *transforms* the one who gave thanks, however feebly.

I am just learning this.

My dear friend, Ethel Wilcox, helped me see it first. Her only son, whom she loved so deeply, was killed in the Second World War. Walking together back to our rooms, across the grounds at the Mound Keswick Conference, where we were both speaking, I said: "You've really had a chance to try Him, haven't you?"

Her smile was radiant, and her voice was quiet with the deep things of God, as she replied: "Yes, I've had so much in which to *give thanks!*"

"Giving thanks always for *all things....*"

This too is a law woven right into the fabric of the spiritual life. Her victorious life proves it.

So can yours if you are willing not only to "pour out unto the Lord" that thing which causes your longing, but to give thanks for the *need* to come to Him in such a deep way.

If your heart is broken, lay it at His feet and give thanks for the broken heart. He will heal it and He will show you how blessed you are above those who live as dully as though they have no hearts!

If you are in confusion, "pour it out unto the Lord" and thank Him for that particular confusion, because if it had not come to you, you would not be seeking Him as you seek Him now!

If you are defeated, make a love-offering of your defeat to the Lord. And give thanks that you failed. Because if you had not failed you may never have discovered the life-changing truth that without Him you can do nothing!

Give thanks for your *need*, as you "pour it out unto the Lord."

Without it, you may never have sought Him as you seek Him now.

20

Early Will I Seek Thee!

David longed.

David, a man after God's own heart, longed with a longing that sprang from the very heart of the God who chose him.

"Ye have not chosen me, but I have chosen you. . . ."

David longed as we long.

God has also chosen us. All of us.

And His great heart longs to have us for His Own. This is also too high for me. I cannot attain to it. But I know that it is true.

David longed for water from the well at Bethlehem. But when he got it, he "poured it out unto the Lord."

Because it was precious to David.

And also because, as with you as you long for a drink from another old well, he did not really want the *water* itself. He wanted what the water meant to him.

He wanted what he had missed being away from where the water was.

He longed for what still lived in his heart concerning that water.

He longed for the *source* of the water.

"O God, thou art my God; early will I seek thee: my soul thirsteth for thee, my flesh longeth for thee in a dry and thirsty land, where no water is."

This same David, earlier in his life, hiding under the wilderness night-sky from his enemy, Saul, called from the depths of his already thirsty soul for the source of the water he needed so much in that "dry and thirsty land where no water was."

"O God, thou art my God. . . ."

"My soul thirsteth for *thee*. . . ."!

And God called back as He calls now . . . "Ho, everyone that thirsteth, come ye to the waters. . . ." ". . . If *any* man thirst, let him come unto *me* and drink . . . whosoever drinketh of the water that I shall give him shall never thirst; but the water that I shall give him shall be in him a well of water springing up into everlasting life."

David longed. And his longing came from God and was for God Himself.

"O God, thou art my God; early will I seek thee: my soul thirsteth for thee, my flesh longeth for thee in a dry and thirsty land, where no water is; To see thy power and thy glory, so as I have seen thee in the sanctuary. Because thy lovingkindness is better than life, my lips shall praise thee."

David longed for God Himself.

He knew God.

And almost the instant he cried out for more of the Lord, Himself, this same Lord flooded David's heart with the secret of the ". . . well of water springing up into everlasting life." When David began to cry out for more of *God*, almost immediately he was caused to remember God's lovingkindness and that it ". . . is better than life."

God showed David alone out there in the wilderness what the inside of His heart was like. And at once, David began to praise Him!

"Because thy lovingkindness is better than life, my lips shall praise thee. Thus will I bless thee while I live: I will lift up my hands in thy name."

David's longing came from God.

David's longing was for God Himself.

And that longing was satisfied the instant David began to *praise* God and to *bless* Him.

"My soul shall be satisfied as with marrow and fatness; and my mouth shall praise thee with joyful lips; When I remember thee upon my bed, and meditate on thee in the night watches."

David praised Him out there alone in the wilderness in extreme danger at the hands of his enemy. And instinctively he knew he would be praising Him when once more he lay upon his bed at night in safety.

But what of the "night watches" during which we lie upon our beds in physical safety but in mental anguish? A woman whose husband had just died told me her most agonizing times were alone at night in the dark . . . in the empty house . . . empty of her loved one . . . empty of sleep for her. Alone. Then one night she began to praise Him and to read aloud David's heart-cry . . .

"O God, thou art my God . . . my soul thirsteth for thee . . . because thy lovingkindness is better than life, my lips shall praise thee."

When at last her heart was turned to Him in gratitude for Himself, her burning grief began to subside. And although her nights remained sleepless for some time, soon she was able to "meditate on Him in the night watches." Peacefully and quietly, without rebellion or fear at being left alone.

She was not alone.

She was *enabled* to cry "O God, thou art my God; early will I seek *thee* . . ." because He was there seeking more of her.

As He is there, seeking more of you.

As He is here, seeking more of me.

And He will never stop seeking. His is the shepherd nature. He longs for all His sheep to be safe at home.

David longed. But he also *sang* . . . "The Lord is my shepherd; I shall not want" for anything which He *Himself* cannot supply.

David longed.

I long.

You are longing and God is longing to give you Himself in the Person of the indwelling Christ. When He comes in, and as you receive Him by faith, your every longing will be met. Because ". . . it pleased the Father that in him should all fulness dwell."

He Himself will be your salvation.

He Himself will be your growth.

He Himself will be your faith.

He Himself will be your constancy.

Your peace.

Your sensitivity, your objectivity, your simplicity, your originality.

Jesus Christ, Himself, will show you what God is really like.

Will give you a look at the very face of God Himself! He will make you new. He will teach you how to meet suffering and failure. He will teach you that He has already taken your uncontrollable self to the cross when He went to the cross. As He is teaching me.

Jesus Christ, living in you, will not only teach you how to live fully, He will live His life *through* you. He will love you and He will love *for* you.

He will fill your every longing. As He is filling mine.

But, there is more.

He *will* satisfy your every true longing with Himself, but He will also, when the time is right for *you*, create in you a still deeper longing beside which all others pale. If you do not see this yet, wait upon Him to show you when it is time.

You may find no words to express it, other than the words David found. But the longing will be new and it will flame white-hot in your heart until you cry, as I cry, once more and still once more . . . and yet once more . . .

"O God, thou art my God; early will I seek *thee*. . . ."

And when it "comes to pass about the spring of the day" that you are yet seeking Him in still dryer land, "lift up your hands in

His name" and give thanks, because the One who created your *new longing*, has done it because He longs for more of *you*.

As He longs to give you more of Himself.

And more. And still more.

"O God, thou art my God; early will I seek thee: my soul thirsteth for thee, my flesh longeth for thee in a dry and thirsty land where no water is."

"O God, thou art my God . . . early will I seek—*thee*. . . ."

About the Author

Before making St. Simons Island her home, Eugenia Price, a native of Charleston, West Virginia, was a resident of Chicago with a highly successful career in the thriving area of radio soap-opera programming. The major networks eagerly sought her creative production talents and Price was well respected in the broadcasting world when her life took a marvelous and powerful turn. God began to use her extraordinary writing gifts to communicate her faith with others.

Price's earliest books—*Discoveries, The Burden Is Light,* and *Early Will I Seek Thee*—gained her enormous popularity as a speaker at religious groups across the nation and across all denominational lines. Her compelling message was not about doctrine, but about new birth. In rapid succession she wrote books dealing with Christian living, women's faith perspectives, and devotional themes. Her masterful rephrasing of the entire Bible, *Beloved World*, went through countless printings. Twenty-six highly personal nonfiction works and fourteen historical novels were ultimately released by the leading publishers of the day.

Eugenia Price died on May 28, 1996, and is buried at her beloved Christ Churchyard, Frederica, St. Simons Island. Following her death, the Eugenia Price/Joyce Blackburn Charitable Foundation was established with Blackburn, also a prolific writer, as president. The Foundation holds all publishing rights in perpetuity. Its sustaining purpose is to ensure the availability of this written legacy for future generations of readers.